The Unfolding Design of My World

About the author

H. B. Dehqani-Tafti is the author of two best-selling books, *Design of My World* and *The Hard Awakening*, recounting his experiences as Bishop of Iran during the turmoil of revolution.

Exiled from his own country, he became Assistant Bishop in the diocese of Winchester. Now retired, he and his wife Margaret live in Basingstoke.

The Unfolding Design of My World

A Pilgrim in Exile

H. B. Dehqani-Tafti

Edited by Kenneth Cragg
Foreword by Bishop John V. Taylor

CANTERBURY
PRESS
Norwich

Dedicated to
Shirin, Sussanne, Gulnar
and in memory of
Bahram,
and also to

the men, women and children who have suffered
because of faithfulness in the face of political
despotism and religious fanaticism.

Copyright © H. B. Dehqani-Tafti 2000

First published in 2000 by The Canterbury Press Norwich
(a publishing imprint of Hymns Ancient & Modern Limited,
a registered charity)
St Mary's Works, St Mary's Plain
Norwich, Norfolk, NR3 3BH

Originally published in Persian in 1999
by Sohrab Books, Basingstoke, England

British Library Cataloguing in Publication Data

A catalogue record for this book is available
from the British Library

ISBN 1-85311-379-4

Typeset by Rowland Phototypesetting,
Bury St Edmunds, Suffolk
Printed in Great Britain by
Biddles Ltd, Guildford and King's Lynn

Was it not I that summoned you to service?
Did I not make you busy with My Name?
Of all those tears and cries and supplications
I was the magnet and I gave them wings.

Jalal al-Din Rumi

Something infinite which talked with my expectation
And moved my desire.

Thomas Traherne

Truths cannot become true till our faith has made
  them so.

William James

I cannot be mine own,
Nor anything to any,
If I be not Thine.

William Shakespeare

I see by glimpses now ... and I would give,
While yet we may, as far as words can give
A substance and a life to what I feel.
I would enshrine the spirit of the past
For future restoration.

William Wordsworth

This is the Lord's doing and it is marvellous in our
eyes.

Psalm 118:23

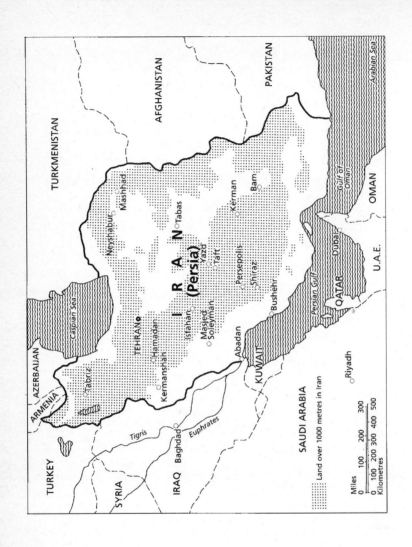

Contents

Acknowledgement

Soon after the publication of this book in Persian, many friends suggested that an English version should also be made available. This seemed a formidable task. However, Dr Kenneth Cragg presented me with a generous and practical proposal: 'If you give me what is in the book, I will edit it for you'! This encouraging offer led to a draft English translation that Bishop Cragg, with some pruning and alterations, soon transformed into the present text, to which he has also added a profound postscript.

His vast and sensitive knowledge of Islam, together with his deep love of Christ, his understanding of the Middle East, Iran and the Persian Church, made Kenneth Cragg the ideal person for this labour of love. Without him this book would never have been produced in English. For that, as well as his friendship and advice over the years, I offer him my most sincere and grateful thanks.

H. B. Dehqani-Tafti

Foreword

In both his earlier memoirs, *Design of my World* (London: World Christian Books, 1959) and *The Hard Awakening* (London: SPCK, 1981), Hassan Dehqani-Tafti's sheer narrative power and lucid explanation of complex situations gripped and enlightened his readers. But they must often have wished, as I have done, for a more complete telling of the strange and costly story of his life's vicissitudes. Here it is at last, from the loving, dutiful Muslim childhood of the boy of Taft, through the triumphs and tragedies of his ministry as Christian, priest and bishop in Iran, to the worldwide friendships and profound inner loneliness of his subsequent exile.

For there can be no doubt that the past 19 years have been a heart-rending exile for Bishop Hassan and, no less, for his heroic wife, Margaret. It has been a great enrichment for the Diocese of Winchester to have had them make their home in Hampshire and to have enjoyed his ministry as an assistant bishop. But, for all the real exchange of love and friendship, there can be no disguising the truth of their essential displacement. The cruellest irony of the Revolutionary Committee's insinuations that they represented hostile foreign interests lies in the fact that Hassan is so ineradicably and passionately Persian. It was typical of him that when their beloved son Bahram was assassinated, Hassan was able to associate it not only with the sacrifice of Christ on the cross, but also with the martyrdom of Hussain, central to the devotion of Shi'ite Muslims.

The homelessness of an exile, like the readiness for martyrdom, is one of the major images of the Christian life. In the

Old Testament also it is the third and last formative experience in the history of the Jews which created their faith, after the exodus from Egypt and the establishment of the kingdom in Jerusalem. Yet Christians have neglected it. How many hymns do we sing about being aliens and pilgrims compared with those on the themes of redemption and the Kingdom of God? This neglect is strange, since every disciple of Jesus Christ is called to be in, but not of, this world, and all missionaries from St Paul onwards have had to try to merge their natural identity in a culture and a language that was not their own.

So I welcome this moving story and pray that Christians everywhere and of all sorts may learn from the experience of Bishop Hassan and the small, scattered Church which he and his successor, Bishop Iraj, have led for the past 37 years, to live in the enduring hope of the spiritual exile. And that is something over and above the other-worldly hope of a 'promised land' in heaven. It is the hope of a return in the here and now of history, brought about by God's action within the hearts of men, when

> he who goes out weeping,
> carrying his bag of seed,
> will come back with songs of joy,
> carrying home his sheaves (Psalm 126:6; REB).

John V. Taylor
(Bishop of Winchester 1975–85)

Design of My World:
An Introduction

In the bye-ways of history no one gets lost.
Ismail Nouri Ala[1]

In his speech, when he received the Nobel Prize for Literature, Alexander Solzhenitsyn said:

> Woe betide that nation whose literature is interrupted by the interference of force. This is not simply a violation of the freedom of the press: it is the locking-up of the national heart, the carving-up of the national memory. Such a nation does not remember itself, it is deprived of its spiritual unity, and although its population supposedly have a common language, fellow-countrymen suddenly stop understanding each other. Mute generations live out their lives and die without telling their story either to their own or a future generation ... This is not just their own personal misfortune but the deep tragedy of the whole nation and, too, a threat to the whole nation. And in certain cases it is a danger for the whole of mankind too, when the whole of history ceases to be understood because of that silence.[2]

To forbear to tell my story would be no heavy loss to my nation, nor would it damage humanity at large. In the course of my life there has been nothing phenomenal or of monumental significance, yet in comparison with the careers of many of my colleagues I realize that my story is marked with experiences that kindle long and hard reflection.

Even strangers to my life story recognize, however vaguely, that it has uncommon features to do with my early nurture and training, and then with the crisis in my religious convictions between heritage and discovery. For it was that spiritual journey which led to the re-ordering of my life and to my vocation first as a deacon, then as a priest and finally as a bishop in the Christian Church. Some, perhaps many, reading this story may think of me as one who has severed himself from his roots, his ancestry, from kith and kin, from his society, and who has been assimilated into an unknown culture, assuming an alien identity.

I must concede the unusual character of my narrative and allow, up to a point, that the course of my life has had a current different from that of my fellow-countrymen. Nevertheless I am convinced that, far from forfeiting my own identity or being alienated from my personal roots, I have come to know them in a wider and deeper way and to possess them more authentically. My Persian identity is enhanced and fulfilled and this has brought me inward satisfaction and peaceful contentment: a harmony of soul that, far from being isolated, has been integrated into living community.

Maybe it is in view of this that friends – and even strangers – have urged me to set my story down almost as a debt or a duty I owe. If I go along with those urgings it is, in the words of Solzhenitsyn, 'that people may be enabled to understand each other'.

To keep silence would be no risk to 'the understanding of history', but it would mean leaving no sign of a true realm of significance for my country.

So I try to elucidate what actually transpired in my life. Otherwise, ambiguous surmise or even dark suspicion might persist which I must dispel at all costs. It is well-nigh certain that distorted assumptions or malicious conjecture cost the life of our only son in the prime of his youthful promise. That he became a sacrifice, a martyr, on account of confused or wilful hostility in our situation compels me now to set down the facts and tell, in further perspective, the significance of all that I briefly etched in 1959 in *Design of My World*.

My intention is to do so in simple terms and in deep sincerity of self-interrogation and explanation, describing the 'me' I was, and the 'me' I remain. We are told by psychologists that nobody is capable of self-expression without some kind of mask. All of us are liable to hide behind one, to conceal ourselves from others and even from ourselves in various kinds of make-believe or unconscious pretence. In any self-telling in words this danger is obviously present.

I know that I am not exempt from such danger, but I have conscientiously tried to ward off all pretence and subterfuge and to aim for complete frankness and honesty. There are mirrors that distort the viewer's image. Let this one prove undistorting. For, as Thomas Hardy said – oh to have known him in my youth – there are also mirrors that speak true:

> That mirror
> Which makes of men a transparency,
> Who holds that mirror
> And bids us such a breast-bare spectacle see
> Of you and me?
> That mirror . . . who lifts
> Throws our mind back on us, and our heart.[3]

Too often, however, our reflecting mirrors are clouded with dust; the glass is blurred and the silver unpolished. My hope is that readers will keep alert for these enemies to truth and discern things as they truly were, so that words will not deceive nor impressions lead astray. In all that follows, I turn to the words of William Cowper:

> 'Tis all Thine own: my spirit is so too,
> An undivided offering at Thy shrine.
> It seeks Thy glory with no doubt in view –
> Thy glory with no secret bent to mine.[4]

In the mid-1950s I was asked by Bishop Stephen Neill to write a short autobiography for his World Christian Books series.

The book would contain the four-sided sequence of my life from experiences of childhood, through to finding Christ, study abroad and ordination. Dr Kenneth Cragg, who happened to be with us in Isfahan at the time, and with whom I discussed the project, suggested *Design of My World* as its title after having visited the famous square on Maidan, historically called 'The Naqsh-e-Jahan' or 'The Design of the World'. He said that the four-sided experiences of my life could well be likened to the sides of that great square at the heart of Isfahan, unmatched for beauty and majesty anywhere else in the world. His suggestion appealed to me.

Leaving all beauty aside, perhaps a human life can be seen as a sort of architecture where meaning dwells. As St Paul said of simple Ephesian Christians, 'You are God's workmanship [*poema*]' (Ephesians 2:10), through the craftsmanship of grace. The Safavids of Isfahan's greatest times used to think that Cairo was one of its suburbs, so that its great Maidan belonged to the world. Through print and translation, it is humbling to think that even an Isfahani student's spiritual narrative can be known across the world. Accordingly, seeing that each of us lives inside the perimeter of distinctive personhood, might I not borrow one 'design' fittingly to tell another?

Forty years later when I wrote a much longer autobiography (the Persian version of this English text), I called it *One Well with Two Sources*. I had in mind the gentle, limpid waters of my village origins. The 'well' was within me, but into it flowed my Persian home and all the benison infused from the other source – my English education and initiation into Christian ministry, according to the Anglican tradition.

The coming together of these two sources of my being has not been easy. Life is a short span in which to learn to be bi-cultural. Diversities of customs and values, traditions of thought and patterns of behaviour merge and conflict inside me, leaving me at times in restful ease, and at other times in turmoil. Even so, the dual waters from separate streams have mingled well and fruitfully. As for the other analogy – do not 'designs' discipline parts into a whole? And may not an unfolding design incorporate what four more decades, heavy with tragedy as well as joy (as told in *The Hard Awakening* in 1981, published by SPCK, London), add to those first dimensions?

In the mystery of birth, despite what Hamlet needed to say in his situation, 'To be or not to be' is *not* the question. Rather, the question is: 'What to be?' Before proceeding to my birth-place in beloved Taft let me duly celebrate all the mystery of 'my coming to be' with the help of the English poet Thomas Traherne in a poem called 'Salutation', where he asks the intriguing question: 'Where was I before I was?' It is hard to know. He continues:

> A stranger here strange things doth see,
> Strange treasures lodged in this fair world appear,
> Strange all and new to me.
> But that they should be mine who nothing was –
> That strangest is of all,
> Yet brought to pass.[5]

That is when all *the design of my world* began.

Chapter 1

Homeland

The heights that separate the Iranian plateau from the plains of Mesopotamia (Iraq) and reach down to the strait of Hormuz are known as the Zagros Range. Some peaks in the Range rise to more than 4000 metres above sea level. At its eastern end lies Shir Kuh, or 'Lion Mountain', 4075 metres high. Its foothills extend to the Lut Kevir – a hot, burning desert. There are many scattered habitations in the undulations of the hills where the climate is less intense and the mountain air salubrious in comparison with the lower reaches where the torrid heat of the Kevir prevails.

The province of Yazd lies at the end of these foothills on the edge of Dasht-i-Kevir. A city bearing the same name is its administrative centre. Yazd ranks high among the ancient provinces of Persia.[1] Its name is linked with 'Izad', the old Persian name for 'God'. Legend holds it to be 'Alexander's prison'. Improbable as it is, the claim occurs in one of the poet Hafiz's sonnets. Where the sandy desert town stands today, there was once – so research has established[2] – a flourishing agricultural community well before Alexander's time.

There is also mention of a Christian monastery here that was destroyed by Zoroastrian fanatics before the advent of Islam. Its name, Reig Dayr, or 'Pebble Monastery', still survives. Taft, my birthplace, lies on the southern slopes of Shir Kuh, some 21 kilometres from Yazd. It has a more pleasant climate than Yazd, being situated by a wide, dry river bed where there once flowed ample water to irrigate Yazd. Save for a few brief weeks during spring, it is now waterless. When surface waters failed both Taft and Yazd had to depend on underground canals or *Qanat*s.[3]

At the outset of my story in the early 1920s Taft was one of the larger villages in the Yazd vicinity with a cluster of lesser hamlets around it. Now it has become a sizeable town.[4] One of the meanings of 'Taft' in Persian is 'a wooden fruit-basket'. It certainly fits with Taft's fame for its wealth of delicious fruits, notably pomegranates, apricots and peaches. In spring, Taft breaks into beauty. The orchards are pink with blossom and the pomegranate trees glisten in the sunshine, their brilliant scarlet flowers aflame in the foliage.

While farming was the basis of the economy, mostly carried out by small landholders, even the craftsmen had their own plots of land, or a garden, to supplement their earnings. The main crafts were carpentry, cloth dyeing, butchery, confectionery and grocery. Blacksmiths' skills were vital, for the entire mobility for goods and persons depended on the shoeing of horses, mules and donkeys. Thus, anvils linked the various villages, not to mention those other smithy items such as spades, sickles and pick-axes that the farmers used.

Another local craft I recall fondly was the making by hand of *giveh*, cloth-shoes for hardy, but comfortable, wear in a dry and sandy world. The shoemakers tended to work in groups to help relieve the monotony of their craft, each having a corner in a shared workshop. Even the soles were works of art, beautifully made. These were usually crafted by men while women weaved the uppers.[5]

My Family

My own family, along with some modest farming and a smithy, had a stake in the making of cloth-shoes, both soles and uppers. Indeed, one of my earliest memories is the steady beat of the mallet (a handless instrument) on a wooden block, where my father and other family members used to work among the cloth-shoe makers. The noise still echoes in my ears. It competes for recollection with the sound of blacksmiths' hammers coming from the workplace where my cousins were busy with their craft. These sounds of manufacture share in my memory with the fragrance of fruit gardens – pomegranates especially – and with the sheep-minding that fell to me in my childhood days.

In our home in Taft was a room called 'the dispensary'. Vividly I remember, from the age of about three or four, women in their colourful 'chadors'[6] gathering in the courtyard, babes in their arms, demanding medicine from my mother. She was a nurse and, despite her scant knowledge of medicines, ran the dispensary.

You may well ask how a village girl in those years in remote Taft could be fulfilling nursing tasks and dispensing medicine. The answer takes me to the very heart of my formative years. As early as 1897 the Church Missionary Society from England had started medical work in Yazd. Philanthropically-minded Zoroastrians made a sufficient grant of land to the Society for the erection of two hospitals, one for men and one for women. For the first time, people in Yazd had access to modern medicine.

My mother's own mother, a literate woman who could recite the Qur'an and so came to be dubbed 'Mullah[7] Zahra', developed eye trouble in old age. With her two daughters, Rubabeh and Sekineh, she made the journey from Taft to Yazd in search of help. The nursing missionaries encouraged both the daughters to stay and be trained as nurses, with a view to help staffing the hospitals. This they did. I think that their training must have coincided with the time of the formidable Mary Bird at Yazd.[8] She was one of a famous breed of women missionaries at the turn of the twentieth century and was remarkable for both her medical knowledge and her infectious faith. The younger sister, Sekineh (who was to become my mother), became a Christian, and gained enough literacy to read the Persian Bible and sing Persian hymns.

The British missionaries had to leave Persia in 1915 because of German and Turkish influences during the First World War, and for a time the hospital in Yazd was closed. Mullah Zahra and her two daughters returned to Taft; the latter both were married. Sekineh's husband was a young relative named

Muhammad. Their first son was Yahya (John), and then in May 1920 I was born in the hospital at Yazd – the place so crucial to my mother's story – which had re-opened after closure. The name Hassan was bestowed on me.

Childhood Memories

The factors that had played so central a part in my mother's nursing aptitudes were soon to have an even deeper importance for me as well. I still savour the memory of it from my childhood. It had to do with a lady named Miss Kingdon who had befriended my mother in Yazd. The day she visited our house in Taft is still engraved in my mind. Miss Kingdon, a fairly tall lady clad in a white dress complete with a white topee such as 'Farangis', as all Western foreigners were known, wore, spectacles hanging by a black cord around her neck, and a metal wristwatch, gathered around her the village women who had come to the dispensary for medicine. Using what seemed to me a very peculiar accent, she told them stories and talked of her Christianity, reading in particular from the Gospels.

My mother's home was open to the missionary because she had been drawn in Yazd to the message. In her simple, impressionable and guileless mind, and thirsty for love, she had responded to what she heard and been captured by a sense of the love of God revealed, as the mission said, in Jesus Christ. She had been baptized and so let her home be used as a base for village evangelism.

It was from this time – or even maybe earlier, as early as my second year – that I remember being in my father's arms. He was standing on one of the flat roofs where we slept during the summer's heat. Standing right on the edge, he was throwing me up and down in his arms. It must have been my childish fear of his letting me drop to the ground below that etched the scene so deeply in my memory.

Going with my mother to the public baths is another of my warm childhood memories. There were days assigned for men and others for women. The noise and the heat, and all that bustling around – these are what stay with me.

Alongside the dispensary, our house had a large rear room with a kitchen off it. Here the pomegranates were stored. The kitchen walls were thoroughly blackened with the smoke of the wood and dried bushes which were used for heat. We bought bread either from the bakeries or the market, or we depended on home baking. For this my mother would use a large, flat utensil rather like a frying pan. The bread it produced was called 'latir bread'. It was truly delicious. On other, special occasions, bread was baked in ovens built in the ground – a kind that would be kept for a considerable length of time and had an excellent taste. The ovens for 'home-baked' loaves belonged to my Aunt Beman, whose house was larger than ours.

A massive water-mill stood near where we lived. Its water flow went down into a deep hole like a well, some four or five metres deep. Under the resulting pressure a narrow aperture at the bottom conveyed the water on to the mill wheel which turned the stone that crushed the wheat. The whole device was called 'Tanooreh'. Families took their wheat to be ground into flour and collected it after a few days, the miller having his due of flour rather than a money payment.

There was no electricity in Taft in those days. We used kerosene for lamps which we called 'lampa'. Local merchants who traded between the village and far-off places like Bombay brought in larger and brighter lamps. These lamps, on loan from the larger, wealthier houses, were used for outdoor religious meetings. We named them 'wind lamps' because they were not easily blown out in the open air.

In the evenings when my father came home from work and my mother had put safely to bed the younger brother I now had, we would sit together around the kerosene lamp. Striking a match to light it, my father would greet the light and call on us to do the same. Only later did I realize that this happy custom remained from Zoroastrian times. Indeed, there was still a Zoroastrian presence in 2 of the 17 districts that made up the Taft region. Fire and light were held sacred in their tradition.

It was through Zoroastrian 'Parsees' that the commerce between the local Taft merchants and Bombay was brought about, stemming from the links they maintained with their fellow religionaries who had earlier emigrated to India.

Having kindled the lamp, with the deference due to the hallowedness of light, my father's next step was to have my elder brother Yahya take up the homework set for him as a pupil of Taft's primary school. I remember well how I watched him with admiring wonder as I pottered around with my proud parents looking on, indulging in their own sort of admiration. In summer we ate and slept on the flat roof, with glorious views of the night sky. The silver gleam of the moonlight drew out my soul in wonder. Then the tablecloth would be spread and, sitting cross-legged, we gathered round it. With these memories I could say with Wordsworth: 'Fair seed-time had my soul'.

After supper, whatever remained would be covered in a large basket, to keep it both cool and safe from the attentions of hungry cats. Now was the time for conversation. I recall my father's narratives about travel and its hazards, especially on remote desert roads, where sudden storms of wind might arise, whirlwinds soaring toward the heavens as if demon-possessed. If one were lost in such journeyings there were the perils of thirst and hunger, the menace of a lonely death. Knowing how to read the stars for directions was vital to survival – not to mention the urgent need to trust ever and always in Allah's mercy.

My father always likened God to light. One night I asked him what God was like. Looking up at the full moon he said: 'God is like that shining moon, but bigger, vastly bigger. Imagine the size of that basket over and over and over again.'

How hard it is to explain to a child of four what we mean by 'God'. I still feel that my father found the best way for, ever since, the words 'God is light and in him is no darkness at all (1 John 1:5), bring back what my Father said to me.

Despite her physical frailty my mother had given birth to four children in some five or six years of married life: Yahya, myself, Ashghar and a daughter, Tooba. The care of the home and the family, the work of the dispensary and the claims of sick women coming from the villages all around took a heavy toll. The day came when she was bedridden with a serious illness. I remember her in her bed on the verandah outside the room below the roof where we children slept. I remember my aunt's periodic visits to her bedside.

One summer night, fast asleep on the roof, I was awakened by the sound of moaning, weeping and wailing. When I saw my father awake, his face drawn with anxiety, I asked to be allowed to go down. He told me to stay in bed. In the morning when I left the roof I saw that my mother's bed had gone and she too – no trace of her, only a heavy, brooding silence filling the air.

The graveyard of our parish was just a piece of desert ground on a mountain slope, at no great distance from our house. All I can remember is my aunt laying a black cloth over my mother's grave, weeping as she tried to console me. The loss of a mother is the most heart-rending experience that a child can undergo, even more so when no one else is there to take a mother's place and to give a mother's care.

Following her death the dispensary was closed. Our family income fell. The market for my father's skills had dwindled and we could hardly meet the costs of living. Our small family farm was sold, but what we accrued from the sale did not suffice to relieve our situation – it declined from bad to worse. Little two-year-old Tooba died six months after my mother's passing. Yahya had to quit school and find a job.

As for me, now just five years old, I used to go to the smithy my uncle ran. His workshop was situated at the crossroads linking Yazd to Taft and Dehbala, a summer resort on the slopes of Shir Kuh. On the way, I passed through dusty lanes with my beloved pomegranates in gardens alongside, their bright green foliage draping over the mud walls. On one occasion as I walked this route I saw a large black snake crossing the road in front of me. The terror that gripped me then stays with me still. I guess the snake had gone down into the 'Pakaneh'[9] to satisfy its thirst and was slithering back to the house opposite.

In my uncle's smithy there were two bellows, one large, the other small. The latter was used for smaller products such as horseshoes and nails. This was the one that my uncle thought was suited to my muscle power. The larger bellows were required for heavier things such as axes, hammers and spades, all beyond my range. The processes used for the larger products of the smithy were fascinating to watch. The youths who worked at them were mostly my cousins. They took their heavy hammers into a pit where the master smith using large tongs removed the piece of molten iron out of the forge-fire, and held it firmly on the anvil while the men hammered it with rhythmic blows into the shape the smith wanted as he manoeuvred it around under their hammers. The tools thus created were then immersed in cold water. I watched with a childish awe the rippling muscles of the men as they toiled, their strong and steady beating of the iron, and the deft skill of my uncle turning the glowing red iron this way and that on the anvil, as sweat poured down their chests and brows.

From time to time my father's father joined us for meals, sharing our familiar diet of soup that cooked slowly from early morning in a ceramic pot hung over the fire, bringing lamb, peas and onions to an appetizing perfection. Grandfather, well on in years, had a grey beard and a bent stoop, marking the twilight of his days. His habit was to go round his sons' work-shops and their garden-plots and to talk as they toiled. His wife, Khayr al-Nisa, 'the best of women' was a kindly soul, and we called her Naneh Khaynesa. I often called on her as they lived in the next house to ours. One winter's day, with snow covering the ground, I went into her kitchen and another vivid memory was added to my store. For as she took the lid off a large pot of cooking turnips, I was greeted with a waft of hot steam on my cheeks. From that cold morning turnips have always been welcome fare, savoured like fresh cheese.

The first day of Aban[10] – known in Taft as Aboomah – was the traditional day for picking pomegranates. One uncle had quite a sizeable orchard of them. On that day whole families, women and men, old and young, would go there with noisy jollity to pick the year's yield. The cone-shaped wooden containers in which they gathered them either went back home with them for winter consumption or to the market for sale. When I was still tiny my memory tells me how eager I was to be among them at this work, especially when every now and then somebody would say: 'What a charming, cute little fellow Hassan is!'[11] My uncle thought I would be better employed watching over a donkey he had tied to a tree well away from the crowd. I remember thinking, as I gazed at the joyful busy throng, what the point could be of watching a donkey that was tied to a tree.

It was this same uncle who used to ask me, now and then, to collect pomegranate skins in bags, with other youngsters. These skins were used to produce a special form of red paint which sold well in the market. His orders were that we had to keep at it until the rays of the setting sun disappeared from the wall opposite. Only then were we to leave. I still remember keeping a steady, wistful eye on the wall, impatient for the sun to go.

In those days the deserts around Taft were dubbed 'fields', for, especially in spring, grasses, wild flowers and even bushes would cover the pebbly ground, providing enough verdure for sheep to graze. From time to time my uncle entrusted me with a few sheep to lead there to graze. As we drifted back homewards, bigger boys used to shake the branches of the trees overhanging the garden walls for the lambs to nibble the falling leaves.

What held Taft society together was religion. Its observances, its rituals and its traditions were the binding factor in our village life. There was the central Hussainieh[12] known as 'Shah Vali', with its historic mosque, but each parish had one or two of these Hussainiehs for itself; and each mosque possessed an Imam of its own discharging the mosque duties that fell to him. Additionally there were other religious leaders known as Akhunds who went from minbar to minbar (mosque pulpits) by invitation, as reciters of the stories of Ahl al-Bait[13] and, most poignant of all, the epic of the martyrdom of Imam Hussain at Karbala. The grandson of the Prophet through his daughter Fatemeh, wife of Ali, Muhammad's cousin and son-in-law, he had been killed by Ummayyad soldiers from Damascus. The memory of the tragedy entered far into the making of Shi'ah Islam. Karbala is commemorated on the tenth day of Muharram. A large wooden structure called a nakhl is hung with ornaments recalling the incidents in the martyrdom, and carried by volunteers in their hundreds, passing it from shoulder to shoulder as they make circuits round the Hussainieh in mourning.

At preaching meetings in Taft, folk would gather to listen to the mullahs, either in the mosque or – frequently – in homes where each and all were welcomed. All sorts, rich and poor alike, would sit together as a family. The 'hosts' on these occasions would freely offer tea at their own expense, either before or even during the preaching. Women would sit apart in a women's area. On these occasions, usually before the meeting, men would take to the roof of the mosque, or a roof nearby, and in a loud, chanting voice recite prayers and religious poems. Like church bells in a Christian setting, these roof recitals informed the faithful of worship calling them.

I recollect one evening before a preaching session in the Hussainieh of our parish. My father took me up on to the roof and, with great pride, I watched him joining in the chanting with the rest. Though he could neither read nor write, he was very intelligent with a truly retentive memory. He knew many poems, both sacred and secular, by heart. So well could he participate in recitals that he acquired the name of Muhammad-i-Akhund among the parish folk.

Pilgrimage (Hajj) was another feature of religious life – the deep desire to achieve it was at the heart of personal piety. Provided they had the wherewithal for the distances and costs involved, people would go either to Qum or Mashhad, further to Karbala and Najaf in Iraq, or even to Mecca itself. My uncle often talked about his pilgrimage to Mashhad. He would also visit Qum once or twice a year to do his duty as required by the Imam to whom he was devoted, having with him the small bag in which he had saved coins for an offering. Cousins of ours who had become relatively rich by working in Bombay all made the Hajj to Mecca. Once my paternal grandmother showed me a bagful of silver coins she had saved in order to travel to Mashhad to honour Imam Reza[14] at his tomb there – an intention she was never able to fulfil, though it had been her life's desire.

My first opportunity to take part in the Muharram Passion Play for Imam Hussain came in the very year of my mother's death. It was decided that I should act the part of the small daughter of the Imam Hussain, her name also being Sekineh. The play re-enacted the drama of Hussain and all his retinue being surrounded by the hostile forces that cut off all water supplied to them so that they were tormented by thirst. I cannot be sure whether it was a camel or a horse, but I was placed on its side in a box or pannier called a paleki, balanced by another child on the other side of the animal. Our part in the play was to moan and plead for water. For me there was no need to act in pretence. I was thirsty anyway and terrified too – even more so when another actor responded to my cries by bringing a cup of water to my lips only to withdraw it and mock me with futile hope. Still to this day I remember the misery I knew then. I wept not only from thirst but also because of the awful sounds around me. Tears poured down my cheeks until finally a strong hand lifted me out of the paleki and put me down under a nearby pulpit. In that partial shelter I quietened down until my father came to carry me home in his arms and my ordeal ended.

Separation

I now come to the bitter story of my separation from home and family and, in due course, Taft itself. It seems clear to me that my mother, before her death, had asked her missionary friend, Miss Kingdon, to ensure that, as far as possible, I received a Christian education. Miss Kingdon's idea was that I should start my schooling in Yazd where the Mission had opened a school. It was supremely difficult for my father to allow his son, or any one of his children, to be educated in a non-Muslim way, but Miss Kingdon had a strong mind and resolution. Thus an impasse developed between my father's opposition and her determined loyalty to my mother. Since she was not minded to concede defeat and he was firm in his sense of the right, a struggle continued between them well into my sixth year. Finally my father decided to consult the Qur'an as a way of settling the issue. This was a common custom in those days in Taft. He went to one of the mullahs whom he knew and set the matter before him, asking for a guidance that would settle what he could not otherwise resolve. The result of the mullah's Qur'an 'consultation' was good. Somehow his 'reading' of the text was taken to be positive.[15] Thus reassured, my father agreed for me to go to Yazd for schooling under Miss Kingdon's responsibility.

The 20 miles between Taft and Yazd seemed such a daunting distance to a six-year-old. I was of slight physique and had by no means a stout constitution. I remember how my father and I departed from Taft after midnight to avoid the heat of the day. At times I walked beside him; at others he would carry me on his shoulders. No roads for cars stretched between Taft and Yazd then. Travel was – if not on foot – only by mule, donkey or horse (camels were mostly used for loads).

There were glittering stars that eventful night, and I was awe-struck by the wide, dark wilderness, but the most vivid of my recollections of that journey is the meal I shared with my father. It could have been in mid-morning or at noon – I cannot recall – but we reached a small, mud-built, dome-shaped structure called an 'Owe Anbarok', a water-tank. Seated on the stones, my father spread on the ground a small tablecloth, on which he laid some bread. Tired by the long trek and alert to the light of the day beyond the hours of darkness, there, eating with my father, my boyish heart was both entranced and apprehensive with things unknown ahead.

Another incident, some time later, when I was in Yazd, comes back to haunt me. I was lost in what seemed a maze of dusty streets under the hot sun. It was one day when my father had taken me to visit hospital folk who knew my mother. As he walked ahead of me I was dreamily following when, at a crossroads, I lost sight of where he had gone. Heavy with anxieties I could not stay still. I trudged around trying to find out where he was, until mercifully I was located by a hospital worker who took me to him.

It had been arranged by Miss Kingdon that I was to board and lodge with a young Persian family employed at the hospital. At last, the hated day of separation came. My father was to return to Taft and I was to be with strangers, I was to start at a strange school, away from home, friends and all my familiar world. It was a hard experience to endure at such a tender age. The sense of this parting in some measure has remained with me to this day, for it represents for me what has more recently come to be called an 'identity crisis' – a situation where what one undergoes raises within one's innermost soul the question: who in the world am I? A certain forfeiture of the past has indeed occurred, and yet that past, being inalienable, abides inside the new identity that, nervously and subtly, is being acquired. It entails much pain, not to say time and patience, before a restful union of old and new, original and acquired, is finally reached and the travail of genuine integration is fulfilled. Doubtless, at that painful moment, I could never have expressed the meaning of what I was passing through. The ache and boyish bewilderment of the moment were enough. How it eventually all became part of me is precisely why I can now be writing in my eightieth year about 'the design of my world'.

The recently married couple in whose home I was to lodge were Habibollah Khan and Habibeh Khanum. They were Isfahanis who had come to Yazd to work in the hospital. As newly-weds they were, of course, much pre-occupied with themselves and, with their own baby on the way, could not spare much attention for their little village boy protégé. I was only left to travel back and forth to school alone, but one day Habibollah, realizing my loneliness from my sorrowful demeanour, mounted me on the crossbar of his bicycle and took me out to the edge of the desert where I could feast my eyes on the road to Taft.

Even the passing years have not clouded that glimpse across the sandy miles with the warm heat of the sun shimmering in the haze. The sandhills seemed wreathed in gold as I drank in the scene one special day that held for me all that belonged to my heart's affections. Habibeh Khanum was also kind to me. One special day she took me to a celebration – I cannot recall whether it was for the birthday of the twelfth Imam or the coronation of Reza Shah – where there were street festivities and illuminations. Lest I should get parted from her in the excited crowds, she told me to cling fast to her chador. I was so bent on doing this, in my fear of being lost, that I hardly noticed the festivities.

The Church Missionary Society had recently started a girls' school at Yazd for both Muslim and Zoroastrian pupils. The Principal was Armenouhi (Nouhi) Aidin, sister to the Principal of another school in Isfahan. Between them they pioneered Izad Payman in Yazd and Behesht Ayin in Isfahan, both destined to become leading educational establishments for girls in the whole south of Iran.

Armenouhi took direct and devoted care of newly arrived children. I remember her holding wooden slabs with separate letters of the Persian alphabet on them as we mouthed the sound. Her accent was slightly foreign, her father being Armenian and her mother Irish. Ezzat Khanum, from Najaf Abad, a small town near Isfahan, told us stories from the Old Testament. They fascinated me, especially that of Joseph and his brothers, though I remember the bitter tears I shed when we came to his 'sale' to the Midianites and his grim exile into Egypt. How comfortless I felt!

Alongside learning the alphabet, hearing Bible stories and reciting verses (from the Psalms especially), we also did sewing during most of the afternoons. I was a glutton for paper and wherever I spotted a piece I would garner it into my store as something for my pencil to cover by and by. What joy it was at the end of the first year to receive – as my very own – a card bearing a picture from those stories. It was also a sort of 'graduation' to Isfahan, for the girls' school at Yazd did not admit boys over seven – the noble age I had then reached. Meanwhile I returned to Taft with my beloved father to await whatever Isfahan might hold for me.

CHAPTER 2

Isfahan

Be I thorn or flower,
I am the Gardener's handiwork.   Hafiz

Fair seed-time had my soul, and I grew up . . .
Much favoured in my birthplace and, no less,
In that beloved Vale to which ere long
We were transplanted . . .   William Wordsworth[1]

In Isfahan I was destined for what was then known as 'the
Colleges' Branch School', where I was to be a boarder. Miss
Kingdon bore the cost of the fees. The Church Missionary
Society had begun educational enterprise in the city as early
as 1869. The 'Branch School' was a primary school attached
to the Stuart Memorial College in Isfahan, which later had the
name of Adab College. The hostel where I would stay was
located near the church. For the most part the richer families
sent their children as day pupils, while the boarding section
cared for children of poorer families unable to meet the fees.
As boarders these children were more involved in the school
life.

So one night at the beginning of the year my father and I
set out from Taft to Yazd by donkey, among numerous other
wayfarers astride horses and mules. Iran and its cities are celebrated for the sheer beauty of their starlit nights. This one was
no exception and is still vivid in my memory, both for the
brilliance of the majesty and also – as at my first school venture
– the company of my dear father sharing the tinkling bells of
the muleteers breaking the deep silence of the dark. In the
enchantment of the scene I found myself all of a sudden reciting

the words of the psalmist as I had learned them by heart in
that first year at Yazd.

> O Lord, our Lord. How majestic is your Name in all the
>   earth
> You have set your glory above the heavens . . .
> When I consider your heavens,
> The work of your fingers
> The moon and the stars, which you have ordained,
> What is man that you prize him so highly,
> The son of man that you should care for him!
>
> Psalm 8:1, 3, 4

My father enquired where I had learned the words – he was
very fond of poetry. With a childish pride I told him: 'At Miss
Aidin's School in Yazd.'

Once again saying a sad farewell to my father, my onward
journey from Yazd to Isfahan was by a truck owned by some
Zoroastrian merchants with whom Miss Kingdon had friendly
contact. My truck journey had to be made on the top of a
20-litre water-container, since the seats were taken by the
driver, his friend and two other passengers. Imagine me, a tiny
figure, perched on a moving throne!

Approaching Isfahan we had first to cross the Shahristan
bridge, then several miles westward came the famous bridge,
Si-o-se-pol, and beyond it the celebrated Chahar Bagh Avenue.
It was evening when we crossed the bridge. How wondrous
and amazing it was for me to see the famed city for the first
time, the bridge bright with electric lights on either side – all
unknown in Yazd at that time. The driver set me down at the
house of Dr Schaffter, then the Head of the Isfahan CMS
hospital, from where I was sent on to the College Branch
School close by.

The Head of the school was called Jalil Qazzaq Irvani. The
name denoted that he was of Cossack birth from Irevan. His
father, Khalil, had emigrated to Iran and found favour with
the then Shah, Nasir-al-Din. Quitting Tehran, he had come to

Isfahan and been recruited to the army of Zil-i-Sultan with the rank of Lieutenant General. After his father's death, Jalil had found his way to the mission hospital as a lung patient and there he also found his way to faith in Christ after much search and enquiry. He had been baptized in 1922.

Jalil, with his Sunni Muslim antecedents, his wide knowledge of Persian, his ability with Arabic grammar and his speaking knowledge of French, English and Turkish, was a most accomplished teacher. He was also a superb calligrapher. A poetry lover and reciter, he also wrote verses of his own. Music also was among his skills. He played Persian instruments such as the Tar. He had married a talented girl named Shokat who had also become a Christian and they had three sons – Ibrahim, Khalil and Ismail. He had proved an ideal candidate to head the College Branch School from the outset, with his wife to share responsibility for the boarding part of the task.

Needless to say, his personality played a large part in the growth of my mind. He was a straightforward man, explicit in speech and act yet ready for sentiment and feeling. He had no truck with hypocrisy, arrogance or flattery. He could be openly critical of missionaries and alert to the danger they were in from obsequious people around them. There was no question about his firm commitment to Christ. His faith was strong and his heart warm. Responding to my homesickness and my frail appearance, he developed a certain fatherly affection for me.

I was glad that there was Persian calligraphy, as well as poetry, recitation and Bible study in the school curriculum. In love with all of these, I made steady progress in them. Jalil began to look on me as one of his successes, even comparing his eldest son unfavourably to me, so that I was in danger of indulging in self-conceit. What checked this, however, was the nervous attitude he sometimes had which made him capable of irrational punishment, which I found hard to take. I began to lose my confidence in him and to temper my good impressions of him with adverse feelings. These led me to something of an inferiority complex – that I had an inability to discern the right and wrong in relationships.

There was one feature of him that I believe was formative for me. He was, perhaps consciously, far better endowed by his prowess in all things Persian – language, literature, poetry, music and writing – than the local church people. Also his Christian faith was deep and articulate in ways that made him exceptional. All this served to make me realize how a strong and intelligent Christianity could truly belong in and with an authentic Persian culture, in a union where both faith and identity could be fully and genuinely inter-active. He taught things Biblical and Christian in a thoroughly Persian idiom. The example made an abiding, tremendous impression on me.

Another person who influenced me was a visitor to the school, Miss Vera Eardley, who had come to Iran in her youth to serve the Church. With gifts of music and a love of poetry, she had learned Persian well and served the faith of Christ in Iran for 40 years. She faced retirement back to England almost like an exile, so loathe was she to leave. She, too, helped to inspire in me a Persian Christianity, one in which I might validly be both Christian *and* Persian.

Fridays and Sundays were the free days in the school week. After Sunday morning worship in church, Sunday school followed which Vera Eardley led. Our motto, 'You are the light of the world' (Matthew 5:14), was in beautiful script on a blue curtain with a star above the words. Here we sang hymns (Vera Eardley playing the organ) and studied passages. During the holidays she ran what was called a 'Joy Centre' for children of all races and faiths which lasted 10 days, with up to 80 or so children attending. Another of her many skills was in the organization of 'Wolf Cubs', or in Persian, 'Lion Cubs'. We wore the 'official' uniform of grey cloth and a grey scarf with considerable pride after we had duly passed the tests and made the grade. This dignity did much for my childhood development!

There were promises to learn by heart and pledges of membership – unselfishness, troth-keeping, swimming up to 50 metres, tying knots, skipping 50 times perfectly, first aid, fire extinguishing, and the like. Familiar enough to many readers, these disciplines stood me in good stead through the years and childhood was the finest time to learn them. Today, in old age, I still maintain skipping to help me keep fit!

I have already mentioned my keen love of poetry. My earliest effort, I think around the age of 11, was a rhyme that ran: 'When still a very small child my mother died.' Later I compiled a book in which I gathered various items of poetry and on which I bestowed the name *Songs of Nightingales*, the second part being from my own ventures into poetry. 'Yazdi' was the pen-name I gave myself. One line ran: 'My pen-name Yazdi: my age seven twice,/Hassan, son of Muhammad, in Taft resides.'

When she became aware of this bent of mine, Miss Eardley encouraged me, urging me to compose hymns for the young that could be sung in church. She would then write the tunes for them. (Many years later I translated a number of famous hymns into Persian. She was very helpful in finding Persian rhythms that could accommodate the English music; when the words would not tally with the customary tune she would compose one herself. She would never allow an English tune to ruin the rhythm of a Persian line. I have run ahead of my chronology by this diversion into cross-cultural poetry and music. Suffice it to say – before I return to my schooldays – that thanks to this partnership the Persian Church has been truly enriched.)

Years later my first published poetry was entitled *The Divine Suffering*. It was dedicated to her when the last of her services to the Church in Iran, prior to departure to her English 'exile', was to provide a hymnbook with music. The first we had, it is still in constant use.

Summer Holidays

The summer holidays from school, except for one year when I remained in Isfahan, usually found me back home in Taft to spend two months with my family. My father had married again some four years after my mother's death. All the daughters of his second marriage died but three sons, my step-brothers, survived. The usual means of holiday travel was by bus. These old vehicles were adapted from old cargo trucks and had no seats. While I was still young my father would come to Yazd and take me to Taft. Since Yazd had no hotels or inns at that time, we used to stay overnight in caravanserai, wayside lodging for travellers.

On some days I would spend my time in my father's work-place; on others I would help my stepmother or make mud bricks for house-building. At other times I would go with a neighbour's sons to explore the Qanats, walking down into the cool water; or we bathed in the Tanooreh – so pleasant to jump into during the hot season, but dangerous too, lest – touching the bottom – one's foot be sucked into the aperture. Releasing it was hazardous. I would also watch bread-making at my aunt's house, relishing the smell and savouring the crusty taste.

My father's workshop, which had been inside our home, had been moved into a communal type of workshop by our local mosque and later to Shah Vali, the central square in Taft. Here, between the ages of 10 and 14, I chatted with all and sundry. I had acquired something of an Isfahani accent – this intrigued the craftsmen and gave me to feel they enjoyed talking to me. One of these men who had little educational opportunity was nevertheless keen on poetry and had taken to composing in the style of Hafiz, with 'Mahzoon' ('Sorrowful') as his pen-name. Occasionally he recited his verses to us.

When not going to my father's place of work, I would take myself off to the orchards of my uncle and my cousins to help with their produce. An aunt of mine (Beman) taught the Qur'an in her house. At my father's suggestion I joined her classes and was soon able to recite the last three chapters to her satisfaction. However, thanks to my leisurely approach I never matched my brother Yahya who could recite the entire Qur'an excellently. He was deeply religious and had the habit – as I understood it – of reading the whole of the Qur'an every week.

As for my own pattern of religious thought and life at 14, it seems to me now to have been like a pendulum. At the outset

of the holidays, the first week or so, I considered myself to be
a Christian and talked about faith and its meanings with my
father, with Yahya and indeed with all my relatives. They
would tell me I was still a child but, 'by and by as you grow
older Allah will enlighten you to a better mind'. Father and
Yahya especially were watching over me and were sincerely
concerned lest I should stray. They took me to the mosque
and taught me how to follow the prayer rite. Yahya was convinced that the mullah at Shah Vali mosque could satisfy all
my queries. I do not recall his name but after each time of
Salat[2] he held a circle of teaching and responding to questions.
I remember – I must have been 12 or 13 at the time – a session
he once had with me when he responded courteously and did
not browbeat me, a mere boy.

It was some years later when Taftis held a religious pro-
cession in the town square, incorporating a 'Shabeeh' (religious
drama). Actors from Ardekan were taking part and doing very
well. On such occasions I would go and watch with my cousins.
In the 'Shabeeh' or Ta'zieh drama, which is about the martyrdom of Imam Hussain, there are various 'characters' including
the arch enemies Yazid and Shimr, but notably a 'farangi' or
European who was reputed to have embraced Islam after witnessing the tragic spectacle. At one Shabeeh much later I was
deeply shocked when it was suggested that I might play this
'foreign' part and take the role of the converted 'farangi'. It
pained me greatly in my deep pride of being Persian that having
a Christian identity made me 'foreign' in their eyes. Even then
I had come to feel a deep authentic kinship between a faith
anywhere at home and everywhere its 'native' truth, though I
did not yet know the famous words of the *Epistle to Diognetus*
in the second century A D: 'For them, any foreign country is a
motherland, and any motherland is a foreign country.'[3]

Other memories from my teenage years concern Qanats,
those underground water canals for which Persia was famous.
They were vital for irrigation in Taft. Each district had its
reservoir fed by the Qanat; each farmer had 'shares' in the
supply and could irrigate his land accordingly. Strict regu-

lations governed water usage. Unfortunately the pools were ideal breeding grounds for malarial mosquitoes, and we children swimming in them were exposed to the disease. One year when I became badly ill with a fever my father took me to our local doctor, Shaikh Muhammad Hussain, who was also a respected mullah. After greeting us he prescribed some herbal drugs for my recovery. When this same mullah preached in the mosque my father would take me to listen. At the time – as I remember – there were religious protests in Mashhad against Reza Shah and his 'Europeanizing' measures in the country. Soldiers fired on the crowd and there were many deaths. In his mosque sermon Shaikh Muhammad Hussain compared the slaughter to the massacres of Karbala, so appalled was he.

I have another grim memory in which he figured. With some other lads, playing near a stream, we suddenly saw a body floating in the water. When the shaikh arrived on the scene, clad in his white robes with a stethoscope hanging round his neck, we watched him examine the body with sombre dignity. Then he stood up and announced in solemn tones: 'Still just alive but not for long.'

He left, leaving us lads glued to the sight as we watched the last hint of life ebbing fast away.

Reza Shah ordered that women go unveiled, and commanded the police throughout his realm, both in town and village, to tear off the chadors from women who persisted in wearing them. One day I was walking along a lane near home wearing a khaki shirt and shorts. At the junction where I turned I noticed a woman washing clothes in a stream some distance away. The moment she saw me she hastily grabbed her washbasin full of clothes and ran for her life. She had mistaken me for a policeman on the way to pull off her chador – even though she was one of my cousins!

Another time, wearing shorts in the central square of Taft, I was stopped by a man asking me why I was wearing them. My reply that I was a boy scout and we dressed that way, left him disgruntled, aghast at my bare legs!

As I became older my father no longer came to Yazd to accompany me back to Taft. Instead I used to take a ticket for Taft from 'Trusty Garage'. How often it belied its name! It was anything but trustworthy – timed for 2 p.m. we usually left around 6 p.m., whims and passengers finally set to go. On another occasion the driver stopped half an hour from Taft on the edge of the road, unloaded my case, told me to get out and drove away to another village. It was pitch dark on the edge of the desert and there was only a tiny tea-house at the spot. Frightened and totally lost I was finally rescued by a youth who shouldered my heavy case and told me to follow him. After an hour's trudging, to my immense relief, we reached home. I have never seen that hero since, but have always been inspired by the memory of what he did.

Wealthy Yazdi families often had houses in resorts high up the cool slopes of Shir Kuh to escape the summer heat. Dehbala was one of these resorts where the Mission purchased a large house for summer refuge, sometimes taking very sick patients with them who were unable to go home. Sanij was a cheaper, more primitive and less popular summer haven. My father used to go to Sanij, sitting to work under some shady walnut tree. I found the place very endearing, with its untarnished beauty and vistas of distant mountains, the trees in foliage and the clear running streams – all spread beneath an azure summer heaven. Walking, reading, musing in this bliss, a poem or hymn was never far away.

At the end of my ninth form, the College proposed an essay competition on the topic 'The Prevention of Cruelty to Animals'. I began writing on the hilly slopes at Sanij, using the device of a conference of animals ruminating over their relations with humans. I won the competition only because there had been no other entry!

Three cousins, grown rich by trading in Bombay, had summer homes in Dehbala. One year, going with them from Taft, I had an overwhelming experience of the mystery of the dawn. A donkey that might have come from my essay bore our baggage and we walked some 20 miles through the night made eerily wonderful by the dark defiles through which we threaded our way under the stars. Dawn announced itself as the sun peered above the rim of the hills and slowly shed its beams across the landscape as we gazed; intensifying as the minutes passed, its wondrous fascination penetrated the inner recesses of the heart.

There was a year when I went with shepherds who grazed their sheep on the sparse grass between the stony ranges. I rejoiced in their simple fare, their ready talk and their characteristic vision of the world. These ventures served also to steel my somewhat suspect physique and, indeed, I exchanged that first reputation of 'frailty' for one of wiriness and strength. I could turn the tables on friends who thought me 'delicate' with the lines of an anonymous poet.

> Do not under-estimate this weak frame of mine.
> Its fleshy sinews oft in trials have been
> Yet never snapping.

Throughout my upbringing in Isfahan the teaching of Christian faith and the study of the Bible were of central importance. There was a strong emphasis on evangelism. I remember one occasion in Dehbala when Miss Kingdon took me aside and opened her Persian Bible to engage me in its sacred text. She made comments on her reading from the Gospels but at some of my questions gave me a look as if to say I should listen receptively. There was no mistaking the zeal with which she cared for my heart.

In addition to the weekly worship in Isfahan there were a variety of evangelistic meetings to which Muslims were invited, held both in the hospital and in homes. The Episcopal and the Presbyterian missions both published books and pamphlets commending the Christian faith. I absorbed much of this pre-occupation with faith-witness, and even in games liked to assume the role of the evangelist, standing on a stool and pretending to preach this precious gospel. Back in Taft in the summer I would talk to everyone I met about Christ, yet still would go to the mosque with my brother and my father. After a few weeks of their influence and the mosque's, my 'evangelism' would falter and weaken, so that on my return to Isfahan for the new school year I felt a big swing back of the pendulum had to come. Then the urge to preach the Christian faith would gather its strength again.

When I was 12 years old my father decided to terminate my schooling in Isfahan. My zeal to witness and persuade others about Christ disconcerted him. The attitude of our other relatives also affected him deeply. I was sent to a Maktab (religious class) led by a mullah in Taft. The man in charge sat with a long stick in his hand in the centre of a circle of pupils of different ages and levels of progress, sitting cross-legged. Little learning passed between him and us and I was repelled at the punishment meted out on a boy who had misbehaved. His face was painted red and black and, garbed with a miscreant's cloak, he was made to sit on a donkey facing backwards. The donkey was then taken the whole way round the central square with its surrounding shops to be the cynosure of public gaze.

I was petrified and appalled. I counted out the hours of the day longing for it to end so that I could escape from the ordeal. After that I was sent to a modern primary school that had recently opened in Taft, called 'Pahlavi School', together with some other local lads. I had only been there a week when letters came from Miss Kingdon and others to my father and me urging me to come back to Isfahan. There was one especially from my beloved teacher, Jalil, in his exquisite calligraphy.

What could so young a boy do in such a quandary? The letters tugged at my heart, but my father was adamant. There was also the appeal of being among those I loved at home and accepting their 'rights' in me. Father stressed my need to be under his authority in the matter, at least till I was 15. He feared the social reproach if he weakened and let Isfahan prevail. Also might any defaulting of his Muslim duty be punished in the world to come? He insisted: 'I cannot let you grow up outside our own faith.'

Miss Kingdon, however, was also resolute in her sense of

her duty to my mother. Despite the negative replies to the letters from Isfahan she despatched two men from the church in Yazd – one of whom was a hospital worker – to try to convince my father. Among their arguments they stressed how English schooling had proved so attractive for other, often richer, families; they were ready to pay for it, whereas what the College in Isfahan offered his son was free. Prohibiting him from what it could offer for his future would be a father's failure of judgement and even of love.

His hesitation was real. For the issue was 'existential' both ways. He fell back on that *istikhara* by the Qur'an that had been his standpoint earlier. When, via the mullah, this yielded a positive result, the die was cast and I could return to Isfahan. It would prove to be my final farewell to my grandmother and my grandfather. I see him now, taking my small face in his two old hands and, kissing me, murmuring, 'Do not give up your religion.' If – at that time – I had any religion it was Christianity. I can say that I have kept his advice.

Stuart Memorial College

On my return to Isfahan, as the College Branch provided education for only four years, I went on to the Stuart Memorial College. It was a secondary school but also provided years five and six of primary education prior to its main function. I had barely registered when an order came from the Ministry of Education forbidding primary sections in foreign schools. Accordingly, the Stuart Memorial College closed its two primary years.

However, the Principal, William J. Thompson, later the Bishop in Iran, went to Tehran and discussed the matter with the authorities there. He was finally able to convince them to allow boys already registered, whom it would be harsh to exclude, to stay for those fifth- and sixth-year classes so that those registered could complete their studies. Gratitude for this reprieve from what might have been, had my Isfahan education miscarried, has remained with me ever since. With the closing down of the boarding section I was housed in Jalil's home and went each day to Stuart Memorial College. After two years, at the age of 13 I received my primary education certificate from the government.

The next two years were among the most agitated of my life. In the early teens, one is beset with adolescent anxieties and the stresses of maturing physically and socially. One needs a steady supply of nurture and nourishment, with regular diet, sleep and relaxation. I cannot say that I passed those years with any such serenity. I was not physically robust – malaria had played its part and I suffered a painful sunstroke under which I became delirious and heard people around me whispering about my being close to death. I had to contend with many confusing fantasies and in the midst of them came the death of Jalil's devoted wife. Poet as he was, he found her passing devastating, and my equilibrium also went to pieces.

I found it difficult to sleep, to dress or to eat properly. Some of my mentors, eager for my Christian activism and urging me to concentrate on Bible learning, verse recital and evangelism, seemed strangely oblivious to the physical and material needs of an adolescent boy. Only Vera Eardley, supplying malt and tonic to me, seemed at all alert to my condition. Such spasmodic acts of kindness did not suffice, and through most of my second year in Stuart Memorial College I was in and out of hospital and incapacitated most of the time.

Having missed the year's exams through sickness, I only got into the third year, the year when preparation for government exams began, by retakes after the summer break.

Things remained critical. Miss Kingdon had returned to England and the Revd Geoffrey Rogers had taken charge of St Luke's Church in Isfahan. With Vera Eardley he arranged for me to be tested for tuberculosis, as it was thought that my mother had died from this disease. Happily the tests proved negative. I went to live in the Rogers' home but in a room on a verandah separated from their family. I took early and late meals in their kitchen, and lunches in the women's kitchen of the hospital, to keep any 'Anglicizing' in proportion. I began teaching Taqi, a servant at the house, from Resht, to read and found much cheer from my success with him when he started perusing the daily paper. I made short work of my lunches in the kitchen, often intrigued by the – to me – hardly intelligible talk of the cook, a village woman named Khadijah. All this was because the College hostel for students proved too expensive. It housed about 60 students at that time.

I became a close friend of Manoochehr Mostashari, a fellow day-boy who took me on his bike to College every morning as he lived on the same route. With some difficulty he taught me how to cycle, but not the tennis and badminton at which he excelled. We developed a curious 'mutual aid society': he liked me to copy out his essays in what he considered my better writing and he then coloured the page with designs and secured better marks. We are still friends to this day.

Scouting at SMC brought the acquaintance of Khushhall Singh, a teacher-scoutmaster, who had recently come from India to teach English and geography. A handsome man and a moderate violinist, he spoke Persian with a marked Indian accent. One Christmas holiday he took around 18 of us on a 3-day walk around the Isfahani villages. We sang 'O my darling Clementine' and other songs en route trying hard to keep up with Mr Singh's pace. A heavy cloud hangs over that memory, for a boy named Amir Dehesh, who had a heart condition and should not have been exerting himself that much, became seriously ill and later died. His untimely death affected me deeply. We were walking during the Ramadan fast and, near the end of our journey, found everything closed when we wanted to buy food. We had nothing left but beetroot.

Another likeable scout-master was the raconteur Taqi Pad Bod who came upon me one day eating lunch in Khadijah's kitchen. He was aghast at my explanation for being there and poured scorn on the logic of keeping me close to my Persian roots lest I acquire 'farangi' expectations that Persian salaries could not meet.

My choice of subjects at secondary level was not science or commerce but literature – partly out of my innate love for literature but also because of my weakness in mathematics, a weakness I was intrigued to find I shared with Rabindranath Tagore! Again I fell ill at exam time but thanks to Geoffrey Rogers' ministrations – both moral and dietary – I was persuaded to sit them, feverish as I was, and came through successfully, much to his delight. This took me on, at 17, to year four. I was keenly Christian but not yet baptized. For this I had to wait till I was 18 and of legal age.

The urgent question was what I should be called. There were Muslim friends who would expect me to forego my name Hassan – so evidently Islamic – and take a Christian name. Enquiries at the Registry Office in Yazd made it clear that the law did not allow me to change my first name but that I could abandon the family name. This I had no desire to do, for I loved my family dearly. So I proposed a second, Christian name – Barnabas, with its rich meaning of 'Son of comfort' from Acts 4:36.

Another aspect of baptism was much more exacting. How was I to inform my father and my brothers of my decision? After much prayer and meditation, I decided to write a letter to them, in which I stressed the freedom of religious faith and how the approach of my eighteenth birthday would end their responsibility for me in both Shari'ah and civil law. Assuring them that my faith was firm, I also let them know how dearly I loved them and how clearly I knew the keen edge of their hurt and sense of woundedness. But I added that Allah did not will that family emotions should constitute a prison to confine sincerity. One's true liberty ought not to be held in a prison of family bonds which, that way, would themselves be falsified. I asked them to respect my freedom and relinquish their sense of responsibility for me. Finally I asked them to read my mother's Bible, which was still in the house, in the hope that they would come to understand my decision better.

Three months after I wrote the letter I was baptized by Geoffrey Rogers in St Luke's Church. I felt very near to God with an overflowing love for all. The joy of that day abides with me still. Sadly, the reaction of my home folk was sad and bitter. When I went back to Taft that summer the atmosphere, so changed from before, was tense and hard. Father, my brothers and cousins, my uncles and aunts, all told me I had made a grave mistake and should repent of it. Old friends refused to talk to me. In the lanes and bazaars of Taft, acquaintances ignored or disdained me. I was like a non-person in their eyes. At home I was like one 'unclean', not allowed to eat with them from the same dish. Yahya especially adopted a strange procedure to mark my 'uncleanliness'. When prayer-time came he would bundle 'clean' garments under his arm and ostentatiously go and change into them lest any contact of mine with him or his other clothes had contaminated him. Despite all this our love for each other remained. I even tried to break through his odd strategy concerning 'unclean' and 'clean' attire. When he had changed for prayers, I would wet my finger and touch him. With a frown he would then go and change again to ensure his proper ritual state.

As for my Father, he talked little. It was as if he suffered in silence, perhaps more from what other people said than from my action. One thing he did say was that when my letter arrived he had a dream in which his right hand was severed from his body, which he took to mean that I was no longer one of them. These words, so hard for me to hear, I tried not to take to heart, nor let my love for them drain away. Relationships never broke down and the love between us continued to the end.

Father was a simple man. There was no fanaticism in his heart. In my deepest instincts I felt he was free in his thoughts, a man with an open mind and a large heart. Always alert for new ideas, he was well able to look for the reason in things.

Among friends in Taft there was a Bahai family, the Anvaris. The father, Mirza Agha Khan, changed his name to Massih when those honorific titles 'Mirza' 'Khan' and 'Agha' were prohibited by the government. A kindly and learned man, he managed the Taft Post Office and also ran a dispensary. The

Anvaris' home was a haven for me and we regaled ourselves with Mowlavi's poems. The family came under much pressure from the mullahs after Reza Shah's time and was dispersed. Years later I met the eldest son, Mehdi Agha, in Abadeh during the early days of the Khomeini Revolution, only to read in the newspapers in England a year later that he had been executed because of his Bahai faith. I wept for him and the memory of our days together in Taft.

After my baptism I had a very full heart for the things of faith and wanted to share my Christianity. Soon there were two opportunities to be open with my Christianity. One had to do with 'turning the other cheek', as Jesus directed in Matthew 5:39. Scouting at Stuart Memorial College suddenly took in virtually the whole school as Prince Muhammad Reza had become head of the Scout movement in Iran and had ordered its massive expansion. Boys who had not been scouts were suddenly involved in all its forms and drills with little or no knowledge. This led to an incident in which a boy who was a year older than I, who had been a scout for years, gave an order which I thought foolish. He grew angry and swore to hit me when the chance came – as it did the next day in class. As I was going out he came forward and slapped my face. I 'turned the other cheek'. He struck that also so I turned my face again, still not retaliating. He went to take a third blow, but stopped, informing me that he was not ceasing out of any shame in view of what I had said about Christ, but had simply left off. I went into the College chapel and sat quietly, wrote a few lines in my diary and prayed for my assailant.

On my way home, friends noted my red face. Inevitably the story got around and Pad Bod felt he had to enquire into it. He told me to relate it to the Principal, Mr Reginald Iliff, as a matter of discipline and 'justice' over an incident of disorder. 'How very hard it is to be a Christian', as Robert Browning wrote.[4] How do we square Christ's way and human 'rules'? I did not want a 'complaint' made, nor the sort of redress that the other fellow's punishment might afford. For several days Pad Bod persisted and finally I had to let it all out before the

Principal who praised my Christian attitude but also needed to take account of unruliness. He, via the College Council, required that the boy apologize, which he finally did. Later when he was ill in hospital I paid him a visit. We are friends to this day.

The other test for my Christian 'integrity' was at the end of the year, when I was passed a copy of some exam questions by a student. I had no knowledge of how he had obtained them. Troubled to keep them or take advantage of them, I handed them over to Pad Bod who was able to prepare an alternative paper. My fledging discipleship to Christ, stemming so mysteriously from my mother's faith, had surmounted the supreme family test and begun to find its way in the perplexing, yet ever exhilarating, world.

Games and Sports

Stuart Memorial College laid great emphasis on sports and offered many for us to pursue. In line with the familiar English tradition there were four 'houses' – blue, red, yellow and green – into which the school was divided, in order to stimulate competition. The Hostel boys were Green. The houses rivalled each other in football, athletics and swimming, all hopes set on the Victory Cup. We were subdivided into seniors, middlers and juniors, each group having its own football fields (the College had very extensive grounds).

Every morning before classes we had 15 minutes of physical exercise, and late afternoon after lessons the fields were alive with teams playing. The swimming gala took place in September at the close of the summer holidays, at Pul-i-Shahristan on the River Zayandah Rood outside Isfahan. One year when the river was too low for this event the civic authorities allowed it to be held in the historic Chehel Sotoon pool, which dates from the Safavid period. Later SMC acquired a pool of its own.

There was also the so-called 'paper chase' and cross-country running in which the three sections ran suitably graded dis-

tances – five, three or two miles – to Shahristan Bridge and
back, Khajoo Bridge, or an aqueduct that was nearer. A senior
from a rich family was once caught by a staff member hiring
a droshky (horse carriage) to give him a lift on his 'run', while
on another occasion a policeman thought boys running were
escaping thieves and arrested them, only to be given the full
explanation later! In late autumn and winter there were football matches between the houses, and a great annual match
for the first team against the American College in Tehran (later
Alborz College). This attracted city as well as rival College
'fans' who regaled each other with partisan songs. Once when
SMC won by a single goal the Isfahani chanted in the local
accent: 'With a goal Isfahan salutes the Capital. How come
your goalie could not catch a ball?'

The Christian Unions in the two homes of learning held joint
meetings in the week of the games. On one occasion dates got
confused. The Isfahanis came two weeks early to Tehran and
so had to return home. I decided to stay in Tehran pending
the event and attended classes while housed in the hostel. At
15, I was somewhat over-awed by the big city, especially when
I had a visit in my room from the famous Principal, Samuel
Jordan. A tall, white-bearded man, he invited me to tour Tehran with him in his car. Seeing Tehran by night for the first
time with its electric lights, heavy traffic and fascinating shops
was a memorable experience. As he chatted with his strong
American accent, I was too awe-struck to respond freely. Such
a gesture from the Principal, sensing the loneliness of a timid
teenager and taking time out of his busy duties to introduce
me to Iran's capital, stays with me as a very fond memory.
The imaginative love that kindles such small acts of sympathy
is surely a mark of true greatness.

As for our Principal, William Thompson, he was strict about
sartorial details. Prior to the government order requiring grey
uniforms in all schools nationwide, we at SMC used to wear
a blazer embroidered with a pocket badge, white shorts and
giveh – the traditional Persian cloth-shoes. Principal Thompson
demanded that shoes have their heel-uppers 'up' not folded

back, and that shirts were tucked into shorts or trousers, not flapping free. This was his idea of tidiness and he kept his eye open to enforce it.

Our College crest had four sections that depicted the Bible, the Cross, and the lion and the sun as national emblems of imperial Iran, together with the pelican from the arms of the Stuart family. The three words 'True, Clean, Thorough' were our motto. Once a week the four houses paraded through the city streets, headed by the College band, or – in its absence – by the Persian games master playing the Persian 'flute' or 'reed' so beloved of the Sufis. Once we showed a short film in a local cinema featuring 'the city of Isfahan and the College sports'.

Shakespeare's plays had pride of place in our extra-curricular activity. During a performance of *Macbeth* I had a crucial, if modest, off-stage role. As a boy scout, I had to ensure that a window on the second floor was kept shut to keep the winter cold out. The play was going well until I noticed two electric wires disconnected from each other. Imagining some mistake needing to be rectified, I carefully re-attached them. Suddenly the whole place was plunged into darkness. *Macbeth* is a dark play, to be sure, but does not call for such technical misdemeanours! Oil lamps were produced and out of the confusion – and my extreme fright – light was eventually restored. I had blown a fuse. By good fortune nobody enquired about the reason for the episode and I kept quiet so that the villainy never became known, until, years later, I told the story in a sermon about 'confession', where it happened that the Pastor listening to me had, years before, been one of the College teachers. He simply gave a knowing smile.

Visitors

We had intermittent visits from notable figures both Persian and foreign, among them Rabindranath Tagore, the celebrated Indian poet-philosopher and man of letters. We did a march-past in his honour, while he stood, an impressive figure with a long white beard flowing over his milk-coloured robe. One of our teachers, an old boy of the College, did a piece about Tagore in a magazine he was editing.

One Persian visitor was Ali Asghar Hekmat, the Minister of Education, who was also opening a secondary school near to us. He exhorted our class about passing the government exams. He too had the march-past honours. We had by then been re-named Adab ('culture' or 'self-control') College, so in addressing the College the Minister recited lines of Jalal al-Din Rami using that word:

> Let us implore God to help us to self-control.
> He who lacks self-control is deprived of the grace of the
>   Lord.

The Earl of Athlone, a British aristocrat, also came our way but did not gain a march-past. Much less prestigious but more significant in my recollection was a priest from England, Mr Wood, who was en route to India. He addressed us on the theme of Sparta and how the Spartans lived to make their city supreme. His peroration ran: 'You of Iran, make Iran glorious!' Perhaps his words move my pen now?

One speaker in assembly whom I still recall was a Mr L. Suratgar, who stressed the importance of 'specialness', of being an 'expert' in some field of study. Another was Jamal Zadeh, an Isfahani who had worked in Geneva and whose theme was culpable ignorance in high places. He drew on James Morier's Haji Baba stories about how Persia's ambassadors in Istanbul had been told to enquire: 'How many tribes are there in Frangi-stan? Are they nomads in tents or do they live in cities? Is England part of London, or is London part of England? What is the connection between England and the East India Company we have heard of? Is it composed of a group of old women or only one?'

I remember from my third secondary school year, one of the earliest Persian films called *Daughter of Lurs*, Lurs being a minor tribe in the south of Iran. It had been made in Bombay by a former student, Abdul Hossain Sepenta. He had been baptized and had even composed a popular hymn about Christian unity. However, travels in India had weakened his Christian faith. Back home one day he came to lecture to us in the College on the art of film-making – a topic we were all zealous to hear about. However, we juniors were barred. We pressured our English form-master, John Wedmore, so hard that finally he yielded and let us go. My chief recollection was of a warning about the danger to the eyes of glaring, flickering cinema lights.

The Effect of Dictatorship

My story takes a sinister turn with the rise of dictatorship. When education by missionary agencies began there was no government system of national education. A few philanthropists had opened modern schools on up-to-date lines, mostly based in Tehran and Tabriz. There were, of course, the traditional 'maktabs' based on the recital of the Qur'an and teaching one or two Persian classics like Sa'di's *Gulistan*. The missionary schools were left largely free to follow their own curricula.

However, with the advent of Reza Shah's national reforms in the early 1920s and the setting up of a Ministry of Education and Fine Arts in Tehran, these schools came under close supervision. Primary schools run by foreigners were closed, and all others were ordered to take Persian names (hence Adab College). The College had to forego its fourfold emblem. The Bible gave way to ethics, while English teaching had to be confined to English literature. All other subjects were taught in Persian; all final exams were to be conducted in Persian.

Inevitably education suffered. One whole afternoon each week was devoted to practising march-pasts for the commemorating day of Reza Shah's seizure of power in Tehran in 1921. Later, another half-day was set aside for practising for the celebrations of the birth of the Crown Prince, Muhammad Reza. A military climate was fostered by a weekly visit by an officer to teach army skills. He would come on a bicycle and accost us if he saw us at prayer or worship outdoors.

Little by little under these pressures the missionary educators grew disheartened and the future of their enterprise grew more dubious. Was it wise to persist under these hindrances? A minority felt that if the original intention in the schools could no longer be honourably achieved, it would be better to close them down. Those of this view thought it confirmed in 1939 when a government decree required all foreign schools to be sold to the State. To them the decree seemed like the will of God.

However, the majority – not least those most responsible for the school management – argued that they should not feebly hand over institutions established for so long and at such cost and sacrifice. In the event, William Thompson (now Bishop) and Dr Samuel Jordan of Alborz College went together to Tehran to negotiate with the authorities. The government agreed to defer implementation of the closure order from one week (as originally stated) to one year.

Several factors influenced the deep soul-searching at this time. Would resistance be wiser than capitulation? Reza Shah might change the order more permanently – if persuadable once, why not again? But the uncertainty, especially for Alborz College, was difficult as Samuel Jordan, near to retirement, had no heart for drawn-out negotiations; there were also those who felt that the schools ought not to resist forfeiture to the State when their true purposes were suppressed. In any event, the take-over by the State was completed within a year. Then in August 1941 the country was occupied by British, Russian and later, American, forces with a view to using Iran as a supply-route for military aid to Stalin, who was locked in battle with the Nazi power. Reza Shah went into exile and a new era began.

Why had he acted so strongly against the schools? One theory was that since there was Communist pressure on him to allow Russian school activity, to preclude that he opted to abolish all foreign education. Another view attributed it to Nazi influence. More probable was the fact that Ali Asghar Hekmat, American-educated, had been removed from office as Minister of Education and his successor, Ismail Mer'at was subject to the mullahs' influence. Reza Shah, impressed by old mission-run schools of high quality during a visit to Tabriz and Rezaieh (Uroomieh), quizzed Mer'at on why the State could not emulate them with its own schools. With Qum mullahs in mind the Minister claimed it could be done, whereupon Reza Shah ordered him to 'get on with it'. It was not an order he could fail to implement. So, sadly, a vital contribution to Iran and to the education of thousands of its men and women was liquidated in summary fashion.

Apart from the French and American school casualties, the CMS ones included SMC (Adab College); Behesht Ayin, a girls' secondary school in Isfahan; Mehr Ayin, likewise, in Shiraz; Izad Payman in Yazd, also for girls; Djam for boys and Itehadiyeh for girls in Kerman; Noor and Sadaqat in Tehran.[5]

These sad developments became part of my own story. It was difficult to experience the end of part of my education in such a harsh way. One could only reconcile oneself to it as being, somehow, within the will of God.

In that final year, since the hostel had been closed, a small group of us looked after ourselves in the College under the supervision of a Kurdish Christian, Salman Bastan, an old boy of Alborz employed by the Anglo-Iranian Oil Company in Isfahan. I left the Rogers' home and became responsible for the meteorological system the College had on the hostel roof, which sent weather reports to Poona twice a day. The payment for this financed my final year's board and lodging.

Despite the untoward occurrences and impending closure, that final year I count as one of my happiest. It was lightened with a number of amusing incidents. The literature class, being small, meant we developed close friendships. Shokrollah Bakhtiari (Shokool for short), whom I mentioned later, had a wry sense of humour telling stories of teachers and playing pranks on them. We had studied an old Persian classic named *Marzeban Nameh*. Shokool had noticed how the teacher had written the meaning of the difficult words in the margin of his book. Proposing one day to spare the class that teacher's lesson, Shokool hid the book. Frustrated in his urgent quest for it, the teacher was invited to use a pupil's copy but quickly suggested that we do essay-writing that hour. We all noticed Shokool's meaningful wink!

I was a prefect and one day putting up a schedule on the wall, the whole wall collapsed in front of me as I tried to push in the pin. It was merely a plaster covering hiding an unused door. The whole class was convulsed with laughter, Shokool loudest of all.

Our Arabic teacher was an ex-chaplain in the Forces who never swopped his religious garb for lay attire. Qazi Asgar used to arrive an hour ahead of time in his mullah's robes and grand turban. He taught from a book called *Majani-al-Adab*. A Bakhtiari boy called Farhad Ahmadi, irregular in his attendance, was asked the meaning of a word that occurred frequently in the book. Not knowing its meaning, Farhad replied, 'Sir, it is the name of the author of the book.'

There was loud laughter and embarrassment for the venerable teacher who set great store by decorum in class.

My habit of frankness got me into a bit of trouble too. Heads of government departments in Reza Shah's time were given to much ostentatious interference in small matters. The Head of the Department of Education had written a booklet on the historical buildings of Isfahan. He recommended it as something examinees should buy. So, as the prefect, I had to fix the conditions for application for the exam on the notice board of the class. The condition being name, identity card number, 6 photos etc., and I then added a note about buying a copy of the said book. The College administrator took me to task and told me to withdraw the extra detail. When I protested that the Minister had more or less told us to buy it, he parried, 'You weren't told to make a show of it!'

Is there not a case for being frank and direct and not engaging in double-speak or subterfuge? Even at the expense of incurring misunderstanding, I have always believed in being straightforward. I once had to write an essay on 'effort and endeavour in life'. I made reference to Reza Shah's rise from very humble beginnings to supreme power. The .teacher reproached me, saying I should have found some other example. Perhaps I was wilful, but why should not one 'call a spade a spade' and have done with mealy-mouthed evasions or suppressions of honesty? I am reminded of the Persian poet who wrote:

> Though truth-telling be precious as a pearl
> It will be bitter, bitter. For the truth is bitter.

I prefer forthrightness. Yet, as Hamlet said to his players, we must 'use all gently', and 'speak the truth in love'. I know myself too often to be too quick-tempered and pugnacious, and then the urge to be frank fails the test of courtesy and grace. As a school report once said, making the best of a bad case, 'He is still trying!' At this late stage of life friends sometimes tell me I have progressed a little!

I must end the good story of Stuart Memorial College. Let me begin its finale with the annual camp, mainly, but not exclusively, for hostel boys, that was usually held in the mountains of the province of Isfahan, at places like Natanz, Isferjan or Abianeh. We relaxed after exams, enjoyed games and long walks, with the opportunity also for spiritual nurture. Because of uncertainty over the future of the College, the last camp was not very full. It took us to nearby Felavarjan, a hot and dusty venue scarcely suitable. It was memorable for me, since it coincided with the good news of success in the exams. With my friend Ata Salmanpur, of the science section, who later became an Under-Secretary in the Ministry of Economics, I had tramped back to Isfahan to learn our fate. Rejoicing in our success we slept blissfully that night under the stars on the senior football field.

Those final exams saw the end of the life of the College. The students dispersed to their homes. The hostel too had its quietus. Just four English teachers remained to watch the handover to the State authorities. My meteorological duties required me to stay on with them, which was good for my English and the subtle business of handling knife, fork and spoon at table.

One of the teachers, Patrick Gaussen, played a large role in my youth. He had taught for 13 years, mainly physics but having charge of a small laboratory of his own devising. He was interested also in practical psychology. He taught us an hour a week on this in my penultimate year. His methods were splendid, well-prepared lessons clearly outlined on the blackboard and intelligently discussed. He familiarized me with the names of Freud, Adler and Jung, in whose theories I took deep interest. We came to share a precious friendship which endured until his death. I was to come upon him again in 1985 when my exile in England had begun.

And so, the Isfahan that had so far moulded me became, next to Taft, the nursery of my conversion and the focus of my heart's affection.

CHAPTER 3

Tehran

I am a stranger in the earth:
hide not Thy commandments
from me.

Psalm 119:19

How was I to move forward after my academic years in Isfahan? At that vital juncture I determined to find my aim in life
and take it up. Childhood, schooling in Yazd and Isfahan,
teenage life chez the Rogers, the church, the Mission, Stuart
Memorial College – all these were part of me but my reading
had been limited. School texts apart, I had only read simple
translations made by the two Mission bodies, CMS and the
American Presbyterian Mission in the capital. Influential as
these were they were relatively restricted, with titles such as
Joseph and his Brothers; *A Shepherd Boy* (about a lad who
spoke the truth and became the favourite of a lady in Switzer-
land); *Sadhu Sundar Singh* (an Indian Christian mystic);
Kagawa of Japan; *The Pilgrim's Progress*; *The History of the
Ancient Church in the Roman and Persian Empires*; *Sacrificial
Love: The Meaning of the Cross of Christ*; *Faith in God in
the 20th Century*; *Science and Religion*; *From Vagrancy to
Salvation*; and the like.

I also read New Testament commentaries inexpertly translated from English and above all the Scripture Union Bible
passages on which I often made my own notes. There were
also evangelistic evenings (with magic lantern) by an Armenian
evangelist with a curious Persian accent. I regularly went to
Sunday School. I was adept at singing hymns and listening to
sermons.

But as my capacity for English grew, new windows opened for me – such books as Harry Emerson Fosdick's trilogy *The Manhood of the Master*, *The Meaning of Prayer* and *The Meaning of Service*. I came upon Studdert-Kennedy's *The Unutterable Beauty* – poems of great power and pathos, also *A Merry Mountaineer*, the story of one of our young teachers, a tireless traveller through Persian villages, who died through typhus infection.

Through all these factors I came to realize in Jesus Christ the most holy, sublime and perfect personality ever to be in this human world. He revealed to me the holiness, wisdom and perfect love of God through his teaching, way of life, death and resurrection. To me he was the perfection of humanity and the meaning of divinity. My whole desire was to follow him. I was eager to be rid of evil thoughts, the unworthy habits of youth and unChristian ways and actions. I had a notebook in which to record my resolutions. They had come to number 77 by the time I reached my seventeenth birthday. I would confess privately to God every failure to fulfil them or occasion to break them, and would seek grace and strength to observe them faithfully. One day, deeply angry with myself at failure, I went, book in hand, to the riverbank to renew my covenant with God. The river was in high flood, right up to the top of the bank. I threw the book into the waters in the hope that my imperfections would be washed away and that I might continue in the way of holiness.

From time to time I was assailed by doubts about the existence of God and issues of faith, and a restlessness would possess me which sent me to people I thought could best help. Among them, Pat Gaussen was a most patient listener; he would give me honest and sincere answers. Passages such as the divine words to Jeremiah (1:4–8) kindled deep thoughts of destiny in me:

Before I formed you in the womb, I chose you and before you were born I consecrated you. I have appointed you a prophet to the nations. Ah! Lord God, I answered: 'I am not skilled in speaking. I am too young.' But the Lord said:

'Do not plead that you are too young. For you are to go to
the people to whom I mean to send you and to say to them
whatever I command you. Fear none of them. For I will be
with you to keep you safe.'

This subject of God's 'calling' was often stressed in sermons
and lessons, always as highly personal and not from far-off
Biblical days but here and now for us. The story of the call of
Samuel became a great favourite, with its urge to us, likewise,
to be attentive to the vocation God had for us. I often mused
on how the disciples heard the call of Jesus and 'rose and
followed' (Mark 1:16–19; Matthew 9:9).

The milieu in which I was living, the sense of these examples
rooted in my mind, together with long reflecting and steady
reading brought me to a certainty that I was called to serve
the Church in Iran. I discussed it with my friends and with the
Church leadership but the general opinion was that it was
premature to think of preparing for ordination and that it
would be wiser to pursue higher studies and widen my education. The Revd S. M. Rezavi, Pastor of our Church in Isfahan, encouraged me to go to the University of Tehran to study
at the Literature Faculty, as the finest thing for any potential
priest to do. He had a very high opinion of the lecturers there;
they were better than anywhere else in the world, he would
say.

His advice coincided with my own deep interests in Persian
literature and after much prayer and thought, I wrote to the
Diocesan Council saying that I believed I had God's call, that
I was willing to serve in any capacity they saw fit, and asked
whether, if they saw further study as my immediate duty, they
could lend me the necessary funds to go to Tehran University.
I would repay the loan if I was not accepted afterwards and
would be ready to serve in any event.

The Council was basically in favour but some members queried whether I might lose my faith in Tehran. They were won
over by the case others made – that risks are to be taken as
part of the maturing process that alone could make a ministry

vital. It was agreed that I should go and I was granted a loan of 360 rials (about £20) monthly.

University Life

And so my story moves to the University of Tehran. Accommodation was an immediate problem, happily resolved when the Revd Jolynoos Hakim, head of the Church's Mission to the Jews, offered me a room in a school he ran in the south of the city, to be shared with two other young men. I was not used to such sharing but did not have to suffer it long because Jolynoos, after just two months, offered me a room in a recently completed flat, close to Rue Amir Kabir (a street named after the reforming Prime Minister of the Qajar dynasty, later murdered by the Shah). My rent here took half of my allowance. I was advised to lay newspapers on the dusty floor to underlie my thin carpet.

I had never learned to cook nor did I have any equipment. Time spent on cooking seemed to me wasted, and I was resolved to live as simply as I could. So I arranged to pay the other half of my loan to another student's mother and the three of us ate together under her provision. This meant that I needed somehow to find funds to pay for everything else. I could translate articles for daily papers so a friend introduced me to the Editor-in-Chief of *Mehr-i-Iran*. I did a daily column for it – a translation from a book on psychology in a sequence that lasted a whole month. That friend proved to be false, for when I went to collect my fee I was told the first month was 'probationary' with no fees payable. He had himself pocketed what was due to me.

This deterred me from further contact with journalists and instead I had the idea that I might get some funds by teaching English. I placed a notice advertising my tuition in the window that faced on to the street. One day two students turned up; there was much mirth when I found out that it was Shokool, my mischievous classmate, who had sent them to discuss terms! He soon followed himself to tease me with queries about where

I would teach and where pupils would sit and the like. When I replied, 'Here in this room, on those boxes' – which had ferried my books from Isfahan – he chided, 'That will never do for a language school.'

I took the notice down. Later I did take on two expatriates, one American and the other English, whom I could teach Persian in their own homes – though the fare to reach one of them took up almost all my fee.

But these were means to ends. Of my own studies, the most important was 'The History of Persian Literature', under the renowned Professor Foroozan Far. He lectured a full two hours without notes. He knew names, dates, lines of poetry – Persian and Arabic – by heart. I attempted to take down everything he said but found the Arabic taxing. Apart from looking at one or two poets' lives, we did very little research (the library had few books anyway); he had scant idea of how to make students think. He would tell us, 'There is nothing "we" do not know of the first four Islamic centuries and nothing that "we" do know after them.' With his prodigious memory, he was kindly and gentle and showed a quiet sense of humour. Once I asked him what could be meant by 'drunken eyes' – a phrase occurring often in Persian mystical verse. He replied with a wink: 'Neither of us know!'

The other important subject was rhetoric, and the study of poetical styles and phrasings. Here the Professor was Bahar, national poet laureate, famous also in politics. He too dictated his lectures and we would take them down to learn by heart for exams – a very unsatisfactory procedure at university level. His love of poetry was infectious. He walked back and forth reciting it, seeming at times almost intoxicated with the music of the words as he ejaculated between whiles, 'Bah, Bah' – 'Wonderful, wonderful!' One line stays in my memory from a tenth-century poet from Balkh (Afghanistan), a line of great if simple beauty:

Have heard Paradise will come to whoever
Enables the fulfilment of another's yearnings

which seems like the other direction of Jalal al-Din's plea in
'The Song of the Reed':

> O for a friend to know the sign
> And mingle all his soul with mine!

There was no written exam for Bahar. Instead he would sit
like a stately grandfather, his hubble-bubble aglow, and listen
carefully as his students, arrayed in front of him, recited ver-
batim what he had said in his lectures during the year. From
time to time he might murmur, 'Well done! Well done!
Wonderful!' Woe betide a student who had neglected his reciting skill.

'Literary Criticism' was perhaps the subject I enjoyed more
than any other – at least for the quality of lecturing. Dr L.
Suratgar – a former student of the University of London –
knew well how to engage our minds and he could be very
humorous. Suratgar had an English wife who wrote
intriguingly about her introduction to Iran in *I Sing in the
Wilderness*.[1] Under Dr Faryar we studied English Literature –
Shakespeare, Dickens and others.

Seeing that most students were intending to teach we had
to take subjects such as 'The Psychology of Education'. This
was taught by a Dr Siassi, later Chancellor of the University.
He had been educated in France and had acquired a somewhat
solemn style; he was self-possessed and always punctual. Dr
Hooshiar taught a course entitled 'The Principles of Education'. In his serious way, he was very deferential with his
'Respected Sirs, or Ladies' as he delivered his material. He had
studied in Germany. 'The History of Education' was the field
of an American-trained teacher, Dr Issa Sadiq, who was very
keen to modernize Iran. 'The Philosophy of Education' was
handled by Dr Reza Zadeh Shafaq, who was considered the
'grand old man of the subject', though there often seemed little
substance to his presentations.

Shafaq also taught us Western philosophy but though he
could speak with clarity, the content was often elusive, not to

say repetitious sometimes. He was succeeded by Dr Mahdavi, recently arrived from France, who was young and relevant, despite his difficulty in matching Western terms and ideals to Persian vocabulary. I remember several occasions when I asked him whether philosophy was compatible with faith in God but he always evaded the issue. Only later did I realize that it would not have been possible for him to handle that topic in class.

For Arabic we were entrusted to the mercies of a well-known Arabist, Bahman-Yar, a Kermani who lacked the teaching skills to match his fine knowledge of grammar. Once, coming on the word 'Rabib', I enquired whether it was derived from 'Rub-abah', a girl's name, whereupon the whole class dissolved into laughter. The group calmed down when he angrily suggested that I was habitually curious and given to much questioning. I am still awaiting an answer to that one.

Fazel Tooni was our teacher of logic. He had discarded his turban but had not adopted a European hat in line with Reza Shah's order about our national headgear. Instead he favoured a sort of weird headpiece that was neither hat nor turban. Likewise his dress – he no longer wore the mullah's robe, nor a normal coat and trousers, but a long habit that draped his odd-looking figure. Though we were never allowed to see the book, he often cited Mullah Abdollah's annotations of Aris-totle's Logic, in the *Organon*.

Another oddity was Qareeb, who taught us the Persian classics. Shabbily attired, he was once mistaken by a student for some College servant. Assar regaled us with 'The Philosophy of the East' once a week. He had been allowed to continue to wear Mullahs' robes. His white turban, long brown robe and neatly trimmed beard bespoke his high dignity, but he had a strange way of speaking that left spaces between words which was disconcerting – at least for me – in comprehending his meaning.

'Composition', or the 'Manner of Writing' – as we call it in Persian – always seemed to me the most important of our studies. It was taught by Professor Iqbal Ashtiani who had recently returned from Europe and was a noted historian and man of letters. Taking some line from the classics, he would ask us to write an essay on it. I recall one instance when he suggested: 'A man's own ill-humour you will always find, if you look well, is where his bitter complaining has its root and spring.'

We were invited to read our efforts aloud for him to criticize on the spot. He urged us to write simply, and to avoid stilted and archaic vocabulary. He was much enamoured of the style of Qavam-o-Sultaneh, the then Prime Minister, who used to write orders to be posted up on the streets of Tehran. Iqbal told us to take them down and study them. Once I managed to do so and found I agreed with the Professor's opinion. The Prime Minister had a fine skill with words.

I turn now to reminisce about my friends at University, and the bonds we shared. Poetry read together, and the joy of rhythm, rhyme and lyricism were great factors in our relationships. A Rashti named Derayeh had an unusual ability to make music, even a sort of dance music, in his recital of poetry. There was one lilting poem of Professor Foroozan Far with which he had us all dancing around to the words. Another student, Dabir-Syaqi, could recite the whole of the famous 'Tarji-band of Hatef', where an enquirer after truth visits a fire-temple, a church and a tavern to conclude finally that 'He is One and there is none but He/There is no god save Him alone.'

Dabir-Syaqi would give us an explanation of any difficult words. Then there was Manoochehr Amiri from whom I heard for the first time Bahar's famous 'Ode to Demavand', and fell in love with it at once. I became a close friend of the late Massoud Rajabnia, a student from Alborz College. We had a common love of English verse and used to recite poems together – among them John Keats' lines:

> A thing of beauty is a joy for ever.
> Its loveliness increases, it will never
> Pass into nothingness.[2]

Occupation

Sadly these idyllic memories of literary joys give way to grimmer things. At the end of my first year at university Iran was occupied by the Western Allies. There had been an uneasy calm from the start of the Second World War but in the summer of 1941 British and Russian forces entered the country. Reza Shah had only recently celebrated the twentieth anniversary of his access to power and we had taken part in the familiar 'march-past' in a vast Maidan in north Tehran. How vividly I remember his imperious face as we streamed past, full of patriotic fervour, never dreaming that within six months his reign would end.

The occupation was prompted by the Allies' urgent need for a secure route by which to get war material into the USSR. The British sought Reza Shah's support and tried to persuade him to expel the Germans working in Iran, but he had earlier affirmed the neutrality of Iran and did not wish to cave in to demands that he abandon it.

Early one August morning, we woke to the reality of a double occupation – by Russia from the north and by the British from the south, violating Iran's neutral stance. The Persian forces made a token show of resistance but gave in after three days. Reza Shah resigned and went into exile, initially to Mauritius and then to South Africa where he died a few years later. His son, Muhammad Reza – under Allied control – succeeded him. Despite the humiliation implicit in the whole episode, the country rallied round him in sympathy for his youth and his difficult role. I remember the spontaneous applause that greeted him en route to the Majlis (Parliament) to take his oath. I stood among the crowd with warm pride throbbing in my heart.

His youth kindled admiration, engendered also by relief at the departure of his father, whose final despotic years had been tainted by the atrocities committed by his secret police.

Great changes in every sphere of life followed the occupation. Not least, was the advent of large numbers of Americans.

The foreign forces virtually ruled the country, albeit indirectly, and maintained the luxury of freedom of expression that we had long been denied. Political parties came into being and there was a spate of new journalism. The Tudeh (Communist) Party came out of hiding and achieved a new popularity among the young. There was open criticism of Reza Shah and of government officials, while debate in the Majlis assumed an unwonted liveliness.

The University was deeply affected by these political and social changes. Tight regulations and the traditional deference from pupil to teacher gave way to libertarian disorder and ill-discipline, which could affect even literary studies. I remember someone returning from France with a book that decried the old traditions of Persian poetry as imprisoning the poetic art. I was initially taken by its ideas but soon sensed how trivial many aspects were. Political poetry with biting satire and innuendo became popular. One student named Qahreman wrote a long masterly poem, a diatribe against Reza Shah, while another writer lambasted the government in words I still recall: 'A young cabinet they have formed/Made up of old thieves and ancient bribe-takers.'

Around this time, the British Ambassador was a man called Sir Reader Bullard, which was too close to the Persian 'Pullad', meaning 'steel'. As the Prime Minister's name Sa'ed could mean 'forearm', the way was clear for a lampoon in one of the satirical papers, using a well-known Persian line: 'Whoever comes into the grip of Pullad (Bullard), bruised on the forearm [Sa'ed] he will surely be'.

As for religion and the things of faith, students showed little interest. I started Qur'an reading in Arabic and English with one of them, comparing the texts, but we did not keep it going very long. It led to much teasing and mockery; we were better off if seen to be busy with Marx and *Das Kapital*, or the Communist Manifesto. The latter I read, finding it to be a powerful piece of writing, with some of which I could readily agree. However, I was in no way persuaded that all the evils of the world could be ended if only a 'dictatorship of the

Proletariat' were achieved. Christian faith identified this for me as altogether too simplistic. The self-seeking explicit in both capitalism and Communism had to measure up to the love of God revealed in the Cross of Christ – a love for all humanity, rich and poor alike. While my own social roots were 'prolet-arian' and I had friends with 'leftish', even Communist, sympa-thies, I could not accept the Communist philosophy.

But enough of Karl Marx, let me tell the story of the shoe. Our much revered Prime Minister had died and on the day he was to be buried, one of our lecturers, Dr Ra'di Azarakhshi, had lauded him to the skies and urged us to attend the obse-quies. The vast crowd prevented us getting into the mosque but when it surged out, bearing the coffin and filling Parliament Square, we were swept off our feet. An Isfahani was at my side, well named Neeroomand ('strong') for only by clinging with one hand to a tree and holding on to him with the other was I saved from being trodden under foot in the mêlée. After-wards hundreds of shoes littered the Square, one of which was mine, torn off in the crush. It was impossible to locate it and I limped back home with one foot shoeless. The story soon got around and a fellow-student produced what became a very popular jingle which began:

> The very day Professor Ferooghi died –
> May God set him in Paradise –
> Catastrophe befell our dear Dehqani, there befell him
> 'Twas a horrific thing. The milling crowd
> Deprived him of his precious shoe!

French was normally the second language, but those of us who spoke English formed an English society which met once a week to hear various invited speakers. While I was its secretary I invited Mary Isaac, our teacher in Isfahan, and on another occasion Reza Zadeh Shafaq who complained to me about how small the audience was (we were small in number anyway and I had not thought to extend it to people beyond the Uni-versity).

The soaring price of food was one of the worst consequences of the foreign occupation. Bread, eggs, cheese and other basic items of the daily diet seemed to grow more expensive by the day. Bakeries often ran out of flour; people had to form long queues and often went hungry. Time was lost from our studies. My room was very cold in winter. I used to warm a brick on a stove, wrap it in old sheets and use it to warm my feet in bed. At times the wrappings would burn and would have to be replaced. The renting of other rooms in the flat made for more and more noise and for noisy tenants too.

Given the soaring prices, I did not think it fair to go on boarding with my friend and his mother. I decided in my second year to share with Manoochehr Mostashari, my class-mate from SMC, who had come to Tehran and lived with his mother and grandmother. He offered to have me at the rate of my loan from the Diocese and I gratefully accepted. The country came to a state of near famine, despite the promises of the occupying forces to bring in bread supplies. There was much hoarding and speculating to the further deterioration of a harsh situation. The so-called 'machine bread' that did eventually reach the market (shaped like a long cylinder) proved almost inedible, being fabricated out of very little actual flour.

The desperate economic situation and the miseries of the country affected me deeply. There were times when I was near despair and found it hard to fight back tears. Somehow the second year passed and the summer holiday in Isfahan allowed me to renew my contacts with the Church. My health and my spirits revived somewhat, though I grew soberly aware of the thesis that had to be written during the coming third year.

At the outset of my third year back in Tehran an old SMC friend called Ahmad Arjumand, a law student, invited me to share his room at the boarding section of the old Alborz College, run by an able educationalist called Mojtahedi, who was from Rasht. He had somehow been able to build a store of rice, so rice became almost our only food – breakfast, lunch and supper. At least we were not left hungry – rice fortified me for my journey (a mile and a half) four times daily between Alborz hostel and my University venue. I shall never forget the kindness I received from Ahmad Arjumand.

It did much to prepare me for the anxieties of the third-year thesis. My first idea had been to write on folklore, but Professor Bahar indicated that I would need old Persian for it. So instead I chose 'Christianity in Iran before Islam', for which I went to Dr Reza Zadeh Shafaq. He listed a number of books but also said that I should widen my scope to take in the Zoroastrian faith, the Manichean sects and other religious forms. So my thesis was re-titled 'The Religious Situation in Iran under the Sassanids'.

I went to work in the Library of the National Bank in Tehran which was well stocked with books, and where, in that cold winter, I could be warm. It was also very quiet with few users. One of them I met was a refugee researcher from Poland, who had escaped the Nazis via Russia and might well have found himself going on to Europe to enlist. He assured me that there were close historic links between Persia and Poland.

My cosmopolitan contacts in Tehran prompted many thoughts about the nature of belief and even the need for religion at all. I grew puzzled and ill at ease about my sense of vocation and the reality of God. What helped to steady me was the advice of Pat Gaussen: that I should never, under such pressures and perplexities, forsake Christian fellowship or abandon the habit of worship. Also I found a warm haven in the Evangelical Church of Tehran, situated in Qavam-o-Sultaneh, whose minister in my first year was the late Dr Yahya Armajani. His sermons were a delight and his personality a strong attraction. He was an Iranian national with an American education, and was gifted with a clear mind to which he could give fine voice.

There was a lively youth group in the Church. I came to know a certain Dr John Elder, whose several books had been translated into Persian. Among these were: *Faith in God in the Twentieth Century* and *Science and Religion*. The translators, not themselves Christians, had done their work well and when

I was able to discuss the books directly with the author I found him both courteous and convincing.

Above all, the ultimate secret for spiritual survival lay in my habit from childhood of a daily 'quiet time' with the Lord in reading and prayer, via the Scripture Union calendar. Another help was E. Stanley Jones' *Victorious Living*, with its reading for every day of the year. Thus, my frail bark was safely steered through the uncertain waters of those years.

> Round our skiff be God's alertness,
> When she try the deeps of sea,
> Sea-shell frail, for all her stoutness
> Unless Thou her helmsman be.

> Traditional Hebridean prayer

CHAPTER 4

Military Service

'This above all, to thine own self be true . . .' Shakespeare's Polonius in *Hamlet* pretended much wisdom but paraded it too pompously. 'Be true to yourself and you won't be false to any' sounds all right if there is a 'true self' to start with! A treacherous self, like Shakespeare's Iago, was grimly 'false' to Othello. The Book of Proverbs was perhaps wiser than Polonius in saying: 'As a man thinketh in his heart, so is he' (23:7). I begin in this way because on leaving university and entering national military service, I was facing another big test of courage and purpose.

I received my degree in July 1943 and immediately wrote to the Diocesan Council offering myself to the Church for ministry. The response came that, in view of my youth, I needed to gain more experience of the world and of life outside Church and University. When I sought employment it became clear that the law required me first to do military service under the conscription rules. These enabled graduates to take the rank of 'officers' and so I registered in the Officers' Training College.

As a Christian I was opposed to war and militarism, yet national service was obligatory. A friend arranged for me to be interviewed by the Chief of the General Staff, who proved to be an old man of impressive mien. When I told him I was a Christian, he took it in a very matter-of-fact way. To my disavowal of war, he responded that Iran was not then at war anyway. When I stressed that because I was against war I would reject battle service but be willing to do any other kind of duty, helping the wounded most of all, he replied, 'You will have to raise all that with the officers at the College.'

When I registered, there was no chance to talk to any officer about my attitude. I found myself with the others, being herded rather like sheep, given uniforms and paraded as if we were puppets on a string. For two weeks we were mercilessly dragooned into porterage, shifting cupboards, chairs, stools and beds, running round fields, and subjected to what seemed pointless lectures.

The normal OTC course lasted for two years for those intending to be regular army officers. My group was among the 'Reserved', who did only six months, followed by another six serving in the ranks as an officer. Second-year students were allowed to dominate us entrants, wielding seemingly total power, demanding instant obedience and actually calling themselves 'the gods of the College'. It had a wretched tradition of ill-treatment and foul language, though by 1943 it was slightly improved, thanks to the national changes that resulted from the Allied invasion. Mine was in fact the first group to be voluntarily registered after the fall of Reza Shah. The foul language and the brutal punishments had been somewhat curtailed, but even so undergoing them was bad enough. Sadistic punishments, such as measuring the football field with a match stick, or propelling oneself along on one's chest, were no longer meted out, but we might still be subjected to such things as standing at attention while holding a stool over one's head.

Reserved students that year numbered around 70, divided between infantry, cavalry, artillery, tanks and financial affairs. I found myself among 19 others with the infantry. A contemporary of mine and a very sociable type, Amir Abbas Hoveyda, always seemed to have friends around him exchanging jokes and laughter, and we were all oblivious of the fate awaiting him.

A few incidents from those days are particularly memorable, for example, the kindness I received from one of those second-year 'gods' when the first days were proving particularly taxing and difficult, and when punishments had neither point nor logic and came so abruptly. This young 'god', it seemed, had had some word about me from Pad Bod, my former teacher, who had lately married into his family. His interventions saved me from much tribulation.

Four second-year men were designated to be our 'sergeants'. 'Torturers', we soon renamed them. The moment any of them came our way we had to stand to attention, salute and greet them as 'Sir', effusively. An Azerbayjani among them by the name of Nejat (which means 'salvation') once intruded unannounced into our bedroom. Singling me out in his Turkish accent as 'Deghani' he ordered me to 'hold the stool', that is, I had to hold the bedside stool over my head until he gave me the order to put it down.

One afternoon they ordered us to run for our tea. One of the 'gods' tripped me up with his foot and I crashed to the ground. I resumed the painful running without turning to look back at him.

The 'gods' had an obsession about making us dust and clean the floors and windows, and drew grounds from this to devise punishments. It happened that the window immediately over my bed opened on to the street that ran alongside one of the Shah's palaces. Its splendid dome brought back wistful thoughts of Shaikh Luftallah's domed mosque back in Isfahan. My window-cleaning tyranny was softened by the sweetness of the memory. I had no knowledge then that we were coinciding with the historic conference of Roosevelt, Stalin and Churchill, which was meeting nearby (November 1943).

The bedroom we occupied was on the fourth floor of the building; it was a long room accommodating 19 beds, each with a cupboard and stool. Early every morning there was 'en cadre', the bed-making drill which left the bedstead looking like a matchbox. Any lapse in this technique could easily result in punishment, however slight the deviation from the perfect 'match'.

One morning who should enter but the Group Captain. The senior student promptly shouted, 'Attention!'.

We all leapt out of bed, pyjama clad, and stood at attention. The Captain called out from where he stood, 'Dehqani, where were you last night?'

Taken utterly aback I answered from where I stood by my bed towards the middle of the room. 'I was here in bed last night, Sir.'

'No, you were not,' came his reply. 'I came in the middle of the night and saw you were not in your bed!'

In my astonishment, my friends came to my rescue, assuring him that I had indeed been in bed all night long. The riddle was solved when he realized that, while my matchbox bed might to his hurried glance look as if it were unoccupied and undisturbed, because my slim form inside was barely noticeable, the cupboards on either side of the beds had obscured my head. Thus he had surmised that I was not there at all!

For our official song, the College had a beautiful piece from the Shah Nameh of Ferdowsi:

Alas! if Iran goes to ruination
And becomes the den of leopards and of lions . . .

However, the following lines now seem to me to be near blasphemy:

Thy love, O King, is our religion and our way,
Our religion is to worship thy Name.

However, we all used to sing it unthinkingly and with gusto as we marched.

So monotonous was the daily routine that we felt as if we were turning, or being turned, like a mechanical wheel. There was just one hour after lunch when we could be ourselves. How I cherished that hour! Sadly even that was taken away. Somehow – I have no notion how – it got about that I could speak English. A captain from a different group asked if I could teach him English. There was no way I could refuse him but the arrangement meant that I had to forfeit the precious hour. The officer in question proved, however, a kindly soul in so far as, realizing my tiredness, he provided milk for me during the English lesson. So I proved the truth of the oft-repeated words: 'If God in His wisdom closes one door, out of His love He will open another.'

Each evening an hour or two was set aside for studying books such as *Know your Machine Gun, Military Tactics and Morale*, etc. The officer in charge seemed unconcerned about what we read, which gave me the idea to devote the fist 20 minutes of every hour to a devotional book which I kept with me, Oswald Chambers' *My Utmost for His Highest*. Those minutes did much to bring back harmony, peace of mind and a quiet heart.

Shared guard duty would also afford useful occasions for reading and meditation. Standing on guard doing nothing for two hours in the middle of the night seemed to me an utter waste of time. So, as I walked or stood around, I would read. One night, as I stood under a somewhat feeble light to read, the officer in charge suddenly appeared and objected to my reading. I explained that since there was nothing to guard I preferred reading to doing nothing. He asked what book it was and I told him it was an English translation from the Russian of Nikolai Gogol's *Dead Souls*. I have no recollection of how this text came my way, nor was I finding it very illuminating, but it was better than a vacant mind. The officer rebuked me and told me to stop reading on guard duty.

So I started instead to put into verse passages from the Bible that I already knew by heart. Favourite among them was Psalm 23. Later Vera Eardley, my early Sunday School teacher, composed a lovely Persian tune for it, suitable for flutes, rekindling the atmosphere of sheep and sheepfolds. It has become one of the favourite songs of our Persian Church. Another passage I put into verse was 1 Corinthians 13, 'The Song of Love', which also came into the Church Hymnal. (The Hymnal does not, however, have a note to let singers know that at the time I was waiting in a queue to have a bath, on the point of fulfilling how 'love bares [bears] all things'!)

Experience had taught me how lack of regular sleep would make me ill, and I sensed that standing on night guard would be a sure way to break my health. I found a way through by staying in College at the weekends when other students went home to Tehran. They needed someone to do their duty to free them to get home to their families, so I arranged to take their weekend turns while they took my night duties during the week. The bargain was beneficial to both parties.

After four months had gone by we were given forms to complete. One question to be answered besides name, family name, identity number and father's name concerned religious allegiance. I realized that to write 'Christian' when my own name Hassan and my Father's name Muhammad were so plainly Muslim would be sure to raise eyebrows. But 'Christian' was what I wrote. To officials it must have seemed unthinkable, seeing that Muslims were required never to change their faith. However, it was unthinkable for me not to be true to myself as a Christian. I took the bull by the horns and tried to prepare myself for any eventuality, but only after long thought and deep prayer.

A few days passed and nothing happened. One night, just as I had gone to bed, one of the student 'gods', called Saghaie, came into the bedroom and, sitting gently by my bed, enquired about my religion. With some fear at heart I replied that I was a Christian. Instead of rebuking me, he gave me some words of praise, saying that he had observed how I was different from the other men. He talked thus at some length. Only later did it dawn on me that he was assuming I shared his 'leftish' sympathies. When I told him my story he became markedly quiet and stole away.

Years later there was an uprising in Persian Azerbayjan. Several officers who had participated in it were executed after the Shah's army had put down the revolt. On the list that was published in the press I read the name of 'Saghaie' and wondered whether it was my furtive night visitor all those years before. It filled me with deep sorrow to think of him and of his family.

A few days later we went to inspect tanks. As we stood around, our Group Captain arrived on horseback and surveyed us for a while. Suddenly he called my name. Stepping out of the row, I saluted him and stood at attention.

He said, 'What is your religion?'

I answered, 'I am a Christian, Sir.'

'How is that possible?' he replied. 'Was your father an Armenian?'

'No, Sir.'

'Then was your mother Armenian?'

'No, my mother was not Armenian but when she was learning to be a nurse in a Christian hospital, she was drawn to Christ through the teaching she heard, and so became a Christian.'

'You ought to have chosen your father's religion.'

'I did not choose anyone else's religion. Educated in a Christian school I grew up with Christians, learned about Christianity and chose for myself to be Christian, Sir.'

'I cannot trust you any more.'

'It is as you will, Sir, but if I were you, my trust would have been increased. How easy it would have been for me to deceive you about my religion – which would have been lying. I could not be untrue to myself or to any one else, Sir.

'Go on with you now,' he chided.

Although this conversation took place in front of them all, I did not feel that their attitude toward me changed in any way.

When our training ended we had to pass exams in military history, tactics, and morale, for example, and the sundry types of weapons, as well as tests in physical exercise and sport. One of these meant lifting a heavy weight called a 'halter' off the floor. With my vest on, I went towards this heavy piece of metal and bent down to lift it up. The more I tried the less it moved. Our sports teacher, Mr Sadaqiani, who was watching from a distance, ran towards me and said, as he touched my bare arm, 'You do not need to do this.'

My marks for physical exercise were as low as 11 out of 20, but higher marks in written subjects compensated for them.

At long last the end came. Forms were handed out asking

us in what capacities we wanted to serve in the army during the next six months which completed our conscription time. I was of two minds. Part of me yearned to be back in Isfahan with the Church and my friends, yet I was aware I needed experience somewhere else where I was not known to anyone. So after much reflection, I wrote that my wish was to serve the Army Division in Tehran. It was not to be. Just before the final days of term several American officers in an advisory group to the Iranian Army asked those of us who knew English to introduce themselves. My good friend from the University, Massoud Rajabnia, to whose home I used to go in free time, was employed by the army as an interpreter. He encouraged me to introduce myself to the Major in charge of interpretation. The upshot was that I had the written commission of 'Staff Officer assigned to the Advisory Department'.

On No Ruz, the Persian New Year (21 March 1944) we went to the Gulistan Palace wearing our Officer's uniforms. The young Shah, who had been on the Peacock Throne only two and a half years, came round and shook each of us by the hand, quite unpretentiously. He had not yet been spoiled by flatterers. We were not saluting him with one hand and kissing his with the other – as came to be the procedure, so ridiculous for serving officers.

Following the holiday I went to the Advisory Department of the General Staff in Tehran and showed them the order I had been given. To my surprise, instead of Tehran where I had expected to be, I was assigned to the Isfahan Army Department to be Secretary-Interpreter to an American Lieutenant Colonel, E. G. Tremane, Jr. He had just arrived from Boston and had been assigned as advisor to the Isfahan Division. It was an extraordinary turn of events. In Isfahan there would be no worry about finding accommodation or arranging for house-keeping. My own room in the Mission compound was empty and there were people around with whom I could share the cost of living. There was even an extra bonus, for, having written on my form at the Officers' College that I wanted to work in Tehran, and finding myself now posted to Isfahan, I qualified for an additional award for working outside the capital, on top of my already good salary as a Second Lieutenant Staff Officer. Not only was I able now to live without anxieties about funds, but I also could begin to save for the future and help my family back in Taft.

On that last point, Vera Eardley (who, incidentally, was housekeeper to our group) reminded me that in helping my family, I should bear in mind that Church salaries, if I came into its service, held no promise of wealth.

Lieutenant Colonel Tremane, it transpired, was a financial and economic advisor whose job was to supervise purchasing and other transactions for the Army in Isfahan. We had an office in one of the rooms of the Isfahan Army Depot, once a beautiful caravanserai in the time of Shah Abbas, later turned into a magnificent hotel called the 'Shah Abbas'. We had to climb a flight of narrow stairs to reach our office. The Colonel had recently read James Morier's book about Haji Baba of Isfahan,[1] which told of him using a caravanserai in the heart of Isfahan. He convinced himself that the very room in which we had our office was Haji Baba's own. Every morning, reaching the end of his climb, he would say, 'Poor old Haji Baba! What a hard time he must have had with these stairs!' This could have been true if indeed there had been a real Haji Baba, and not simply a creation of Morier's mind.

The Commander of the Depot was a very well educated Persian Colonel called Kayhan, who had studied at the Sorbonne, in Paris. As he knew only French, I had to interpret for him when the situation involved Colonel Tremane (he lived very near to me in the Iran Tour Hotel). I joined him every morning at 8 a.m. and together we went in his jeep to the Depot. One day we had to halt at the entrance. Junior Persian officers in the car behind started impatiently to sound the horn loudly. An angry Colonel Tremane got out of the jeep and wanted me to translate his rage and rebuke to the offending occupants of the car. My rendering lacked some of the force of his anger but was enough to mortify them and assuage his wrath. Was this perhaps 'culture-clash'? In Iran it is quite normal to blow a horn when an obstruction occurs; they may not have meant it harshly.

My natural curiosity made me interested to know how Colonel Tremane was advising the Army over financial and economic matters. Once or twice I attended meetings with him at which bidders for contracts were interviewed. There seemed little for a translator to do – the Colonel's silent presence sufficed; it was as if – pardoning the disrespectful analogy – he was a scarecrow in a field.

Generally he was, in my view, much too voluble. On his bedroom wall he had fixed the prayer: 'Lord, help me keep my big mouth shut'. He did not give the good Lord much chance to answer it. He would start talking the very moment we sat down together in the office. I had to go through the motions of listening, albeit impatiently, wanting all the while to get on with translating various pieces of correspondence. Seldom did he halt the flow of words.

His topics of conversation varied widely: comparisons between Persia and America, people, streets, buildings and the like. He waxed eloquent about his home, memories of the First World War and so forth. Doubtless he was homesick and talking relieved his loneliness. I tried to interest him in the Church but he was very childish in his reactions and would say, 'I will come if I have a letter this week from my wife.' One afternoon I invited him to tea with Dr Howgate and Vera Eardley. His endless flow of words wearied them. His great anxiety was for the opening up of 'a second front' to be expedited by an Allied invasion of Europe. One day the event actually happened. On 6 June 1944 we heard that the Allies had landed in Normandy. Overjoyed, he posted a map of Europe on the wall and every day he traced the progress of the Allied forces.

By September my year's conscription was due to end. General Razmara, who later as Prime Minister was the victim of an assassination, was then Head of the General Staff. He ordered all 'end of service certificate holders' to present themselves to Tehran. When I flew there to be at the celebrations, I had to wear long boots, a thing I had never done working in an office. I was advised to go to the workshop and try to borrow a pair, but found no one could supply me – everyone was too busy making them.

Then an untoward thing happened. As I hung around looking for someone to help me, the Divisional Commander, no less, entered and a sergeant called the place to attention, a duty that was properly mine. The Divisional Commander, with the rank of General, reproved me in evident rebuke. I saluted and, when asked to which section I belonged, replied 'The Advisory Department of the General Staff'.

He dismissed me contemptuously saying, 'Ah! Advisory Department. Ugh!', as if its members were quite incapable of calling attention when a General appeared. By the time I reached the ceremony, still bootless, the certificates had all been handed out and I had to retrieve mine from a mere office!

Now with a certificate saying my conscripted service was completed, I informed the Diocesan Council that I was ready to enter the service of the Church. The response again was that I should continue gaining experience in the wider world. Bishop W. J. Thompson, who earlier had been my Headmaster in SMC, held strongly that young people, as potential clergy, should work in non-Church circles to understand society more fully before entering the ministry. Only in this way could they come fully to know the world they would be serving, its ups and downs, its cares and woes.

Colonel Tremane held this opinion of the Bishop's in very high regard. He had grown familiar with my ways and would have found it hard to work with a new translator from Tehran. He was eager for me to go on working in his office and to accept a contract as a 'civilian interpreter-secretary'. The salary and benefits were the same as those of a colonel in the Iranian Army and identical to what I was already receiving. Either side could terminate the agreement with a month's notice. Stressing to the Colonel that this provision was very important to me in view of my pledge to the Church to answer its call whenever it came, I signed the agreement with a glad heart and continued my pleasant duties in that office.

CHAPTER 5

Answering the Call

If thou art the man of the way, know that the way is through blood, and that distressed, despised, daunted thou must go. Set thou foot upon the way, asking no question. The way will reveal itself in thy going.

Farid al'-Din Attar (mystic poet, died 1229)

It was a few months after I had signed my contract of employment with the army that a letter reached me from the Archdeacon of the Diocese, inviting me to become a full-time recruit as a youth and literature worker. Since Bishop Thompson was in England, Archdeacon John R. Richards was in charge of the Diocese. His ideas differed somewhat from those of Bishop Thompson and he believed that if there was a deep sense of vocation anyone so moved by the Spirit should get into training straight away. As for further experience in the world, that could take care of itself as the claims of equipment for ministry were taken up. (Of Welsh blood and temperament, the Archdeacon was soon to return to Wales where he became Bishop of St David's.)

On receipt of his letter I informed Colonel Tremane of my intention to terminate my contract. He tried hard to dissuade me, saying that he was happy working with me, that he would be returning to America after a while, and that he did not want to have to become accustomed to another assistant. However, I could only answer that my commitment was to the Church whenever its call came. There were others, too, who urged that deferment would be wise, seeing as I was still young and had built up no financial assets for the future. Continuing a while longer in army employment would allow me to do this, if only modestly.

I had the same pressure from my father and my brothers, for whom army service was not only more lucrative but gave me, and them, some prestige and standing in society. They saw work for the Church as something inferior, unworthy of my level of education.

Hard as it seemed, I was inwardly sure that I should keep my promise. In my heart of hearts that was where the call of duty lay. Also I had a fear that if I refused the call then it might become more difficult to take it up later. How long would army earnings take to be 'enough'? We have a quirky idea about saving. The more you save, the more you think you need to save. The habit of acquisition feeds on itself. As for 'more worldly experience', Bishop Thompson's estimate of its value stemmed from his own background. Prior to his ordination he had been an engineer, seen military service and taught in schools, so he did not readily approve of his Archdeacon's initiative over my immediate recruitment at the cost of terminating my army contract.

I, meanwhile, had no knowledge of this difference of opinion between them. One thing only I knew, and that was that my pledge had to be fulfilled once the door was opened. I had known others whom the Church had helped through education who had reneged on their promise to serve in the Church in return and had gone their own way, and I had no intention of copying them. Despite the opposition of my family and the dissuasion from many around me, was my army resignation accepted. I was wistful about the disappointment of the Colonel, with whom I had established a sort of friendship. Sadly, a few weeks later he was involved in a bad car accident and was flown home to America. I did not see him again. I continued to live in the same house, exchanging 8000 rials per month for 1200 rials as the designate youth worker of the Diocese and secretary of its Christian literature committee.

What was the 'call' and who was the 'caller'? It was vital for me to have the true answer, for it would be the thrust of my whole future. It had come, to be sure, from the Church via its appointed means, but these were only instrumental in what, with all my heart, I knew to be the call of God alone. It was from the Lord Jesus Christ that the summons I was heeding had come. The Church set out the ways and means of obeying the claim that stemmed from him alone.

To explore this supreme reality I look back afresh on the inner course of a spiritual journey, the ups and downs of a soul pilgrimage through childhood towards maturity. As far back as my first conscious thoughts I remember musing about the whole mystery of things, why I was here, and where I was going. Like our poet Nezami of Ganjeh (died 1217), I queried my being and meaning and how they held together:

> From here – where bound? We do not know!
> Why have we come? Why and whither our going hence?

Was not Nezami akin to the English poet, Thomas Traherne (1637–74), enquiring 'where he was before he was' and wondering why it had come to pass?

> A stranger here strange things doth see
> Strange treasures lodged in this fair world appear,
> Strange all and new to me.
> But that they should be mine, who nothing was –
> That strangest is of all,
> Yet brought to pass.

Like Nezami I had to agree how

> Mind, philosophy and intellect their utmost do –
> But, unresolved persists life's baffling riddle.

I could only conclude that I had to go beyond where intellect could take me if I were to reach the answer that I sought. As in Dante's 'darkling wood', using only your mind finds you wandering around in a tangled maze. But by letting faith decide the day, a way through the maze, and the depression it often kindles in the soul, can be found.

Thanks to my childhood in Taft, I had grown up in an atmosphere of 'faith in God' – a benison further confirmed by living among Christians and becoming familiar with the Bible. One of the immediate consequences for me was the liberating realization that faith in God did not, need not, mean I had to follow rigorous regulations or superficially religious rituals. Rather, faith in God had to do with the whole of life, more inwardly ordered by grace than by outward acts of conformity. God's call was to yield the whole of life to him in answer to his commissioning love. This enfolded all else in a single purpose – studies, career, profession, and any choice about a life partner. To yield a whole self in these terms was not only to learn peace of mind but also to be taken up into divine employment for the furtherance of God's ways.

My next discovery through reading the Bible was the principle of divine 'choice' of people for ministries in the divine economy. Doubtless all believers are 'called' and 'chosen' by the Lord in love, so that all they do belongs within his design for the world. But it is also clear from the pages of the Bible that there are special vocations for people, both corporate and personal. Being 'chosen' by the Lord in this way does not imply that such vocations make 'chosen ones' more worthy than others. There is no favouritism in terms of merit or advantage. It all consists in responsibility and the fulfilment of a divine end and purpose. I read how 'the children of Israel' were chosen in this divinely purposeful way, but failed in not comprehending their real role under God. Personalities such as Isaiah knew themselves summoned to serve:

The Lord called me before I was born, He named me from my mother's womb ... the Lord formed me in the womb to be His servant ... I appoint you as a light to the nations so that my salvation may reach earth's farthest bounds ... the Lord who is faithful has chosen you (Isaiah 49:1, 5, 6, 7; REB).

Such chosenness for God's service can entail hardship, suffering, and even agony like that of Jeremiah, for whom the sharp reality of prophetic vocation was laden with grief and pain.

> Before you were formed in the womb, I chose you and before you were born I consecrated you ... Ah! Lord God, I answered, I am not skilled in speaking, I am but young. But the Lord God said: Do not plead that you are too young, for you are to go to whatever people I send you and to say whatever I tell you to say (Jeremiah 1:5, 6, 7; REB).

So heavy was the task, so hard the way of vocation, that Jeremiah thought he had been deceived about vocation under the weight of persecution and despair. He cried in anguish to God:

> You have duped me, Lord, I have been Your dupe. You have outwitted me and prevailed. All the day long I have been made a laughing-stock, everyone ridicules me ... A curse be on the day I was born, the day my mother bore me, may it be for ever unblessed! ... Why did I come from the womb to see only sorrow and toil, and to end my days in shame? (Jeremiah 20:7, 14, 18; REB).

Yet, despite all his tribulations, Jeremiah remained faithful to God and held steadfastly to his vocation.

At my baptism, Vera Eardley presented me with an English Bible in which she inscribed Jesus' words to his disciples: 'You did not choose Me. I chose you. I appointed you to go and bear fruit' (John 15:16). I sincerely believed that God had called me to serve him in the Church in Iran, in whatever capacity the Church should choose. I had no illusion that this would be easy. It would be an unpaved road, rough and stony with many a hazardous turn. If God's invitation was clear an unknown future could be left in his hands. I recalled how strongly I was moved by a poem quoted by King George VI when he spoke to his nation at the beginning of the Second World War. I felt the words somehow speaking directly to my

situation. I translated it into Persian when, at the beginning of
the Persian New Year (in 1945) I entered the service of the
Church in Iran. When later a tune was fitted to it, it became
a popular hymn for No Ruz (the Persian New Year) in our
Church Hymnal. It always reminds me of the time I accepted
the call of God. Wherever the path of life has taken me, I have
carried with me a beautifully inscribed copy of the hymn:

> I said to the man who stood at the gate of the year: 'Give
> me a light that I may tread safely into the unknown.'
> He replied, 'Go out into the darkness and put your hand
> into the hand of God. That shall be to you better than a
> light and safer than a known way.'

It was my conviction that I was called. I was accepting God's
invitation to travel the vale of this world with the purpose he
had set for me. As the poet 'Attar wrote: 'Though the way be
through blood, step forth upon it asking no question. For the
way itself will tell thee how thou shouldst go.' My whole duty
was to put my hand in the hand of God and walk in trust with
him, whatever might happen.

But what was the responsibility I was receiving from God's
hand? It was to interpret Christ's way to my fellow Iranians,
by the way I lived, by word of mouth, by ink and pen. Though
I had grown up with, and into, the Christian faith, I had not
found unshakeable faith. Doubt has always been part of my
sense of faith, as my deep querying of belief during my studies
at Stuart Memorial College showed. The genuine crisis of faith
I knew then persisted throughout my university career. 'Lord,
I believe, help Thou my unbelief' has often been my cry. But
in all my oscillations between faith and unfaith, between assur-
ance and agnosticism, my trusting sense of God has been sustained by the love revealed in Jesus the Christ as being God in
his own credentials, the divine self-disclosure on which it was
essential to rely. This was the sufficient ground of my call, the
warrant of my obedience to it.

Other factors helped my faith become mature. I noted earlier how belief in God was taken for granted at home, and how my father told me that 'God was Light'. The names of God and his attributes were constantly recited and rehearsed: 'God is great'; 'God is gracious'; 'God is merciful'; 'God is almighty'; 'God sees and knows'; and so on. Later I learned about the negative and the positive aspects of God. 'He is not contrived of parts [*murakkab*], nor is he corporeal [*jesm*] nor visible [*mar'ie*], nor is He localizable [*mahally*]. None is partner to Him. He is altogether inexplicable. He is the Creator, utterly and unneedingly rich [*ghani*].'

Yet for all the emphasis of these dictates of theology, I found the calm sea of my being tossed with storms of doubt and cynicism. Schooling told me not to accept credulously all that we were told unquestioningly. Was there not that ancient Latin precept *Sapere aude*, 'Be bold to think'? Exercise a critical judgement of your own. A readiness to interrogate putative 'truth' was the first ingredient of honest belief. We learned of the Cartesian notion of an all-inclusive doubt that led to the firm conviction: 'I cannot doubt that I am doubting.' But obviously such all-inclusive doubt could only be hypothetical, and even Descartes needed rigorous interrogation. He might better have said: 'I am and so I think'; or 'I suffer and so I am'. But at least his hypothesis of inclusive (if also dubious) doubting allowed one to discern how confidence against scepticism could begin to repossess a valid world. In Persian poetry we had a sort of Descartes, a mystic who wrote: 'I do not even know what "do not know" can mean.' There, surely, was an inclusive reach of sceptical honesty.

It was doubt about the reality of God that made me so anxious and restless. Nature had unutterable beauty but could also prove relentlessly harsh, barren of all mercy. All the superb potential of human goodness could be overtaken by a savagery unknown even among beasts. In such musings I queried why God had not created a world immune from such tragedy and a human nature of total goodness and beauty, whereby the human scene could be bathed in happiness, carefree joy and peace.

What, too, of those dire calamities in which hapless folk undergo desperate loss of life or limb or house and home? What could be the point of all those inexplicable human woes visited on the weak, the helpless, infants and the aged, depriving them of all hope and succour? What creator was it who could countenance the Holocaust, and allow the enormity of gas chambers and their millions of victims, killed by other humans capable of such atrocity?

My whole being seemed consumed with vexing questions about God, meaning, life and its enmity to life. What was the meaning behind creation? To what end was it contrived? Had it been 'contrived' at all and, if so, why and for what? My mood was captured in the lines of the great Persian poet and traveller Nasser Khosrow (1003–83):

I cannot believe, nor can I give my ear
To the following of excessive ascetic pieties of devotees.

Had you wanted one who would never question You
You ought to have made me merely animal.

O God, to speak truly, the wickedness lies at Your door
Yet fear holds me from arguing against You so.

Had You had no vile evil end in view
Would You ever have let Satan be?

You ordain the deer to run,
The dog to go in chase.
You require of us that we worship You
Yet You give leave to Satan to vex us sore.

I pass my days in an abyss of fear and hope
And know no peace of mind or heart.
If bad or good I be, Yours is the creating so
A good creation, only good, You should have made.

We should not be counted guilty in Your service,
Bad we be, as You should not have made us.
Halt! Nasser. Your intellect is far from wisdom
Thinking so. Cut off at root this line of thought.

I, however, could not cut off this line of thought. It dogged
me constantly. I may not have been akin to the English poet
A. E. Housman, who 'thanked whatever God or blackguard
made the world',[1] but my restless queries I could not quell.
Nevertheless, I maintained my fellowship with the faithful and
wise folk whom I trusted, and pursued the studies permitted
me in those days. In the end I came to accept that the being
of God must transcend and surpass our whole capacity to
understand him. Had not one of our poets expressed this attitude in the lines: 'If a twig might sound the ocean depths/Then
might intellect fathom the divine nature'?

It was at this bewildering time that I recognized that if God
were real and desired his creatures to know him, it would not
be enough for only 'messengers' to be sent to tell of him.
The only sufficient way, surely, would be for him to rend
the concealing curtain and reveal himself, so that his human
creation might know themselves conversant with him in authentic terms.

Doubtless any such confidence would still be mysterious but
could resolve the deeper, harder mystery of an unmitigated
hiddenness. When one of our Persian mystics, Khajeh Abdullah
Ansari of Herat (died 1088) wrote 'There be some who lay
wait by Your door with some plea!/Here I come desiring You
alone, to know You for Yourself', he truly echoed the yearning
prayer of all humankind. All that scholastic, religious language
about God as never 'compound', incorporeal, invisible, and
for ever self-sufficient, and utterly unlike all else in being 'peer-
less', can never satisfy the lonely, the bereft, the broken in
spirit, the victims of poverty, injustice and sin.

I grew convinced that faith in the reality of God must incorporate active compassion, sympathy, empathy with the human
creation, in a sharing of suffering. I was drawn to many of the

sayings of our mystics, such as Sayed Ahmad Hatef of Isfahan (died 1783), describing God as the friend disclosed in all things by his own love:

From door and wall, unveiled, the Friend shines radiant,
O ye who have eyes to see!
Thou seekest a candle whilst the sun is on high: the day is
very bright whilst thou art in darkest night.
If thou wilt but escape from thy darkness thou shalt
behold all the universe the dawning-place of lights.
Like a blind man thou seekest guide and staff for this
clear and level road.
Open thine eyes on the rose-garden, and behold the gleaming of the pure water alike in the rose and the thorn.
From the colourless water [are derived] a hundred thousand colours: behold the tulip and the rose in this
garden-ground.
Set thy foot in the path of search, and with Love furnish
thyself with provision for this journey.
By Love many things will be made easy which in the sight
of Reason are very difficult.[2]

Or there was Forooghi of Bastam (died 1858) singing of the omnipresent Lord:

When didst Thou depart from the heart that I should
crave for Thee?
When wert thou hidden that I should find Thee?
Thou hast not disappeared that I should seek Thy
presence:
Thou hast not become hidden that I should make Thee
apparent.
Thou hast come forth with a hundred thousand efful-
gences
That I may contemplate Thee with a hundred thousand
eyes.[3]

The minds of these mystical poets and writers are summarized in the allegorical poem by Farid al-Din 'Attar, the 'Conference of Birds'. Thirty birds under the leadership of Hoopoe decide to set out for the Simurgh (an allegory for the Truth of God). They continue their quest and pass in succession through seven valleys – search, love, knowledge, independence, unification, amazement, destitution and annihilation. Ultimately purged of self and purified by their trials they find Simurgh, and in finding it find themselves. The literal meaning of Simurgh in Persian is 30 birds, and so the 30 seeker birds, by annihilation in God, find themselves. The allegory ends like this:

> They besought the disclosure of this deep mystery, and demanded the solution of 'we-ness' and 'thou-ness'.
>
> Without speech came the answer from that presence, saying: 'This Sun-like Presence is a Mirror.
>
> 'Whosoever enters It sees himself in It; in It he sees body and soul, soul and body.
>
> 'Since ye came hither thirty birds (*sí murgh*), ye appeared as thirty in this Mirror.
>
> 'Should forty or fifty birds come, they too would discover themselves.
>
> 'Though many more had been added to your numbers, ye yourselves see, and it is yourself you have looked on.'[4]

Such mystical writings fascinated me but failed to satisfy my yearning for a personal encounter, truly 'finding' God himself.

Although the beauty of nature could warrant our positing beauty as divine, it would fail to convey knowledge of God into one's soul. The beautiful sayings of people who lived holy lives, captured my interest, but they resembled a gentle breeze caressing one's face and fleeting away.

It was in coming face to face with the life and significance of Jesus that I found what my whole being yearned for. Seeing him through the pages of the Gospels, it seemed to me that he had no concern to start some new religion. His aim was to change people so as to bring about a new society. While he spoke about the prophets, he did not rank himself among them. He seemed to have within himself a more than ordinary power but he did not employ it to prove a claim or to recruit disciples. He healed the sick but urged them not to publicize it. When they wanted to make him king he took leave of them and went his way, not craving power over people. Rather than forming an organization and issuing rules and regulations, he befriended an inner circle of 12 followers, simple folk for the most part, in order to infect them with his mind and spirit, intending them to be pioneers of a new people. As for books, he never wrote – except reportedly one day in the sand, writing which footprints soon erased so that no one knew its message.

Those disciples of Jesus – Jews to a man – were as strong in their confession of the unity of God as any Muslim has ever been. However, a divine self-disclosure in human form has always been regarded as anathema in Islam. It was only through experience of Jesus that his disciples eventually came to that conviction about the Incarnation. At the outset they knew him as their 'Master' and a 'prophet' – the one from Nazareth, a city despised by front-rank Jewry. Like many of their compatriots the disciples initially looked to Jesus to fulfil himself as a political Messiah, set to drive out the Romans and liberate his people.

He dissipated those notions by his steady practice of ministry, his disinterest in worldly power, his refusal to defer to people of influence and prestige, whose hypocrisies he fearlessly condemned, discounting the enmity with which they rewarded him. He was tireless in the care of the poor and defenceless and of the sinful outcasts of a self-righteous society, whether male or female, Jew or Gentile, native or alien. His active love disowned the barriers of caste and kind, its confidence being in the transforming power of grace in all reaches of society, despite the exclusions devised to secure privilege and prejudice.

Thus Samaritans, whom Jews scorned as unclean, lepers, aliens and rejects were counted among his friends; they were humans worthy of the dignity his caring gave to them against the odds of a censorious society. He gave a sense of purpose and significance to those who crossed his path. From all of this his immediate disciples came to a new and revolutionizing perception of his identity and role. When one of them pleaded 'We know not the way [to the Father]', his response was: 'I am the way, the truth and the life' (John 14:6). To their request, 'Show us the Father, that will be all we yearn for', he told them: 'Have I been with you so long and still you do not know me? He who has seen me has seen the Father. How then can you still be asking to be shown Him?' (John 14:9). From his words 'I am in the Father and the Father is in me' (John 14:11), his disciples came to recognize this truth of him, to read in the 'I am-ness' of Jesus the very nature of the God from whom he came, in whom he lived and whom he revealed to them. Resolute 'unitarians' as they were – and we must say remained – they yielded to the fuller truth of the divine unity enshrined in the divine initiative of revelation which his very person held for them. In Paul's words, 'God was in Christ reconciling the world' (2 Corinthians 5:19).

These deeply won convictions meant that God had made his sovereignty discernible in human form in Jesus, so that we might relate to him in personal terms. For as 'knowing *whom* we have believed' is a reality far beyond saying *that* God exists, in external, credal terms. This distinction was vital to my perception of what faith holds and what holds, or enlists, faith. God's own self-revelation to us in human terms, which we could comprehend, seemed to me no more than a corollary of the belief that God exists at all.

Moreover, how could the living God be imprisoned in a logic or a philosophy? Like the first disciples, I came to the conviction that Jesus, present in the human world of time and place, brought to humankind the revelation of what it means that God is God. It was this that drew me to him. It might therefore be said that I came to believe in God because of Jesus Christ. Through him I learned a new and attractive concept of the divine nature, of God as known in Christ.

I had strenuous difficulties, however, with some Christian ter-
minology, especially with 'Son of God'. This was indeed hard
for me to accept. 'Child of God' would have been easier, but
its particular meaning would then be at risk in that we are all,
in creaturely terms, 'children of God'. 'Son' and still more 'only
begotten Son' were initially stubbornly irreconcilable with my
Islamic awareness of the indivisible, inalienable reality of God
as God alone. How could the 'Son of God' be 'begotten' –
being from eternity? I came to appreciate that this language
expressed the conviction I had reached that the 'text' of Christ
is 'authored' in the very being of God. It was the way the
disciples in the early Church expressed what they had experienced in Christ and related it to its source. Just as a son
'reminds' us of a father, so Jesus 'reminds' the world of God.

No physical connotation was meant. There are similar analogies in Islam, when Ali, Muhammad's son-in-law and cousin,
is dubbed 'the hand of God', or when the beggar who receives
alms from Zakat is dubbed 'the son of the road' (*ibn al-sabil*)
because he is customarily found there. In Persian, the verb used
for the generation of electricity is an Arabic derivative *tawlid*,
the same root as yields *mawlud* for a child born. The Qur'an
uses the term 'begotten', insisting how it can never apply. 'He
[lit.] does not beget: He is not begotten' (Surah 112), where
the sense is entirely literal and in no way analogical. The point
Surah 112 makes is entirely Christian also, inasmuch as Christian theology never meant to say that the Eternal had marital
relations and 'fathered' offspring who were his 'begotten ones'.

That thought is outrageous for all theists. In Christian terms
the reality (in our human history of time and place) of Jesus
as the Christ derives, issues from the very being and nature of
the Eternal. Properly 'exalted above all we could associate'
(which is the case, even while analogy is indispensable to all
theology), we might say it happens just as the musician's symphony or the dramatist's play derive and issue from being and
nature. They are the clue to each in his own author's very
persona, because they are the token of who he is in the very
capacity that constitutes and fulfils his identity.

Therefore faith affirms that Jesus was 'begotten' in something of the same sense that the composer and the symphony belong together. God made himself available to us in and through the person of Jesus and all the capacities in which he lived, cared, healed, taught, suffered and redeemed. This is how the problems I had about 'the Son of God' were resolved. However, I am well aware how difficult a theme it is for Muslims to understand or allow.

. My other difficulty lay in the term 'Trinity'. How, I had to ask, could one God be 'Father, Son and Holy Spirit'? Hatef of Isfahan, in his well-known 'Tarji-band', has a dialogue with a Christian girl in a church:

> 'How long (will you continue) not to find the way to the divine Unity? How long will you impose upon the One the shame of the Trinity?'
> 'How can it be right to name the One true God: Father, Son and Holy Spirit?'
> She parted her sweet lips and said to me, while with her sweet laughter she poured sugar from her lips: 'If you are aware of the secret of the divine Unity, do not cast on us the stigma of infidelity.'[5]

The poet went on to explain the mystery of the Trinity in his own mystical way. I realized that 'Trinity' was about God and God is a mystery whom we cannot fathom, nor confine in our logic. I came to understand that 'unity' is not always simple (as in a 'unit'). A single stone is a unity only in being a unit: we can break it into many smaller bits, but it remains stone. Crush a single flower and you spoil its unity; it is no longer a flower.

Humans have many constituent members: limbs, intellect, emotions. It is precisely our multiplicity that comprises our unity. God's unity is no less manifold and rich than ours. So it came to me that belief in the Trinity explains – if it is not necessitated by – the mystery of the unity of God, and does so better than insistence on a numerical oneness. It deepens the sense of divine personhood. Worship in these terms seems fuller, truer and worthier than worship in purely 'unitarian' concepts. The mystery remains, but for me the difficulty of the term 'Trinity' was lifted.

The 'greatness' of God was another problem I had. *Allahu akbar*, 'greater is God', had from childhood been repeated daily. I had taken it for granted that 'God is the greatest', but when doubts pervaded my mind the concept of 'greatness' also came under scrutiny. What did 'greatness' mean? What did it imply? I understood that to be 'great' normally meant to exercise power over others, to dominate and perhaps intimidate in will to impose one's will on others. Power seemed intrinsic to greatness. The more power, the greater its possessor. So what was the meaning of 'greatness' when referring to God?

Was it like an ability to reward those who served it well and to requite those who disobeyed? Was it like the most powerful forms human power had taken in history? At first it seemed to me logical that it must be so, yet that seemed spiritually useless. For I was well aware of how frail and weak I was, lacking control over my innermost thoughts, thinking and saying the wrong things. I sensed only too well the weaknesses and wrong-doings that mere orders from above, sheer power from on high, could not alter or correct. Rather, such power would only lead to fear, depression and despair.

In frailty and self-distrust what one needs is a spiritual enabling and a strengthening sympathy. I knew in my heart that belief in a divine almightiness, in an unlimited greatness, would never save me from evil thoughts, nor overcome in me hatred, vengefulness, jealousy, hypocrisy or – worst of all – pride. When one is dispirited, bereft, broken in heart, inwardly wounded or lonely, how will knowing God as 'great' bring comfort?

Such questionings were set at rest when I came to realize that Christ had revealed that the greatness of God was fulfilled in service, his almightiness in unselfish love. 'The power that reigns is the love that suffers.' Discerning and describing the power of God in and through the love of Christ gave me a complete and satisfying reassurance.

It may all seem too good to be true, a paradox beyond belief. God is, indeed, all that for so long we assumed he could not be. When the Isaiah of Chapter 53 was beginning to think in these terms of sacrificial love being the divine insignia, he asked in incredulity: 'Who has believed our report, to whom is the arm of the Lord revealed?' 'Report' has the double meaning of what we are saying and what you are hearing. It is like the double meaning of the Christian term 'tradition', that is, what was passed to us that we must pass on to you.

The Gospels show the greatness of God in the likeness of a 'good shepherd' who leaves the 99 sheep and endangers his life to find the one that is lost (Luke 15:4). God is like that father in the parable of the prodigal who respects his son's freedom even at the risk of losing him to 'a far country'. He is vulnerable to the boy's waywardness and while he strains under the pain of it, he never abandons the ties of love – the ties which, in due course, enable the self-centred wanderer to 'come to himself' and to say 'I will arise and go to my father', the father whose unremitting love, through the unbroken pain, is the crux of redemption and reconciliation. Those open arms, the costly robe, the fatted calf – and the love that underpinned them – were Jesus' analogy for 'God most great'.

This belief that God does not enforce conformity and good behaviour but concedes to us autonomy even at such cost to his love, is the foundation of democracy, the sheet-anchor of liberty. Is this why that ideal has taken root wherever the Christian theme of God's greatness in these terms has prevailed? Some countries may have taken a long time to learn it and have also passed through long cycles of religious despotism and tyranny – even oppressive dictatorships – but the seed of freedom has been there and has surmounted adversity and suppression to bear its proper fruit.

These thoughts lead to the import we draw from the word 'sin'. In Christianity, sin is not only that we disobey some divine command; rather, it is that we break a loving relationship and turn away from God. Sin does not merely disobey a law; it separates us from the Lord. It follows that repentance is not when we fear the retributory power of God but when we realize the hurt to his love and go back to him. We are then met, not with a clenched fist but with wounded hands; not with threats and punishment but with words of grace and pardon, available for us only through costly love.

All this was proven to us by Jesus in his 'love to the uttermost', the love shown in the Cross and Resurrection. This realization brought great comfort to my heart. There are many Biblical references to the power, majesty and omnipotence of God, but ultimate majesty and glory are in view they are identified not in limitless force, but in meekness, humility and suffering love. The advice to disciples is that they follow their Master in an *imitatio Christi*.

> Take to heart among yourselves what you find in Christ Jesus: He was in the form of God; yet he laid no claim to equality with God, but made himself nothing, assuming the form of a slave (Philippians 2:5–7; REB).

I became well aware of the shame, blight and awesome blemishes of Church history, things done in the name of Christ, things of unspeakable horror and guilt, using deceit, treachery, cruelty and murder in the pursuit of sinful power, of criminal self-will. These enormities shamed not just the Church but humanity itself. I knew that these deeds had all flouted and treacherously violated the way of Christ, his teaching, his life example. Though parading his name and sign in the Cross they utterly denied the meaning of the truth and love that Cross had signalled.

This problem of evil I too found grievous to ponder. Our hearts and minds are all burdened with the injustice, cruelty, sordidness and sin in the world. I could only conclude that no final answer was available to intelligence or reason, not least vis-à-vis the suffering of the innocent, of children and the helpless. I found the passage in Isaiah 53:2–5 the most adequate explanation, the more I understood how the Christian faith finds its ultimate meaning in Jesus and his Cross.

> He grew up before the Lord like a young plant
> whose roots are in parched ground;
> he had no beauty, no majesty to catch our eyes,
> no grace to attract us to him.
> He was despised, shunned by all,
> pain-racked and afflicted by disease;
> we despised him, we held him of no account,
> an object from which people turn away their eyes.
> Yet it was our afflictions he was bearing,
> our pain he endured,
> while we thought of him as smitten by God,
> struck down by disease and misery.
> But he was pierced for our transgressions,
> crushed for our iniquities;
> the chastisement he bore restored us to health
> and by his wounds we are healed (REB).

It has been said of these words that 'They show us intolerable things yet carry us on a flood-tide of inner peace'. Whenever I read them I find that to be true. It surely lies beyond logic and reason but it is because I feel the suffering God near me that I find peace within. It is as the hymn has it:

> And when human hearts are breaking
> Under sorrow's iron rod
> Then they find that selfsame aching
> Deep within the heart of God.

In my many travels around the villages of Iran, I have encountered heartbreaking scenes. For example, some sick baby burning with fever, crying its heart out in a parent's arms and quivering with pain. No medical relief is near, no doctor is to hand – the only 'help' is the emergency itself, the tears of the mother and the babe, the one absorbing the other's cry. This shows for me a deep parable of what Christians believe concerning what God has done for us. The very Creator himself, Lord of the universe, has – through Christ – borne our afflictions and carried our sorrows, restoring us to himself, and healing us by his wounds. It was the majesty – should I say, the magic – of this divine love that I found to be an irresistible reality. As the hymn says, only 'my soul, my life, my all' could be the proper response. I resolved to surrender my life to the Lord's service within his Church.

CHAPTER 6

Learning the Ministry

You will know the truth and the truth will make you free.   John 8:32

The convictions I have just summarized were to inform and undergird the entire ministry to which I knew myself called. My account of them may owe something to the subsequent experiences I now recount, but these would never have ensued had I not let myself be taken captive to Christ as I have described.

That vocation, however, certainly needed and keenly awaited that which would equip it for the task it had assumed. Ministerial training, from the time of the first disciples of Jesus, has always been crucial in the life of his Church. But where to train? Choosing a theological college was no small problem. The Near East School of Theology in Beirut, Lebanon (part of the American University), was nearest to Iran. However, there was a query whether, at that juncture, it was the right place for a young Persian. Several colleges in India, with excellent credentials, were also considered but it was thought that there were too few contacts in India to provide a nurturing environment for a stranger, an inexperienced youth, embarking on a new and untried venture.

What of England, still recovering from the aftermath of the Second World War, only slowly bringing its economic and social fabric back to normality? There was much to be said for choosing one or other of its lively colleges, given that many friends and retirees from Iran lived there. So, after two years serving the church in Iran, the Diocese decided to send me to Ridley Hall, Cambridge. This was preceded by a period in

Cairo en route so that I might arrive in England in time to join a group bound for Norway to attend the second World Youth Conference convening there that summer.

Cairo

We are now flying above the Mediterranean Sea. This is my first view of the ocean which is gleaming back at me in a deep blue colour. The scattered clouds seem like snow-covered peaks. The reflection of the sunlight is creating wondrous images as if thousands of white woolly sheep were sleeping in a close huddle together. As I look down on the ocean, the waves look like the wrinkles on some old man's face. Where the sun strikes the water directly it is as if there were a channel of gold leading down from the silver hilltops which are the clouds to greet the waters. As far as the eye can see is a panorama of light, colour and the ocean's face. What a world of wonderful contrasts the Lord has created – all those vast miles of Arabian desert and this watery spread of vivid blue and gold!

The capital city of Egypt falls into two parts – the new with its high, majestic buildings; and the old quarters where filth and poverty abound. The dress code for men is a mixture of trousers and jackets, or a robe that flows like a skirt, wide and cool, akin to what our Iranian women wear at home. Such attire is cheaper and more comfortable than jacket and trousers in the extreme heat (20 June 1947; diary extract, en route from Tehran to Cairo).

In Cairo, I was the guest of Dr Charles Alexander King of CMS. I had stimulating conversations with him, savouring his interest in Christian Socialism and his lively way of discoursing about world affairs. He deplored the wiles of high finance and the exploitation of the poor and disadvantaged by capitalist economic self-interest. He held strongly to the concept of the welfare state and society's responsibility to organize a free, just and compassionate order. Such social provision against ill-health and poverty he saw as essential to true spirituality.

On the Sunday I attended the church of 'Jesus the Light of the World', situated within the grounds of the Old Cairo Hospital, built and dedicated in tribute to the great ministry in Egypt of William Temple Gairdner, whose death in 1928 had deeply bereaved the people he loved and served for 30 years of strenuous and imaginative ministry. The priest in charge was the Revd Adeeb Shammas, later Archdeacon in Egypt. It was also my first encounter with the Coptic face of Egypt – those Christians, from their origins through the apostle Mark, who had survived the Islamic invasion of their land in the seventh century. Their present condition as a minority reminded me of the Armenians in Iran, faithful to their Lord despite cycles of persecution. I visited several Coptic churches with a local friend and found myself almost sensing in their walls and doors the marks of blood, the travail they had endured. I visited the famous Cairo Zoo – my very first experience of such a place. I feasted my eyes on lions, tigers and elephants, snakes and turtles and even noticed a young couple having an intimate discussion inside an empty cage into which they had secreted themselves. The wry thought came to me that a zoo would be incomplete without human exhibits, since we too are animals. The zoo was quite cosmopolitan, for the creatures too had their nationalities. I identified no explicitly Persian specimen except myself and a very beautiful gazelle, whose slender and beautiful legs brought some lines of Hafiz to mind:

> O Wind of morning, rise and tell
> My love, who like a wild gazelle
> For ever loiters proud and free,
> That she shall no more torture me.
> Because of her, this summer day,
> Across the desert sand I stray
> To find, when the day at last is done
> The Vale men call Oblivion.
>
> (trans. J. C. E. Bowen)

My sightseeing tour took me to the pyramids, which lie west of the River Nile on the edge of the sprawling city. I marvelled at the skill of the huge construction and wondered at the thousands of toiling hands that had been employed in assembling the massive stones and transporting them to this place. I was stunned by the thought of their great age and the pride of man in this defiance of mortality. For such the pyramids were surely contriving to be, as a bid for immortality via enduring stone. Those unknown thousands of workers had lacked all modern equipment. I had the same sense of awe at the pyramids that I have always felt at our own Persepolis. What should one think of the Sphinx – or of that tale about Napoleon having shot a gun at its nose, explaining its scarred appearance.

Toward the end of my sojourn in Cairo I visited the famous museum with its treasures taken from Pharaonic tombs. Ancient Egyptians mummified their noble dead, believing that after death the soul still required the amenities of earthly life. There before my eyes was the mummified corpse of the renowned Tutenkamun, as discovered by a British archaeologist. My reaction was to wonder why, if they could look after their dead (or the high-ranking among them) so well, we could not care for the living with an equal thoroughness?

After two weeks in Cairo, I left for England via Malta. Flying over France I was fascinated by the greenness and the cultivation I could see below. There was no sign of dry desert, and England, from the air, looked even greener than France. Not an inch, it seemed, of uncultivated ground! Though it was 8 p.m. the sun still seemed high in the sky, though dulled by a lingering haze. It hinted that I would rarely see brilliant sunshine – that brightness only the desert has to offer – as long as I stayed in my new territory.

The former Headmistress of my first school in Yazd, Miss Nouhi Aidin was there to greet me. She took me by tube to Richmond to stay with relatives of a former head of the Djam School in Kerman. While in England I visited several places, as my diary records:

Oxford

I travelled with Reginald Iliff, my former Headmaster at
Stuart Memorial College, to visit Oxford and for the whole
50-mile journey I did not see dry land! To my Persian eyes
all was vivid green. The whole stretch of England seemed
to me like a single garden. I noted the absence of high walls
around the dwellings and pondered how different Isfahan
would seem without them. Old and young, men and women,
walked freely in the streets, boys and girls on bikes going
hither and thither and children playing in streets as if these
were home to them. All was total calm and liberty. England,
I thought, is no bigger than our province of Khorasan, yet
its 58 or so million people seem well able to live in harmony.
Each pedestrian seems at ease in the busy thoroughfares and
even the police patrol with an impressive dignity and are
readily accessible to each and all, even children, who have
something to ask of them.

Such impressions, of course, were not the whole story, as I
was to learn full well. The British population is not a heaven
of saints! I knew that there were many dark parts of their
history and the evils of poverty, crime, bribery and squalor
still persisted. I had not yet seen Hogarth's grisly portrayal of
drunkenness and lechery, even in high places. But in my first
impression of the land and its history I happily attributed all
the grace, beauty and well-being to the influence of Christ and
Christianity.

I came to understand that perhaps only ten per cent of the
population was then actively Christian. If, I wondered, even a
fractional Christianity can achieve so much good for all, how
much better still would all things be if their number were
increased! It was all a matter – in Jesus' words – of being 'the
salt of the earth' (Matthew 13:5). And salt is useless when it
has lost its flavour.

I noticed that the ordinary folk were ready enough to help
one another. I attributed this mutual spirit to the long centuries

of the Christ-factor in their tradition and their history. With industrialization and the spread of technology, there were intelligent, educated people committed to a lively faith and free of superstition. All that I learned about the clergy and the Church heartened me and made me realize how faith and culture could enrich each other, and how important it was for religious faith to shake free from superstition, demagogy and polemic. All these had within them a corrupting malaise conducive to bad faith and enmity in society.

My first acquaintance with Oxford at close quarters was from the high windows of a restaurant overlooking a busy street. What intrigued me there was the sight of turbaned Indians, and Afro-Caribbeans in their colourful attire. I could identify Europeans too in the crowded street and counted ten or so clergy with their 'dog collars'. It brought Qum to my mind – a place always alive with mullahs in their distinctive garb.

I had heard about the ancient buildings of Oxford and Cambridge, but nothing prepared me for the sight of Magdalen College. I was filled with awe, as I reflected on the long centuries these buildings had stood and the haunts they had afforded for generations of scholars. How venerable those walls, doors and windows! They seemed to me like the wrinkled face of an old man showing his age in the lines of his countenance. 'Read here,' they seemed to tell me, 'the text of centuries, the tale of studious enquiry and the timeless record of learning. Let them be your tutor now.' I thought of the stream of educated youth, empire-makers some of them, moving across the world from these hallowed precincts. The British, I felt, were not embarrassed by antiquity: they revelled in it as a thing of honour.

London

Another first and telling experience for me was the lawns and gardens, with grass like silk and neatly manicured flowerbeds. Then there were the endless cyclists! People's strange composure impressed me. One day in London, for example, when the train came to a standstill in a tunnel, nobody worried or protested, many just buried their heads in a book or newspaper. In fact the only noise was my Persian friend and me talking!

Reginald Iliff accompanied me to London Zoo one day. I found it compared well with that of Cairo. Reg burst into some lines of poetry in Persian when we noted how inferior the deer in Iran were compared to those in London Zoo:

> The deer in running learned from Thee,
> To shy, to pause, to glance behind,
> As kindled, flaming, blooming wide
> A candle, winged fly, flower too learned from Thee.
>
> Traditional

It seemed odd to me, since camels were so familiar in my desert land, to find a long queue of boys and girls waiting for tickets for a camel-ride. One plainly old and not yet decrepit lion I especially noted. As he peered back at the circle of human eyes surveying him, he seemed to say: 'You have come to feast your eyes on me, a captive caged. Little do you realize what caged animals you are yourselves. Your self-worship, your proud self-esteem confine you more than my cage does me. My spirit is not imprisoned here. It is you who need to free yourselves from chains.'

E. G. Browne in his book, *A Year Amongst the Persians*,[1] tells how one day he ate his lunch in a flat in Taft. A crowd quickly gathered to peer at him through the window as he ate. What intrigued the onlookers was his use of a knife and fork. Although he was not alarmed by their attentions, he thought of the lions in London Zoo and how they had to endure such staring every day while eating.

The rail network in and out of London amazed me, with its throngs of commuters. Dr Donald Carr, whom I visited early on, lived near Aylesbury. He had served for 30 years in Iran and had founded both the Isfahan hospital and one at Shiraz, travelling tirelessly between the two. On several occasion he had been attacked and robbed. It was he who introduced the first bicycle on the streets of Isfahan and, later, became the first resident to use a car (thus fulfilling his name!). Before the time of petrol stations supplies of fuel in barrels had to be sent ahead by camel so that at set points the car could refuel. One of his two daughters returned to Iran after her education in England and married William Thompson, future Principal of Stuart Memorial College, who, in due course, was to become my father-in-law after becoming the third Bishop in Iran. However I had no hint of this when I paid my memorable visit to Dr Carr's rural home in leafy Buckinghamshire. Even so, I was received with overwhelming hospitality – perhaps a sign of things to come. His home was truly a haven of peace and joy.

Following that visit, I was due at the headquarters of the Church Missionary Society in the heart of London. Founded in 1799, it had maintained a flow of servants of humanity – doctors, teachers, architects and engineers – through Africa (its first area of activity), Asia, Egypt, the Sudan and elsewhere. There, in Salisbury Square, off the famous Fleet Street and close to the Thames, I met Geoffrey Rogers, in whose house in Isfahan I had lived for a time. He lived 12 miles out of London at Loughton, near Epping Forest, and cycled the distance daily to his office. He took me to see St Paul's Cathedral; its vastness moved me deeply but I had little admiration for the numerous statues there. Too many of these, and too many tombs detract – in my view – from the simplicity of worship. A sanctuary should not become a museum! Yet I was impressed by the thought that there had been Christian worship there since the year 713.

Returning to Loughton, I had my first experience of a moving escalator. I quickly had to learn the art of stepping adroitly on and off, while watching the faces and expressions of everyone else. It was 10 July 1948 and the papers that evening announced the engagement of Princess Elizabeth to Philip Mountbatten. Here as elsewhere I had my 'ration book' which every host needed to keep me fed in those post-War years. The skill of the English in economizing – so necessary then – can seem like niggardliness to a Persian mind. Yet it was a quality that contributed to survival in war circumstances, ensuring a fair share for everybody.

Travels Further Afield

So on after these cherished visits, I set out for Oslo and the Second World Christian Youth Conference. I was to represent Iran among 1300 delegates from around the world. I embarked at Newcastle-upon-Tyne for the journey across the North Sea and into the Skagerrak. I met some intriguing fellow-travellers from Burma, Africa, India and Sri Lanka. Our boat, the *Stella Polaris*, was sumptuous, being a holiday ship. Aboard was a lesson in human heterogeneity, a diverse array of physiques, hairstyles, colour and expressions. The blue of Norwegian eyes made me think of Persian skies at home. 'Let every tongue confess that Jesus Christ is Lord' (Philippians 2:11) was the theme of the Conference, but how to achieve this in a world that war had so desperately ravaged? Daily discussion topics included the breakdown of moral values; the theological confusions of the young; freedom and socialism in Europe; post-War hatreds; and the divisions between Christian churches. As for 'hatred', I remembered the French saying: 'Hatred means that in not regarding the other as a fellow human, the hating person forfeits his own humanity.'

As for Christian disunity, I was stunned at the ruling from Bishop Stephen Neill (later to become a dear friend): namely, that Archbishop Geoffrey Fisher saw the event as a Conference and not as a full 'Church' occasion, and therefore at the final Communion Service we Anglicans were not to receive Communion, since it was being celebrated by some whose 'Holy Orders' were not of requisite validity.

This I took grievously to heart. For me there was not an issue. At home we took part in others' liturgies and they in ours without demur or hesitation. I stood up and said I could not obey this directive and intended to receive with *all* my associates in Christ. Some were discomfited but others took my side. It was only later that this issue became such a thorny topic. It had been sharply divisive in the South India Reunion scheme – an enterprise impeded by many obstacles of prejudice and contention. Sadly, there were those who thought that 'inter-Communion' ought not to precede a resolution of all that was between us concerning church order, otherwise it would obscure what was at stake. Others held that 'inter-Communion' ought not to wait for 'final' steps but could rather be a means to expedite them. The debate continues today.

After my stay in Oslo I went to the University of Lund in Sweden where there were meetings chaired by Dr D. T. Niles, a leading thinker and priest from Sri Lanka. Other meetings followed in England about Bible distribution and Christian education, prior to a holiday with the Rogers family at Clacton-on-Sea, in a tiny bungalow that could have fitted easily into my bedroom in Isfahan. I spent hours sitting on the rocks down by the sea. The water seemed to flow into me, shaping my thoughts. How varied are the moods of the sea: fearsome in storm, gentle in calm and mysteriously ruled by tides, shores, winds and weathers! How fine is Robert Frost's image of a 'bay' as 'holding the curve of one position, counting an endless repetition'.[2] I fondly imagined my host nation, an island people, sharing with the seas that surrounded them the same qualities of reverence, beauty and order.

After all, peoples are shaped by where they live. We Persians are surrounded by dry deserts and rocky mountain ranges. It is these which breed in us the Persian qualities of mind and soul. Does British insularity – in the physical sense – explain their reticence, their characteristic reserve, even their ambiguity? Then there is the normal cloudiness of the English sky. Rarely are the sun or stars visible for long, as in Iran. Perhaps the contrast between our Persian openness and the English reserve can be traced to those encircling waters that make for the insularity of an island and the clarity of our Persian skies.

Cambridge

When I arrived in Cambridge I was overcome with awe and admiration – the sheer glory of the buildings, the peace of the gardens and the unmistakable sense of history. This is how I described it to friends in Iran:

> It is autumn; the colours here are spectacular – tall majestic trees in golden leaf and the shimmer of sunlight casting on the ground the shadows of their branches. The carpet of the grass here is like velvet and so carefully kept and trimmed and rolled for centuries. The river running behind some Colleges, known as 'the Backs', is a haven for graceful swans and busy ducks, not to mention punting humans. I feel inspired by the ancient feel of studies here and am eager to begin my own.

Ridley Hall was to be my venue. Entry required a degree from some university. Mine from Tehran was recognized, and seconded by a commendatory letter from my Bishop in Iran. The date was 12 October 1947. Dinner in Hall found us surrounded by portraits of former worthies. Grace was said in Latin. After the meal there was coffee in the Common Room and then an invitation for new students to retire to the Principal's house. Faulkner Allison welcomed us with sound advice to help us adjust to what lay ahead. I was struck by how relaxed he was – no talk of rules, but of customs and traditions we would inherit. For example, he did not say 'The rule is that you attend Morning Chapel every day at 7.15 a.m.,' but instead, 'Our custom is to . . .' He did, however, stress that the Hall door closed every evening at 10.45 p.m., and that if we wanted to stay out later there was a way in over the wall at the rear. The second ruling was that guests were admissible to our rooms but that, if they were women, they would have to be out by midnight.

Cambridge College buildings bore some resemblance to the madrasas of Isfahan, with individual student rooms around a central court and larger lecture rooms in the precincts. There were three main terms in each academic year with a fourth shorter one in the long summer holiday. We had lectures on the main subjects – Biblical interpretation, philosophy, ethics, pastoral care, Church history and doctrine – and there were also sessions outside the Hall with various, often famous, University Professors. I found Christian doctrine the liveliest, involving many deep issues for discussion. Professor Elmslie's lectures on 'How Faith Came to Be' were especially memorable. Years later I translated some of them into Persian under the title *Men of God* (Noor-i-Jahan Publications, Isfahan, 1962). Professors C. H. Dodd and H. H. Farmer were others whose lectures I attended.

I had to prepare myself over 2 years for examinations in 14 subjects, by listening, taking notes and wider private reading, and – most of all – through the personal tutorial system. Each of us had a teacher to whom we read our essays and who kept track of our progress and needs.

The Vice-Chancellor of Cambridge University (the really important administrator and mentor, the Chancellor being a more honorific figure) was Professor Charles Raven, a man of remarkable gifts and a great moral leader. He addressed us once at a retreat in a small village three miles away, to which we had to cycle in a heavy rainstorm. When we arrived we were so soaked to the skin that we all needed a hot bath. Alas! Ridley Hall had only four tubs and a hot water supply quite inadequate for our corporate (and corporal) needs. The only solution was for us to use the same water! As I took my turn in the now murky, lukewarm water, I thought of how my brother in Taft used to think he was 'unclean' if just my wet finger touched his forehead – yet here I was undergoing the Ridley version – by baptism – of 'the communion of saints'. A piece of Persian verse came to mind:

Wine from an alien cup in the hand of Zarathustra
Is unclean, forbidden and unclean!
– Dark as night it be, to be shunned, to be shunned,
To be shunned.

Should I have been saying, Shylock-style,

> I will buy with you, sell with you, study with you,
> but I will not lave with you, nor wash with you!?[3]

Perhaps I shed the final traces of my brother's near fanatical cleanliness in those turgid Cambridge waters?

Study and exams apart, the University had ample facilities for sport and recreation and also for the art of oratory. Indeed, parliamentary skills are honed in the Cambridge Union where students organize political debate. I was taken to one when the motion was: 'This House considers the Conservative Party weak and, if they ever take power, will never fulfil what they pledge.'

There were MPs from both parties sharing the debate which was conducted by the students with all due decorum and lots of 'cut and thrust' of argument. In the event the Labour side lost the Motion by some 200 votes.

I was taken along to the Oxford/Cambridge Boat Race one year and, gratifyingly, Cambridge not only won but beat the record time – not because of my presence, but because of the strong tide! I tried my hand (and feet) at tennis and squash but found neither congenial, so I took up athletics. Every Tuesday and Thursday afternoons we ran as far as Grantchester. I enjoyed the green and gentle turf underfoot and got much needed exercise until one day we lost ourselves in dense fog. Such are the vagaries of the English climate!

Another highlight for me at Ridley Hall was a meeting with 30 German theological students, still prisoners of war, whom we invited to a lunch. Among the many thousands still awaiting repatriation and eager to reach it, despite the chronic state of their country at that juncture, was Jürgen Moltmann. He became a Christian while in prison camp in Scotland and subsequently a celebrated theologian. We gained pastoral experience and a sense of what evangelism meant by annual ventures into industrial areas of England. My first trip was to Mansfield, a mining town in Nottinghamshire and to a parish of about

4000 people. We were housed with local folk. It was our task to visit 60 houses and give our witness, and there were also worship and group sessions. Four of us were initiated into what coalminers undergo. Suitably rigged out in miners' clothes and 'hard-hatted' we went down in the 'cage' more than 550 metres. At the foot of the cage a small train took us a mile or so to the coalface – all that distance had been cut away laboriously yard by yard since the shaft had opened, the tons of coal drawn back to it and taken up to the surface. Some of the miners were from Latvia and Poland. I talked to one Pole who, aged 14 when his country was invaded, had made his dangerous way to North Africa and then on to Britain. We watched the miners work with pickaxes and even had a go ourselves, but quickly tired.

The following year our venue was Manchester, but my hardest pastoral experience of those years concerned a sorrowful home in Leicester. During my years at Stuart Memorial College, I had a couple of penfriends: one in the USA, and the other in England, a chap called Raymond. War conditions had disrupted our exchanges. When my stay at Ridley Hall had been arranged, I sent word to Raymond hoping to meet him. A reply came from his father. It said that Raymond, a prisoner of war in Japan, had perished in a transport ship sunk with no survivors. The father urged that, nevertheless, the family would love to meet me as a friend of their loved son.

The visit remains one of my sharpest encounters with the reality of grief. Raymond's mother opened the door and I quickly realized the depth of her brokenness of heart when she talked about the criminal futility of war, fearing still for younger sons, their National Service duty, and the anguish of her desperate loss. I felt keenly the strange infection of her tears and mused that were the world run by mothers, wars would be no more.

The pathos of those moments was worlds away from the thrill and magic of the royal wedding. I well recall listening on my radio to the nuptials of Princess Elizabeth and Prince Philip, and following their pledges in the same vows that for centuries have graced Christian marriage. Here were two people in mutual, free and trusting dedication of 'either to other', by giving and receiving of a ring and by joining of hands, so endowing each other with the new and abiding 'status' (if we can use so formal a word) of 'wife' and 'husband'.

There was another Princess I encountered while at Ridley Hall – not, this time, merely on the radio! Princess Aida Desta of Ethiopia was a student nearby at Newnham College. She had come to England with her grandfather, Emperor Haile Selasse, after the Italian invasion of their land. I was introduced by a schoolfriend of hers and invited her to tea. She accepted graciously and we had a memorable conversation. Years later she suffered imprisonment and years of hardship after the Communist Revolution.

About the same time, Queen Elizabeth (now the Queen Mother) came to the city to mark the 500th anniversary of Queen's College, and to visit the girls at Newnham College. It happened that my room at Ridley Hall overlooked where she was to walk en route to Newnham. Mary Isaac of the school in Isfahan and Margaret Thompson came to share my window and to see the Queen.

In the summer of 1948 General Smuts was elected Chancellor of Cambridge University and came to visit in the company of Winston Churchill. The streets were lined with eager crowds. Determined to see the great man I climbed a railing and hung on there for a good hour. I was rewarded. The pair walked right in front of me, Churchill beaming a broad smile with the famous 'V for victory' sign. Friends now, the two had been bitter foes during the Boer War.

Royalty and celebrity apart, I had a long ambition to see those other stars – those in the heavens – by means of a powerful telescope. My wish came true when a friend with contacts in the Cambridge Observatory invited me there. It was a summer evening with long hours of daylight. We were ushered into a tiny room with a dome-like roof which could be manoeuvred in different directions by ropes and wheels, and equipped with a small window. The actual telescope, dating from the eighteenth century, with a 12-inch diameter, had been used in the discovery of the planet Neptune.

My friend positioned it and I had my first glimpse into space through this powerful lens. What I saw reminded me somewhat of the dry deserts and mountain ranges around my hometown of Yazd. The brilliant moon showed no sign of life but had a hard and frightening beauty, bold, spiritless and dead. It had its luminosity reflected only from the sun. It was this, too, which gave its contours a special splendour. How keen a parable of what God's grace can do with people. We also had a good view of Saturn and its 'rings'. I recalled a Persian poet, Negami, celebrating the glory of the moon, and stars, as witnessing to the majesty of God:

Do you know why these pilgrims of the universe
Go circling round this perimeter of earth?

What seeking they in their orbit's thrust
To what intent their pilgrim turnings thus?

Like the needle of the compass move they on
To find the secret One who gave them motion's way.

From circling realms of light in heaven's dome
What has their vision far save this encircling round?

Vain query. Wisdom's heirs do know
For everything that turns a mover rules them round.

During my two-year stay by the Cam I had hoped to encounter Professors of Persian lore, ancient or modern, but only near the close of my studies did I have the chance. Dr Reuben Levy, who had lived in Iran for many years and had been a pupil of Edward Browne, was in charge of Persian Literature. Professor

Harold W. Bailey, an Australian, presided over the ancient languages of Avesta, Sanskrit and Pahlavi. I had long discussions with both of them, especially about Christianity in Iran before the advent of Islam, and – a matter that much concerned me – whether any part of the Bible existed in the Pahlavi language. Professor Bailey informed me that, of late, a script of Mani, dating from Sassanid times, had been discovered, showing the influence of Christianity. He also showed me parts of the Bible in the Soghdi language from the north-west of Khorasan, and had information about the four Gospels (perhaps the Diatessaron?) in Persian dating from 1549 and so three centuries prior to our present version. I found his humility and modesty a touching lesson. It seemed to me a characteristic of the learned people in Cambridge. He had such impressive credentials. His library, too, was superb, with books by Purdavood and Malek-al-Shuraiy-Bahar. In one of his texts I found lines from Jami, printed in Russian, citing 'Abdallah Ansari:

Thou art the One, Thy very Name a fount of love,
From Thy message and Thy Book Thy love doth flow.
Whoever comes where Thy dwelling is to love is turned.
Yea, love from where Thou dwellest all abundant flows.

My time at Ridley had its darkest moment in the tragedy that befell the family of the Principal. His nine-year-old son, Tony, was swinging on the College gates. Heavy and somewhat rusted with age, the motion caused them to collapse on top of him and he was killed instantly. The entire Hall was plunged into grief, though day-to-day activities went on. For a few days the Principal was absent from Chapel and Hall meals. Then normality had to resume.

Part of such normality in the summer term was punting on the Cam. For the reclining passengers punting is most relaxing, the more so in that the 'pilot' is exerting his muscles and risking his balance on their behalf. One day, Mrs Meg Thompson and her daughter Margaret, on a visit to Cambridge, came with me to the river after tea in my room. I had the chance to repay the hospitality I had known in their ever-gracious home whether in Iran or England.

It was intriguing to recall that Edward Browne had rhymed the river with a town in the south-east of Iran when he wrote:

> From far Kerman and the confines of Bam
> Returned I again to the city on the Cam.[5]

There was music, too, in Cambridge other than the love-dreams on the river and the ripples round the prow. Colleges organized concerts and I was taken by Cyril Bowles, Ridley's Vice-Principal, to one at Emmanuel College. He, too, was a man of quiet charm and gentle modesty, who made me realize that true humility is always oblivious of itself. One item at a rather more ribald concert in Ridley Hall made fun of me as one coming from – or was it into? – exile. This followed more serious musical pieces but I have wondered since whether it was prophetic of what was to happen to me.

At length, my two years of studies came to an end, and 9 June 1949 saw the last of my final exams. On my last Sunday, I attended Morning Prayer in King's College Chapel with its soaring fan-vaulting stayed on great external buttresses, where 'light and shade repose and music dwells'.[6] I had a last punt that afternoon with friends and on the Monday morning left a place and time of unforgettable memories. There was one great temptation – apart from a trauma to which I must come – to which I was not able to succumb. One of the professors in the Persian Department invited me to stay on to work there. It was an attractive opportunity to deepen my love of my land's cherished literature and to work in one of earth's paradisal academies. But I had pledged to serve the Church in Iran and the invitation had to be rejected.

Final Days in England

Before leaving for Iran, I spent some time in Bermondsey, a poor area of East London. My quarters were in a youth club situated between two railway lines, where the odour from two tanneries mingled in the air with local grime. I was certainly out of the ivory tower, finding the folk uninterested in the things of faith. As my Vicar guided me, I became accustomed to pubs that functioned like tea-houses in Isfahan. There was little outright drunkenness but endless poverty, unemployment and drug-taking. I had seen something of this in south Tehran where, however, addiction was unrelieved by the kinds of loving ministries I saw at work in Bermondsey – the parish, the Salvation Army and units of student volunteers from both Oxford and Cambridge.

While there, I got acquainted with the tannery and could admire the chemistry that turned tough buffalo hide into charming leather goods. A Polish worker there responded to my query about what most impressed him about England. When he cried 'Freedom! Freedom!', I heartily concurred. When, unhappily, my Vicar fell ill, all the duties of the parish fell to me for a momentous week; during which, as the local paper had it, 'Persian student baptizes English babies'! I was learning precious lessons about the realities of life, enhanced by visits to the Old Bailey and the Law Courts. Jack Hoare, a lawyer and former missionary in Iran, escorted me, and gave me some clues about the British legal system, emphasizing its long, slow development. I was impressed by the dignity and rigour of the proceedings. In a rear room I witnessed the judge donning the black cap worn when pronouncing the death sentence – as was still legal in 1949. I also watched the proceedings in a divorce court – sadly now a much briefer formality. Jack Hoare crowned his goodness to me with a trip on the Thames so that I might admire its many stately bridges; but I pronounced them inferior to our own in Isfahan (Pul-i Khajoo and Sio-se-Pol)! His kindness to me that day was unforgettable and was all of a piece with the self-giving generosity with which he had served in Iran.

I briefly visited the famed British Museum, and on leaving came upon my dear old scout master, Pad Bod; sadly, we had no time for more than a quick greeting. I did find time, however, for that so-called 'Royal Peculiar', Westminster Abbey, where the Diocese of London has no writ and Dean and Canons are appointed by the Crown. Impulsively, I made for 'Poets' Corner' where the great literati lie: Browning, Dryden, even the notorious Byron, and their peers. Sadly we have no such poetic mausoleum for our lyricists in Iran. There is dear Hafiz in Shiraz with Sa'di, but Ümar Khayyam and Farid Din al-Attar are far away in Neyshapour.

But there was more than poetry – or better the poetry of sacrifice – to arrest me in the Abbey. For example, the grave of Livingstone inscribed with the words from John 10:16: 'Other sheep I have which are not of his fold: them also I must bring and they shall hear my voice and there shall be one fold and one shepherd.' Also written there, quoted from his last journal entry, was whether he should invite 'English, American or Turk' to join him in the liberating of the slaves. That '. . . or Turk' in his day was the usual synonym for 'Muslim'. How might religions in their differences be one in their common compassion? I had heard of Livingstone in Sunday School back in Isfahan, and I sat at his tomb a long time reflecting on the meaning of mission and Persia's part in it.

On No Ruz, the Persian New Year, I was invited to the Persian Embassy by His Excellency Taqi-Zadeh, our Ambassador, as was the custom for all Persian subjects in their British 'exile'. Each person entering was announced by name, and then greeted His Excellency. We mingled together for refreshments, enjoying the elegant Persian carpets underfoot.

I was also invited to Coventry by Canon Howard to see how they had reacted to the near destruction of their cathedral in the German raids. The gaunt and roofless walls stood open to the sky, a grim but eloquent contour. At the east end, the sanctuary, stood a bare stone-cum-brick altar and, reared against the outline of the vacant window, there stood a cross of charred timbers saved from the fire. The stone bore the two words 'Father, forgive' – a plea that acknowledged a mutual guilt, a single, common yearning. Crosses made of salvaged nails were available, some of which have found their way to cathedrals and churches all over the world. They bear the same petition concerning reconciliation that is 'not overcome by evil' as Paul wrote in Romans 12:21. I took the one given to me that day by Canon Howard to Isfahan, keeping the piece of paper explaining its history in my Bible. I hope that those who took everything from us in Isfahan in 1979 have found and understood it. The splendid new Cathedral built some twenty years after the tragic destruction nobly captured the truth of resurrection.

I could not possibly leave England without a visit to Strat-ford-upon-Avon, the birthplace of William Shakespeare. I went and paid my homage to the great Bard and surveyed his bride's cottage and the church where he is buried. I also bade farewell to several friends who had served in Iran, among them my beloved teacher Pat Gaussen who was about to marry (I had the joy of being present at the wedding); Miss Kingdon down in Devon whom I found calm and serene in the prospect of a terminal cancer, and who gave me her diary describing her village evangelism in my home territory and to whom, under God, I owed so much in my faith-story; and Dr Donald Carr, gentle as ever in his old age in his Aylesbury home and who told me how he took the first X-ray contraption for the Shiraz hospital on camel from the port of Bushire. Finally it was 19 August 1949, and I was boarding *Bardistan*, the ship that was to take me back home. I was accompanied to the harbour by the Rogers family, who had on so many occasions tended my long sojourn in England with love and hospitality. The boat usually took cargo to the Gulf, but on this occasion had berths for a few passengers.

By 1 September we had reached Port Said. Then came the passage through the famous canal, with the statue of De Les-seps, its French builder, proudly adorning its entry waters. During the six-week journey I was able to review the whole experience of studious exile. Among the books I read was

Trevor Huddlestone's *Naught for your Comfort* and Alan
Paton's *Cry, The Beloved Country*. I also found time to translate the prayer used at Pat Gaussen's wedding, for which my
friend Mansoor Amiri later composed a fine tune (it can now
be found in our Persian Hymnal).

The thrill I had at Bandar Shahpour seeing my native shores
was marred by a sorry altercation with the Customs officers. A
foreign fellow-traveller, giving himself airs, was waved through
without a hitch, where I was subject to tedious delays and
prevarication. 'What was in my cases?' 'Books.' 'What books?'
'Theology.' I was against 'oiling palms' and this resulted in my
missing the train from Bandar Shahpour. At closing time they
wanted to go, so a junior officer took me to his house in order
that I could catch the morning train. En route, I stayed a few
days with the (then) Anglo-Iranian Oil Company Chaplain at
Abadan, and then made the long trip to Tehran. A few days
later I took the bus and savoured again the beauty of Isfahan.
I felt like Sa'di when he wrote: 'What is it to have anew the
sight of old, old friends? It is like a laden cloud distilling its
rain upon the thirsty soul in the dryness of the desert.'

I was one with Sa'di in the sweet emotions of that blithe
reunion with Isfahan and all the dear folk there.

Spiritual Turmoil

Despite many rich and varied experiences in England, I must
confess to a number of inner tensions and stresses there that
thus far I have not disclosed. These emotional and spiritual
upheavals sifted and tested the very core of my being and my
faith.

I related earlier my deep pain at the time of the first separation from my father. New dimensions of this 'wound of
absence' were to come in the very exhilaration of the new
experiences I had, attending sundry conferences, learning in a
world-famous university, encountering new scenes, fresh cultures, and widening vistas of the world. Great excitement had
gripped me. I wanted to savour everything, to participate and

belong, to see all I could, to know and appreciate all I met, to open my whole self to every encounter. But amid all this wealth, this diversity and this thrilling episode in my life, who was I? Was this excess of new experience threatening, displacing or querying my own identity, unbalancing the equilibrium of a genuine selfhood?

The first few months passed quietly enough but then an inward disquiet supervened, a restlessness of perpetual self-questioning. In my depths I felt alone and estranged; I felt acutely the loss of my mother when I was just four and then the isolation from my father, from my home, my relatives and all that I held dear. Yes, kind and gentle people had sheltered me as a teenager but what I seemed to have forfeited was irreplaceable. Those people were not my people. This vacuum within me figured in my dreams; I yearned for love for love's own sake and on its own terms. I became tearful at times and my distress intensified, when a friend whom I had deeply respected committed suicide.

My very faith in God and, with it, my sense of vocation, came into question in my heart. 'Who am I and what am I doing here?' I found myself asking. Why had my mother died when I was so young? Why had Miss Kingdon taken me from where I was 'me'? Back in Taft I might well have found studies to equip me for life without all that had happened to me via Isfahan. Was God real? I had not yet discovered how suffering actually ministers to maturity, so my thoughts were inconsolable. Nor could I tell how – as Malachi phrased it – divine grace 'would sit as a refiner and purifier of silver' (3:3).

The first effect of this disquiet was insomnia. Unable to sleep at night, I would be languid in the daytime with a serious loss of concentration. This gave rise in turn to an inhibiting self-pity, and I would think of the poet Nezami's lines:

> Forlorn I am. Hidden my wounds within!
> Friend of all forlorn, Thou knowest it well.

Worse than all this was the feeling of helplessness and despair when I could not fulfil the goals for living I had set myself since my teenage years. I felt that a Christian should be able to say with Paul: 'I can do all things through Christ who strengthens me' (Philippians 4:13). Thus my plight was deepened when I found my resolutions like ruins around me. I realized I was far from the grace Paul experienced and doubted how all my failures could be resolved. Why was my Christ not like Paul's?

It was all too easy, in this condition, to grow cynical about others. There were perhaps unconscious influences too from the xenophobia which had seeped into me in my youth and especially from army service and the university in Tehran. Even what one is not consciously harbouring can disrupt one's equanimity and cause even minor irritants to be magnified beyond reason.

For instance, in my first year at Ridley Hall I had the usual two-room quarters, a study and a bedroom. However, in my second year the staircase was altered and I was allocated a single room in which to study and sleep. I was inclined to read into this a deliberate annoyance or belittlement, 'foreign' as I was. The reaction was foolish but as no one explained any reason and I never asked why, the matter rankled in my mind. In communal life there are ample occasions to read ill-will in others if one is so minded.

These inner stresses became more spiritually perilous because they remained submerged. I somehow was able to go on working, do my studies and even take an exam. Yet I felt as if I was heading toward some sort of breakdown. Friends to whom I could partially offload myself answered me in familiar clichés: such as 'I will lay me down in peace and take my rest. For it is Thou, Lord, only . . .' (Psalm 4:9), and 'Tell all to the Lord, surrender to Him, and peace of mind will be yours.' In my turmoil, however, these meant nothing – I had known these palliatives since I was a child.

What if I were to quit my studies and go back to Iran? What use would I be to the Church? Where, How, When could I recover those halcyon days when I had answered my divine call? The struggles went on until one day a student suggested I write to Bishop Stephen Neill, who, he said, had helped many at a time of mental strain. I had, in fact, met Stephen Neill briefly in conferences and knew he was in Geneva working for the World Council of Churches, so I ventured to write. He replied quickly and suggested a time to meet when he would be in Cambridge. In mingled excitement and trepidation, I went to see him at Trinity College. For about two hours he simply listened to me as I poured out my heart to him, unashamed at times about the tears I could not restrain. I kept back nothing consciously and came to feel in him, his demeanour, his whole being, that there was someone who would understand, who could comprehend me better than I could myself, who could lead me to wholeness. His very dignity drew me, as did a sense of his wisdom and integrity. Perhaps he was – I later thought – filling the role of a father-figure, satisfying the need stemming from my separations in Yazd?

After that first crucial 'rescue' of my soul, we met again inter-mittently before my return to Iran, maybe some six times in all. Our friendship endured right up to his death in the summer of 1984 when he was living at Wycliffe Hall, Oxford. He be-queathed his pectoral cross and episcopal ring to me as Bishop in Iran. Gratefully I wore them up to my retirement in 1990, and passed them on to my successors.

We wrote frequently in the crucial months following our first meeting. His responses were always prompt and pointed. Though the actual letters were all lost when our home was looted in Isfahan at the time of the Islamic Revolution, some excerpts survive from my own writings where now I draw on them.

Now for your question why some are called to experience descent into dark depths of despair. First, I think in order that they may be privileged to understand one part of the work of Christ which is hidden from those who have never had such deep experiences. Second, in order that they may be able to help others who through circumstances have to suffer in special ways. God does not waste His material: if He gives a special vocation of suffering He gives a special reward in special opportunities of service. I think some men have to fight against these temptations to despair all their lives, but if they are sure that God is leading them all the time they win through: others are set free from them completely . . . Yes! Everyone in the world needs to be broken-hearted at some time or other – with some it comes before conversion, with others after but *no Christian* can escape this experience.

Worrying has become so much of a habit with you that it is difficult to stop it easily, but I think you are making progress . . . Never make any promise: simply say to yourself each day: 'Now today, if I am faithful to God and trust Him, He will keep me from evil.' We can't live more than one day at a time, and often your failures are through trying to live further into the future than a man can do . . . There is a great difference between wanting to know and being impatient to know: some things God will never show us, and other things He will show us when His own good time has come. In either case we must be patient and let Him do as He wills.

At one of our sessions Bishop Neill suggested that I read the Book of Psalms and the Book of Job quietly and calmly, and to do so in Persian – that language being likely to 'reach' me more deeply. In this way I identified myself with Job's complaining about suffering. Some verses exactly expressed my own physical and mental turmoil:

After this, Job broke his silence and cursed the day of his birth. 'Perish the day when I was born . . . why was I not stillborn? Why did not I perish when I came forth from the womb? . . . If only the grounds of my resentment might be weighed and my misfortunes placed with them on the scales! They would outweigh the sands of the sea . . . I cannot hold my peace, I must speak out in my anguish of spirit . . . I am sickened of life, I shall give free rein to my complaints, speaking out in the bitterness of my soul . . . My kinsfolk hold aloof, my acquaintances are wholly estranged from me, my relatives and friends fall away . . . I am become an alien in their eyes

... Why do the wicked live on, hale in old age, and great and powerful ... the rod of God's justice does not reach them ... One man dies crowned with success, lapped in luxury and comfort ... another dies in bitterness of soul never having tasted prosperity ... Today my thoughts are embittered ... If only I knew how to reach Him, how to enter His court to state my case before Him and set out my arguments in full.'

It was when I reached chapter 38 that a transformation took place. It was as if I had emerged from dense fog – the fog of conceit that had covered me so that I could not see, the fog of egotism, vanity and pride. In part, how I had grown up in the atmosphere of the Church contributed to it. I was for a while the single individual being groomed for ministry and the Church's future, the only one who had done university and military service, and was now sent abroad for further education. This had all made me a conceited fellow, teaching and preaching since his teens and not able to see his own defects, his many frailties, while seeing those of others only too well! Pride was the ultimate factor underlying my doubts about God – I could not accept anything unless satisfactorily proved *to me*. God, for my sake, ought to be more forthcoming about his alleged evidences.

So my latent hypocrisy continued until I detected it for what it was. God did prove himself in the end though not – as with the leper Naaman – on my own terms, but on his. Through these verses in Job, he melted me in the crucible of humility:

Then from the heart of the tempest, Yahweh gave answer to Job: 'Who is this obscuring My designs with empty-headed words? Brace yourself like a fighter. Now it is My turn to ask questions and yours to inform Me. Where were you when I laid earth's foundations? Tell Me, since you are so well informed! Who decided the dimensions of it, do you know?'

Then replied Job to Yahweh: 'My words have been frivolous, what can I reply? I had better lay my finger on my lips.

I have spoken once, I will not speak again: more than once I will add nothing.'

'I know that You are all-powerful: what You can conceive You can perform. I am the man who obscured Your designs with my empty-headed words. I have been holding forth on matters I cannot understand, on marvels beyond my know-ledge. (Listen, I have more to say, now it is my turn to ask you questions and yours to inform me.) I knew You then only by hearsay, but now, having seen You with my own eyes, I retract all that I have said and in dust and ashes I repent' (Job 42:1–6).

The truth was that I needed repentance; not in a pietistic sense but deep within, a U-turn from self-centredness to centredness in God, repentance not from this wrong or that but from the whole edifice of my self-esteem, to know myself as a speck of dust before the unimaginable reality of God. I came down from my imaginary palace of conceit to dwell in the lowly place where there was rest from the striving of self-will. I felt a process of healing was under way within. Tensions were relieved and I began to find release from the tendency to enmity, resentment and suspicion to which I had been prone, not least toward foreigners. I began to sleep more normally and took up breathing exercises before sleep, as Bishop Neill recommended (I did not then know from what long insomnia he himself suffered).

Reading the Psalms as he suggested inspired me no less than the book of Job. Before this time words like 'trust' and 'faith' had for me a purely mental import in an intellectual exercise. Now, from the psalmists, I realized that 'trust' meant entire self-surrender.

Blessed are they that put their trust in Him (2:11)
O Lord my God in Thee do I trust (7:1)
In the Lord put I my trust (11:1)
Trust in the Lord and do good (37:3)
What time I am afraid I will trust in Thee (56:3)

In Thee, O Lord, do I put my trust let me never be put to
confusion (31:1)
Those who trust in the Lord shall be as Mount Zion, which
cannot be moved but abides for ever (125:1).

Just as at dawn the growing light spreads across the dark face
of earth and heaven, lightening all things, so in my heart did
a darkness give way to a light of divine trust. This was the full
meaning of *Tavakkul* – a total trust and confidence in God –
I had heard about at home among Muslims. How incredibly
simple it all came to seem. In one of my meetings with Stephen
I asked him 'Can it really be that simple?'

He answered, 'Yes, that simple.'

From that time on, I let anxiety, fear and suspicion retreat
before the invading peace of God. As a result I grew happier
and at rest with my soul. I once said to Stephen that it seemed
to me as if I had never believed before. 'Yes, you have,' he
replied, 'but not deeply enough until now.' He explained his
view that there were three stages in Christian faith: first, an
emotion prompted by whatever arouses it; secondly, an intellectual grasp whereby doubts are handled with a will to get
beyond them, lest faith remain falsely sanguine and complacent; thirdly, an entire spiritual self-offering that is beyond
logic, argument and rationality. Only in this way will the whole
person be Christ's so that practical discipleship in all its claims
takes over the self.

As I set all this down now, half a century has passed.
Recalling those vital meetings now, I do not remember Bishop
Neill saying anything that someone else could not have said.
The crucial factor in my whole experience stemmed, I am sure,
from who he was: the grace, wisdom and gentleness of his
whole persona. He had a brilliant mind, excelling in all things
academic. He had turned from a sure and distinguished career
as a Fellow of Trinity to be a missionary in India. His scholarship, leadership and spiritual ministry was esteemed by all.
Yet this great man's generous openness to me was, for me, a
soul-transforming example of pastoral self-giving, for which I

am eternally grateful to God. He took me beyond all my sadness, hidden grief and into an acceptance of my life and vocation. In quiet hope I went beyond pining over what I had read as adversity or tribulation – as my introverted self-pity had supposed them to be.

Among the things that I wrestled with was my Persian-ness and how it related both to the Islam which, historically, had overtaken it, and to Westernism. All Iranians have a sense of *Ahuraii Iran*, that is, the Iran prior to all things Islamic, and then the divergence of our Shi'ism from the dominant Sunni Islam elsewhere. These two dimensions of our identity are deeply prone to tension and to some extent are at odds with each other. It is a situation from which Arab Muslims are exempt. As for Westernism, most of the outside influences in my life had come from English folk who were mainly evangelical. The Church to which I came to owe allegiance was Anglican. I could not take its identity lightly. I wanted to be loyally sincere and sincerely loyal but it was not easy. The failure to hold Persia, the Shi'ah in Iran, and English Christianity together correctly could lead to a split selfhood. There had to be unification in the soul. Had I not travelled through 3000 years or more of history in the 30-odd years of my odyssey from the village simplicity of Taft to the complexity of the West? These stresses were only faced when I learned to trust in God completely. 'Acceptance' was the word to describe all I had undergone – acceptance in Christ. His truth would be the sieve through which I had to pass all my reactions; all my yearnings only He had the power to realize within me. I had to respect and possess everything good and valid in *all* my heritage, so that joy might take over. The thing to banish all self-pity and self-esteem was the suffering love of Christ and him crucified, he whose resurrection was the wellspring of hope and power for the unknown future. This healing in the Holy Spirit, the fruit of all my anguish away from home – which was also my re-making – found me ready and eager to return to Iran, in all humility, to begin service in the Church.

CHAPTER 7

Life's Aspirations

My longing to be where thou art
Is no strange thing.
A thousand like me, strangers all,
Thy abode do ever seek.   Hafiz

My yearning to serve the Church, the aspiration of my life, is
best exemplified by Jesus when he said: 'The Son of Man is
not come to destroy . . . The Son of Man is come to minister
and to give His life a ransom for many' (Matthew 20:28).
Jewish faith and ritual were familiar with official 'priesthood'
offering daily ritual sacrifice on the Temple altars. Jesus' offering was himself, in the midst of daily life, as he taught, cared,
healed, suffered and so redeemed. His whole being was thus
'consecrated' to the design of God. The element of 'sacrifice'
was not that of artificial ritual but a readiness for the whole
cost of what his ministry brought upon him of burden and
travail – what Paul later called 'a living sacrifice', which meant
'presenting ourselves alive'. The dimension of surrender was
there, no longer the involuntary subjection of an animal to
slaughter, but instead the free self-surrender by the person, of
personality, wholly and gladly.

This in Christianity is what our selfhood is for: not for
self-forfeiture in a mystic sense as if 'we' were no longer there,
but self-finding in a selflessness that still needs its selfhood –
as St Francis was present for there to be any 'poverty' with
Christ. The self-entity we all have is not elided or suppressed
(for then no 'surrender' would be possible); rather, it is held
wholly on behalf of God's will and design for it. This is what

Jesus meant when he spoke of the disciple both 'losing' and 'finding' his life in this way.

This vocation and destiny are open to *all* disciples in Christ. However, in the early Church, particular forms of ministry began to develop and leadership emerged. It had been there already in the 12 disciples. Christians travelled far and wide and were customarily given refuge; however, as the Church was also much spied upon by ill-wishers, these travellers needed credentials that showed they were bona fide brethren or sisters. Who but some trusted local leader could issue or assess such letters of commendation? So in this way functions developed that referred to special 'orders' of ministry, such as a house-holder – like Philemon making a place for the Church 'in his house'. Had it not been in an unknown disciple's 'guest room' (the Greek for 'an upper room') that the first Holy Communion had been held? Was it not such a 'guest room' that the inn-keeper in Bethlehem had to tell Mary and Joseph was taken?

So it followed that caring for the distribution of alms to widows and the poor, etc., as well as presiding at Holy Com-munion, came to be entrusted to particular people who were ordained to this trust and task. Thus what came to be the 'Orders' (threefold) of deacons, priests (or elders) and bishops (overseers) emerged. It was in this context that my sojourn and training in Cambridge had been planned, leading hopefully to that ministry so tenderly described in the Gospel under the analogy of 'shepherd' (John 21:16, Acts 20:28, 1 Peter 5:2) – hence the terms 'pastor' and 'pastoral'. My ministry would incorporate administration, study, teaching, preaching, under-pinned throughout by caring.

Early Ministry

In the traditional Anglican way, it was as a 'deacon' that I was called and ordained first. The date was 18 October 1949, in St Luke's Church, Isfahan, and the 'laying on of hands' (the traditional phrase from apostolic times) was performed by our then Bishop, William Thompson. As former Principal of

Isfahan College, he had known me from my earliest days. Deacons normally work under supervision, at least initially. I was posted for two months to Kerman, under Nasrallah Solhi-Kol and then to Abadan for some six weeks to be acquainted with the English as well as Persian people there and to gain more experience. I then came back to Isfahan to work under the Revd H. C. (David) Gurney, an Australian and a noted watercolour artist who – in that pursuit – deeply loved the Persian mountains and the landscape. He encouraged me to take up his hobby, to my endless gratitude.

Coinciding with my ordination as priest in August 1950, there was a large conference in Shiraz of members of both our Churches in Iran – Episcopal and Presbyterian – comprising both Biblical studies and social and clerical issues. The service was held in St Simon the Zealot Church, a rare structure in a Persian style, and a worthy work of art. The congregation that day was joined by seven clergy from four nations. Two friends of my childhood, Abdol-Masih Shirvanian and Dr Fathali Azali, later head of the Christian hospital in the city, were present to support me. A few months later, during the time David Gurney was on leave in Australia, I had responsibility for St Luke's.

One incident of those early days of ministry comes to mind. A schoolteacher and an army officer called on me and, after the usual formalities, asked what I did for a living. When I replied that I was a priest in the Church, they were aghast. How, they wondered, was it possible, credible even, for a man with a university degree, an educated fellow, to pursue such a calling in that day and age? I tried to explain the nature of Christian ministry and why I had found it such a compelling and authentic vocation. For all my warm sincerity, I feared they remained quite sceptical; I felt that all my words had fallen on deaf ears.

Their disdain brought home to me the difficulty the Christian faith encounters because of the association with missionaries and the prejudice they can arouse in being seen as alien. The Church and its institutions for health and education were inevitably linked in the popular mind with things political, with the economic and military activity of Britain in Iran during the nineteenth and in the first half of the twentieth centuries. Thanks also to T. E. Lawrence and his role in western Arabia, and to the South Persian Rifles in Iran, Iranians looked on the British with suspicion and dislike. I realized I would be facing this atmosphere and that it could well be a prolonged and arduous dimension of my vocation.

Certainly, most people welcomed the ministries of school and hospital which the missionaries brought, especially in the early years. As I noted earlier, the mullahs opposed the opening of Christian schools, but the more perceptive and well-disposed among them recognized their worth and sent their children to them. By and large, however, it was only travelled people, those who were well educated and familiar with the honest principles of the missions and their role in other lands, who gladly recognized their worth and approved of their presence. As for fanatical people, they never lost an occasion to vilify and denigrate the Church.

Behind the reaction I had from my two visitors that day was their doubt that I really was a priest and not a planted agent with a hidden agenda, dabbling in secret activities. Throughout my service in Iran this issue and the tensions it caused were like a thorn in my side.

I loved Iran. I was enamoured of Persian literature and language. I was loyal to my heritage with my whole heart. While I readily acknowledged what could only be reproached about political Britain and its role in Iran, I resisted all hostility and disdain directed against individuals, whether they were my own compatriots or foreigners. My faith in Christ, the compassion he taught and the vocation he had granted me all meant that I should aim for an inclusive love across ethnic and political lines. My whole goal in life was to interpret the Christ I loved and be ardent in relating him to all, to socialize and care in a spontaneous way, without prejudice – in short to love and to be loved.

Yet all too often I felt that people did not accept or take me on these terms; rather, they would regard me with suspicion and mistrust. Convinced as I was of my calling in Christ, there was no question of letting the situation deter me. I firmly believed that I must read it as the path I had to follow, even if it meant pain and suffering. To undertake this would itself demonstrate love in Christ and would fulfil what he had meant when he said, 'If anyone would be my disciple, he must renounce self, he must take up his cross and follow me' (Mark 8:34). Thus to face suspicion and hostility fell within the mission granted me by God.

Very soon after I had begun my ministry in the Church in Isfahan the crisis over oil developed. A few people from the National Front came to the Church at that time, making what might be called verbal intimidations by means of sarcastic remarks and gibes; I myself was in agreement with the principle of oil nationalization. The situation deteriorated thanks to the mutual intransigence of the Anglo-Iranian Oil Company and Dr Muhammad Mossadeqh, our Prime Minister. Anti-British feeling and propaganda intensified and affected our work adversely. Return visas were denied to personnel from Britain who had gone on leave there, but locally we carried on our duties. The Detective Bureau of Police regularly visited the church to listen to my sermons. The man introduced himself as 'Mojtabah' ('chosen', if not 'choice') but behind his back we used to call him 'Eshtebah' ('mistake'); every time he left we would encourage him to make a donation to charity, which he frequently did.

Love and Marriage

'In the spring,' they say, 'a young man's fancy turns to thoughts of love.' Spring or not – and perhaps, at 30-plus, I was not so young – my thoughts often turned to whom I might marry. The loneliness I faced in the ministry, betwixt and between the two worlds I have described, only made the question more – as they say – existential. There was also the complication of the local tradition on such matters, whereby marriage was very much an inter-family arrangement and personal freedoms were therefore limited. While I had been in the staff department of the army there had been suggestions from those who wished me to be a member of their households. When told, however, of my priestly vocation, they would promptly become cold towards me.

How was I to negotiate between the two worlds of my identity, my being integrally Persian and my incidental 'Englishness' in the inclusive context of my calling in the one Christ? My quandary was well-caught in the lines of Jalal al-Din Rumi:

'From where art thou?' I asked.
The mocking answer came:
'A half from Turkistan, a half from Farghaneh,
Half mud and water me, half heart, half soul.'
'Then be my friend,' I said. 'My "me" relates to yours.'
'What means "relates"?' came the answer.
'Related', 'unrelated' are all the same to me.[1]

Given the mutuality between peoples that is implicit in Christ, and given the onus to live it out in a setting that would always test our will to it, I knew that my wife would also need to be bi-cultural, 'half Turkistan, half Farghaneh', unless I were to opt for celibacy and forego the ideal of marriage. But as I sensed in my bones and in my heart, foregone it was not to be. However, I will content myself here with the simple fact: a girl appeared on the horizon of my life who was thinking along the same bi-cultural lines herself, and she gave a positive reply to my proposal.

In phrasing love's mystery blandly in this way, I realize that I have used an incorrect analogy, for 'horizons' recede as you approach them. Happily, it was not so with this horizon, nor of the meaning of Christian marriage.

Margaret was the third daughter of Bishop and Mrs Thompson. Born in Isfahan, she had also been educated in Iran for her first schooling. Whereas her older sisters had been sent to

England, this had not been possible for her owing to the onset of the Second World War. However, when the War ended she did spend four final years in an English school; she had then returned to Iran. Her time in Tehran Community school and her whole upbringing meant that she spoke Persian fluently and was in effect a bi-national.

On my return from Ridley Hall and England, she was living with her parents in Isfahan and we used to see each other from time to time. Very soon, however, she left for England to train as a nurse. Our friendship continued by exchange of letters until, in the summer of 1951, we announced our engagement. This was a time when anti-British feeling was running high thanks to the altercations over Dr Mossadeqh's policies. Inviting friends to our engagement celebration, we quoted this from Sa'di: 'If there be enmity and war between the Arabs, Love and joy abide between Lailah and Majnun.'

Her parents had approved, though they would have preferred her to complete her nursing training. She and some of her friends, however, saw the situation worsening so rapidly that it would be better to return to Iran quickly. I warmly concurred with this opinion.

The immediate problem was the return visa. She had often travelled before between the two countries without any visa problems. This time the Iranian Embassy in London refused her entry, and stated that, as she and her mother had been born in Iran, she should not be presenting a British passport at their Embassy. This was a delaying pretext.

The obstacle had to be overcome. No imagination is necessary to understand the urgency and zeal with which I besieged the offices in Tehran until, after some two months travelling to and from Isfahan to the capital on this holy errand, the order was sent to the London Embassy to issue the visa. Margaret flew back to Iran in early May 1952, and the marriage, conducted by her father, took place in St Luke's on 6 June. It has been for over nearly five decades a saga of joyful fidelity.

We were well aware of the problems often said to be involved in inter-ethnic marriage and both of us had been advised by friends to let those issues deter us. Our faith was that God in his purpose had brought us together, for otherwise how could such a union, fraught with immediate political adversity and many other hurdles, have ever transpired? Our antecedents might be very different, but the bond was authentic and was meant to be trusted.

As Jalal al-Din had sung, disparities are fit to be ignored when – as marital logic says– 'one plus one equals one'. Certainly, it was a long way from Taft/Yazd to Clonskeagh Castle near Dublin. It was there that Margaret's father, William Thompson, had spent his childhood, his father having been a member of the landed gentry. In his boyhood he had been accustomed to all that goes with that measure of elegance and status in the community, but had forsaken it when he became a missionary teacher in the land of his adoption. Meg Thompson, too, could boast similarly well-connected social credentials. Her father, Dr Donald Carr, came from the landowning 'Carrs of Holbrooke', and her mother, Agnes, was a great-granddaughter of the famous Elizabeth Fry (1780–1845) of the Fry chocolate family, a celebrated social worker and reformer of prisons. Agnes Carr was also related to the great Florence Nightingale (1820–1910), the pioneer of modern nursing.

These antecedents are of interest not only in indicating the devotion that brought the missionaries to Iran but also their capacity to give their generations to the land of their adoption. It was not the social stature that mattered but its loving investment in the paths of gentle ministry. In all our years together, I have never known Margaret refer to her ancestry, nor did my parents-in-law ever fail in their warm acceptance of their new 'son'.

It is well known that love readily turns to verse. How many lyrics have been composed by the lovelorn! I myself wrote a hymn in Persian which was duly sung in this translation by Norman Sharp:

O God, Triune, transcendent!
　　Love's spring, for ever flowing!
Upon Thy love dependent,
　　Love be from us outgoing.
　　　　By Thee is love implanted;
　　　　By Thee each boon is granted;
　　　　Where praise of Thee is chanted
　　Is Heaven, joy bestowing.

For Love's delight and pleasure,
　　O Lord, we magnify Thee;
For gladness without measure,
　　O Christ, we glorify Thee.
　　　　Our future pathway brighten;
　　　　Of harms and hurts that frighten –
　　　　Of danger, us enlighten –
　　Of wrong that may defy Thee.

These two, O Lord, do Thou view;
　　They both their troth have plighted –
Are joined in one, as Thou too
　　Art with Thy Church united.
　　　　Through all life's toil and trailing,
　　　　When young – when frail and failing –
　　　　Thy gracious aid availing,
　　Their love be well requited.

In times of tribulation,
　　When ways and means are slender;
In pain and in privation,
　　Renew our heart's surrender;
　　　　In hours of jubilation,
　　　　Success and relaxation,
　　　　For Thine aid and salvation,
　　Our gratitude we render.

These two, O Lord, enable,
    Their welfare coalescing,
In Thee be strong and stable,
    Each other's heart possessing.
        Their bond with Thee unites them;
        To faithfulness incites them;
        Until death's call invites them,
    Grant them ever more blessing.

With two tunes composed at the time, the hymn is now included in our Persian Hymnal. If the English version seems a trifle awkward it is through the exigencies of the tune; the Persian is much more singable.

Beyond music and poetry, what of the sacramental meaning of this wedded troth, the stature each bestows on the other in the total trust of a love that, in its true possessiveness, wants only to deserve to be possessed? What does it feel like to have a bride, a whole personality through all the transactions of body, mind and soul, pledged to one's own being as a husband? There is a passage in George Eliot's *Adam Bede*, which says:

> He called his love frankly a mystery . . . He only knew that the sight of her and memory of her moved him deeply, touching the spring of all love and tenderness, all faith and courage within him . . . He created the mind he believed in out of his own which was large, unselfish, tender.[2]

Only brides and wives can tell the mystery from the other side of the male world but in a Christian sacramental sense of 'this holy estate' it is surely identical: trusting to belong and belonging to trust. Life-longness, having death as – maybe – the only feasible rupture, is no more than the reality of authentic love.

The arch in architecture offers perhaps the best analogy for wedded troth. It springs from two separates – the walls or pillars that will constitute its being. Marriage does not cancel idiosyncrasy, it recruits and hallows it. But those separates have 'a tendency toward' as the arms of a potential arch that reach out towards a completion for which they are meant – a completion that is sexual and spiritual, in the body and in the heart.

Marriage, then, is the keystone that is dropped into the thrusting arches that await it and which alone uphold it. Correspondingly, the keystone, the pledge and troth, bind them into one. In so doing they create space for family and hospitality; they hold up the very world of home. Then, by the strange paradox of this engineering in stone, an arch finds itself solidified precisely by the weight it carries. Thus what it needs to do becomes the very deed in the doing. The wedding ceremony says to us: 'Be what you have now become and from the being is the becoming.' As in ordination, the dignity conferred is the vocation to achieve – not one without the other.

My story, from a wedding transacted in these Christian terms, becomes the story of a partnership. Margaret's personality and influence need the tribute of what words cannot well convey. What Paul tells in Galatians 5:22, of 'the fruits of the Spirit', describes what we have sought and found. I have continually thanked God for the gift she has been to me in all the vicissitudes we have passed through together. Her strengths have counterbalanced the weak points in my make-up. Her calm demeanour, patience, silence and unfailing affection have countered and disciplined my restless and impatient ways. As Solomon reportedly said (Proverbs 31:26) of his 'ideal wife', 'She opens her mouth with wisdom and in her tongue is the law of kindness'.

Hence the gratitude I have always kept for her tranquil spirit and her unassuming ways. Mothering our four fine children drew out all her patient skills and gentleness. She gave herself unstintingly and intuitively to them, to their well-being in home and school and beyond. Sacrificially she ensured for us all that family cohesion and unity of heart so often disparaged or denied in contemporary attitudes unready for the patient cost of it in nurture and in grace. We have been able to pass on to our children the same ideals, the Christian traditions around home and household by which we were guided. Such effective legacies are benediction indeed, a theme of my steady admiration and abiding thanksgiving. The narrative yet to come, with its tragic crises, will only corroborate and deepen this testimony. She stood squarely with me in my own costly stand against the tyranny, calumny, deceit and tribulation of those dark days.

Difficult Times Ahead

From these reflections on our 'To have and to hold, from this day forward' of that blissful June in 1952, my narrative must renew its meandering way. The oil crisis deepened. There was a sharp impasse between the obdurate Mossadeq and the intransigent Anglo-Iranian Company, and the relations between the two States worsened ominously. During the first half of 1952 many oil personnel, unwilling to be employees of the new National Oil Company of Iran, left the country. The Imperial Bank of Iran saw its concessions lapsing and terminated its long years of activity in the country. The British Consulate closed in Isfahan and finally diplomatic relations between Iran and Britain were broken off. The USA began to gain an interest instead, partly via President Truman's 'Point Four' policy, which brought in large benefits in welfare, agriculture and cultural relations. For the first time we acquired an American Consulate in Isfahan, manned by John Hall Paxton, who with his wife attended St Luke's. After she became a widow she continued in 'Point Four' work for several years.

A different experience of my first year came with my journey to India to be Iran's delegate at the Third Christian Youth World Conference meeting in Kerala, together with Parviz Hakim of the Evangelical Church. Kerala was chosen because it had the largest proportion of Christians in its population among Indian states. I was impressed at that time with their attitude to the issues of 'foreignness' that so tested us in Iran. Having just attained independence, their patriotism, exuberant as it was, seemed free of grudges against aliens. In criticizing their British legacy they were free of rancour and capable of appreciating what was worthy of credit in their long history. This was evident in the Conference when it came to discussing the aftermath of a long period of imperialism, and aspects of legitimate reproach. It was so different from the mood in Iran. One of the Indian delegates, a grocer I think, got up and commented: 'After all the bad things you have alleged about the British, why not reflect on how it would have been with us if, instead of them, we had had the Nazis here. Would they not have liquidated Mahatma Gandhi and his followers forthwith?'

Learning that I was from Iran, one of the Indian men took me to a small rural church in Kottayam, an almost all-Christian town and headquarters of the Mar Thoma Church. Inside the church he showed me a cross carved in the stone which he said was locally known as 'the Persian Cross'. It was due, apparently, to the influence there of an ancient Persian Christian community. In the visitors' book there, I wrote that just as Christian Persians had gone to India and one should rejoice, so too it would be apt for Indians to come to evangelize in Iran.

From Kerala I went to visit the well-known Theological Seminary in Bangalore, Mysore State. I had been asked to discover whether it would be well to send there, rather than to England, any recruits to ministry we might have forthcoming in Iran. After taking stock and talking with the staff at Bangalore, I felt it could prove a very appropriate place for our people, with the advantage of the Asian environment, and in hope of being free of the automated culture of the West. Furthermore, they would be hopefully rid of the notion that Christianity was a Western religion. And indeed, on my return, our Church in Iran did make Bangalore the chosen, preferred venue for our ordinands.

Prior to that, I had a sojourn in Lucknow, a city with ancient links with Iran. There I listened to a speech by Jawaharlal Nehru, Prime Minister of India, addressing a meeting under the World Council of Churches. He was greeted with applause when he referred to the services that missionaries had rendered over many years to the people of India. From there I went to world-famed Agra and marvelled, as millions before me, at the majesty of the Taj Mahal, surely the most superb tribute in architecture of the love of man for woman, of Shah Jehan for his dead wife, Mumtaz Mahal. No Persian could fail to thrill with pride on reading the verses in Persian, beautifully inscribed on the marble stones. At one point there is a mistake, said to have been deliberately made on the Shah's orders, lest the perfection of the mausoleum be absolute – which no earthly edifice might ever be. Perfection belongs to God alone.

In the same city I visited St John's College, which was designed and built by Bishop Thompson in his younger days. His name is inscribed there on a copper plaque. En route home I had an opportunity to pass by New Delhi and Bombay, where my brother Yahya and three of my cousins were working. They either managed or worked in restaurants, building up assets for their future. This family contact was welcome. During a hiatus at Karachi about an ongoing flight to Tehran, whom should I see, sitting quietly in a corner outside the main passenger hall, but Bishop George Bell of Chichester, a founder spirit of the World Council of Churches, and one of its Honorary Presidents.

I approached him and we began to talk. During the Second World War he had striven to maintain brotherly contact with the isolated Confessing Church in Germany, and had sharply criticized the Allies for saturation bombing of German civilian populations. It could be that his courage in this precluded him from appointment to the Archbishopric of Canterbury where, earlier, he had been a very innovative Dean in developing religious drama and the arts. It was a benediction to me to find in so significant a Christian leader this keen interest in the arts.

Back home our situation grew ever more strained. The National Front and the Tudeh Party together fomented anti-British passion, deeply affecting the climate of our lives and our fellowship within the Church. Our Bishop was ordered to leave the country and did so in May 1953 amid keen sadness. No reason was given. The loss of them (Mrs Thompson also left her birthland) was sharply felt by his numerous former students at SMC.

Still greater pressure against the Church followed. Opposition to the hospital intensified, partly abetted by local physicians who seemed to resent its work. The Department of Health decreed that the hospital should close with six months' notice. Headmistress Nevarth Aidin was summarily dismissed from her headship at Beshest-i-Ayin School where she had presided, much loved, for many years.

Nevertheless, the Church continued steadily in worship and prayer. One day I was summoned with two colleagues to Police Headquarters where they began compiling files against us. As I recollect now, one of the interrogators seemed to have some sympathy, even encouraging me to be free to negate what might be incriminating. This in honour I could not do. So when asked, 'Do you know x?' – actually a young man who had attended services and with whom I had taken a walk or two, his family having been familiar with the church for a long time – I replied, 'Yes. I do know him.' It transpired that he had made charges against us. Rumour also had it that there had been talk in one of the households in the city of a plot to assassinate me.

It was a tense and disheartening climate in which to go on hoping for normality and an abatement of the hostility. We favoured oil nationalization and could not understand why political enmities should be foisted on the Church. As for the long tangle of Allied–German wars and tumults and their repercussions on Iran via the Tehran Conference and Rashid Ali's role in Iraq and the fall of Reza Shah – all this, I thought, could be divorced altogether from the work and being of the Church. I had been in Germany, at Willingen, for a conference about the mission of the Church and had met Dr Martin Niemöller, famous for his opposition to the Hitler regime and all its works. Our ties were ecumenical and not uniquely British. When he enquired about the Church in Iran and I reported on the strained climate and the ugly auguries he said, 'Nothing can destroy the Church except disloyalty by those within, its members. Even if one, two, three or four stand fast, you should have no fear.'

What he meant by such consistent loyalty was clear from his other famous remark, 'First they came to arrest the Jews and I did not protest because I was not a Jew. Then to arrest the Communists and I did not protest because I was not a Communist. Then union members and I did not protest because I was not a union member. Now when they come to arrest me, there is no one left to protest against my arrest.'

We were immersed in perplexity in the summer of 1953 as to whether or not the Diocesan Council should be convened. Opinion was divided because there was widespread unrest across the provinces and turmoil in Tehran and Isfahan. Statues of the two Shahs, Reza and Mohammad Reza were overturned. On Mordad 28th (19 August, 1953), with the wailing of the sirens of Isfahan's weaving industry, we realized that something was afoot. A coup had overthrown Dr Mossadeq, enabling the Shah and Queen Soraya to return from their exile in Rome.

In point of fact the 'popular' coup had been a foreign conspiracy, engineered by the famous, or infamous, Kermit Roosevelt, of America.[3] Cunningly, the coup was so handled as to delude the nation that it had been spontaneous, an act of the self-liberating people who, with the assistance of the army, had toppled a troublesome upstart and restored the country to itself. Like most people, that was how we understood the event in its immediate aftermath, though the truth about it could not be so readily digested later.

Mordad 28th coincided with the end of the six months' notice of closure on the hospital. A letter came from the Department of Health that we were free to carry on. Returning missionaries, with visas now available to them, began to arrive to resume their sundry ministries. That same year, on 30 October, our first daughter, Shirin, was born; 14 months later, to complete our joy, and theirs, her maternal grandparents were back home.

The devious turn of the political wheel is history now and

need not be rehearsed again here.[4] American and British intelligence services had contrived to bring back the Shah but the memory of the subterfuge behind his new tenure of office deeply compromised his claim to it. The contretemps may well have contributed to the success of the Ayatollah's campaign against the Shah 15 years later.

Day-to-Day Ministry

Because of these ambiguous circumstances, their truth still to unfold, we were able to continue our work in easier conditions.

At the heart of any 'shepherd's' life in ministerial priesthood – or priestly ministry, the two are as one – is the nurture of personal faith and understanding among the people in his care. This means continued study, reading and prayer, so that – out of the wealth of his own meditation – he can mediate truth and wisdom to every range of listener. This interplay of mind to mind and soul to soul is no easy task. The clergy wrestle in their studies with meanings and queries they cannot always readily interpret effectively to folk accustomed to more workaday things. R. S. Thomas, the Welsh clergy-poet, wrote of his sheep-keeping, often inarticulate hearers, in the pew: 'I preached to them the everlasting Gospel and our eyes never met.'

'Eyes have to meet' in the sense that meanings are recognized and love in them exchanged. This is the meaning of 'the ministry of the Word'.

It is even more exacting where another faith dominates culture, concepts and also vocabularies, so that the gospel may be misheard or half-understood. Great pains are necessary over 'the sense of the Word' in any and every context. Pains mean patience. This 'ministry of the Word' transpires in the setting of worship, of Holy Communion, the gathering around the bread and wine. Here the sacramental situation needs to be fully understood. This is no ordinary meal, nor is it a bare spectacle. 'Take and eat this in remembrance . . .' Eating is a wonderful analogy for personal faith, for it is never something for which there can be proxy. 'The Son of God loved me . . .' we say inwardly, as we partake in our own hands of 'bread and wine'. But what is deeply personal is also corporate: sharing 'one bread and one cup' we celebrate our unity.

Furthermore, by so doing we are calling to mind the central fact of our redemption – not repeating what was 'once for all' but recalling its once-for-all-ness in the broken body and the shed blood of the Cross. In this rite we are also linked back to creation and the human trusteeship of the good earth. For bread and wine are inclusive symbols of 'man over nature', of 'nature via man' through the whole economic order. So we learn to consecrate all our powers and techniques in the offering of ourselves as 'a living sacrifice'.

These wondrous meanings of the Eucharist, familiar enough, need constant interpretation so that they are ever fresh within. I found that fulfilling this ministry as its public servant in sanctuary and study meant keeping close to the Lord in quiet meditation. I tried to remain in a quiet place at noon every day for about 20 minutes, and these times became to me both precious and indispensable to peace of mind and to perspective in the stress of events. Take deep breaths and focus on God in awareness of his love. The result can be calming and perhaps transforming too.

Such were the regular ministries. In Isfahan we also had informal meetings that any were welcome to attend with friends, in which topics were raised and questions aired. Friday evenings brought a course on the life and teaching of Jesus, with slides to illustrate, held inside the church.

Those who wished to enquire more deeply were received on a one-to-one basis, for they differed so widely. Some were genuinely 'asking to understand' (the original sense of that Greek word that gave us 'proselyte'); others perhaps had ulterior motives, such as spying on behalf of intelligence services of the State. However I felt, I made a point of not allowing any suspicion on my part to tarnish or compromise my attitude. That would have made my relation with them insincere. If one looks for 'good faith' one must always offer it.

We would often have trouble from the Tablighat-i-Islami, or 'Islamic propagation' group, whose members posted themselves at the door of the church and took stock of those who came and left. These they might later threaten or attack. Alternatively these activists would come inside and try to disrupt the meeting. Their level of activity often depended on how strong or how weak the central Government was. Whenever those in charge of the country's affairs lost their grip or neglected the demands of law and order there would be an increase in disruptive behaviour on the part of these elements. Likewise, when central control was strong their influence diminished.

I recall one incident of a painfully puzzling character. I accepted an invitation from a bunch of people who came periodically to our meetings to go with them on an outing outside Isfahan. They took me into the hills east of the city in a big car. We left the car and started to walk around. I noticed them talking furtively and whispering secretively as if pondering where to go or what to do. In the event, it was soon suggested that we return to the city, and they took me back home. Later when I talked about this with one of my Persian colleagues, he expressed astonishment that I had gone in the first place and warned me off ever doing so again. He believed they had intended to kill me and had changed their minds at the last minute.

In all my pastoral and teaching work, I sought to speak clearly about Christ and faith and to keep close to the Bible, without reference – critical or otherwise – to other belief systems, Islamic, Zoroastrian or any others. My name and family were, of course, Islamic, and because of this certain mullahs urged the fanatical people to get rid of me. There was some security in civil law, as long as it was recognized and obeyed. That had been so in the case of Ahmad Kesravi, whose assassins were caught and sentenced to death. He had explicitly criticized Shi'ah Islam. This led me to believe that no one would really want to kill me. From time to time I would be stopped in the street and asked why I was wearing a priest's collar.

Preparation for the great Christian festivals occupied much

time. Every Christmas, the Bishop invited the Governor General of Isfahan and local government officials and prominent citizens to the church hall, and then to the church itself for carols and hymns. I took great care over many weeks in the preparation of the sermon that followed the singing. Some would comment that they had discovered meanings they had not hitherto realized and expressed appreciation. Among those who came was Prince Akbar Mirza Mas'ud, the son of Zell-i-Sultan of the Qajar dynasty.

At Easter, to celebrate the Resurrection, we would go to church 'while it was yet dark' with dawn at hand (as in the Gospel) for Holy Communion. Then, in the early light of day, we would go into the hills around the city or beside the River Zayandeh-Rood to watch the rising sun from the steps of Khajoo Bridge. We would sing the dawn hymn (*sepideh dam*) and return homewards for breakfast together.

Another joyful task was to co-operate with Bishop Stephen Neill in the production of the 'World Christian Books' series which he was supervising from Geneva. It was a project of the World Council to provide simple, readily translatable Christian books, classics or new writings, destined hopefully to be translated into a variety of languages across the world to stimulate study and equip preachers and teachers. A panel of authors and a team of advisors were recruited, among whom I was one. We were to conduct research on what was needed and decide on appropriate publications. This meant much reading and assessing of possible items. I was also interested in the Persian translation of some of them. The composing of hymns was another welcome exercise and during the 1950s and beyond I composed a number of them which were published in Nur-i-Jahan publications and have found a home in the Persian Hymnal.

Our second child, a son named Bahram William, was born on 22 September 1955. His name linked him with his native land and his maternal grandfather. From very early years he gave signs of his keen intelligence and zest for life, bringing great joy to our whole community and endearingly to ourselves and home. None could have then known how men would tear away the petals of his youth.

Service in Yazd

Almost two years later I was transferred to serve the Church in Yazd where there had been a large drop in membership, but where a fine nucleus remained. Sadly, the men's and women's hospitals where my own mother had won her nursing skills had gone. It was a hard thing to be serving where I had first gone to school. The church built by Norman Sharp, once a beautiful Persian structure, had gone, together with the old bookshop. The reason for the sad changes there and the forfeiture of its earlier liveliness had been a devastating flood that had swept through the town destroying many other buildings in its path. The very dryness of the region makes the incidence of sudden downpours that rush down from the foothills all the more catastrophic. Only part of the men's hospital could be salvaged and afterwards it became the church and clergy house into which we moved with our two small children.

I count the six or so months I spent there into the spring of 1958 the happiest of my whole ministry. Childhood memories were renewed. The walls and doorways of the city, the streets and the bazaars, the shops and the pedestrians, the smell of water sprayed on dry dust, the aroma of sundry spices on stalls on the suqs – all these were like nectar to my lips, a medicine to my soul. Yazd was only 20 kilometres from Taft and from time to time with Margaret and the children I would go there and meet my father and my brothers. On one occasion when Bishop and Mrs Thompson visited Yazd we all went over to Taft and had a delightful inter-parental visit with my father. At Nosrata-bad, a village near Yazd, a number of Zoroastrians had become Christians and nearly every week we went to see them, conducting a simple Holy Communion service with them.

It was, appropriately, while at Yazd that I got to work on the small book *Design of my World*, mentioned in the Introduction. An incident in Yazd reminds us how significant a greeting can be. Margaret and I were walking along one day when two young boys passed by. One of them said to me, '*Salamu alaikum*', 'peace be on you', which is the Muslim greeting and customarily given only to Muslims. I reciprocated his greeting. We had taken a few steps further when he turned and shouted, 'I wasn't saying *Salam* to you!'

Meanwhile, his friend had told him I was a Christian so he wanted to take back his greeting. The incident was a sort of commentary on Jesus' meaning in the Sermon on the Mount when he referred to this kind of restricted greeting prevailing among Jews (and later between Muslims) whereby a recognized form (*Shalom*) will only be used among 'the faithful' and will be withheld from others and – if used mistakenly – will be withdrawn. Hence Jesus' words: 'If you salute your brethren only what are you doing more than others?', and the further obligation: 'Be ye inclusive as your heavenly Father is' (Matthew 5:47–48). For 'inclusive' is the meaning here of that otherwise puzzling translation that would have us be as 'perfect' as our Father. The Greek word *teleios* has the sense of 'unstinted' and 'hospitable', hence the instance of heaven's 'rain on just and unjust alike'. There is no apartheid in the Kingdom of God.

If there was a certain pain in having a Yazdi boy by implication disown me, I had cause to recover my pride in Yazd's reputation for honesty. I had collected my suit from the cleaners and the following day a young boy came to the house with a crumpled 20-rial note in his hand which he said he had found in my trouser-pocket and was returning to me. I was gratified at the significance of this incident and prayed that this might long endure as the quality of Yazdis and be the benison of all Iran.

During this time our second daughter Sussanne was born, not in Yazd but in our hospital in Isfahan on 9 February 1958. Just two weeks later mother and child returned by bus to Yazd to be the theme of a truly enchanting picture taken under the glorious yellow foliage of a Yazdi garden.

By the time the family returned to serve in Isfahan, the jubilee of St Luke's Church was due to be celebrated. Standing between the two hospitals, it had been consecrated in 1909. The commemoration took several forms. The north wing of the church became a small chapel named after St Thomas and had a cross shaped like the 'Persian Cross' I had seen in Kottayam, India. It was decided to remove the rows of pillars which had impeded the view down the centre aisle. This meant a measure of reconstruction and incorporated changes to the roof, with new wiring and electric chandeliers. We invited the veteran American missionary, William Miller, spending his farewell term in Iran, to hold a week of special services and we published a guidebook recording the history of its 50 years. I composed a jubilee hymn for the occasion, and all was crowned with a 'general Thanksgiving'.

High points like jubilees come and go, but the steady task persists. One important dimension of ministry was, from time to time, to take advantage of visitors to the city who might be willing to meet the community informally and share their faith and wisdom. Bishop's House was open on such occasions to local dignitaries and friends. One of these welcome guests was Professor Arnold Toynbee, author of the ongoing and monumental *Study of History* in – ultimately – 12 volumes. Unlike many historians who only felt academically secure in limited fields such as 'The Sewerage system of Rome under the Antonines', or 'The English Civil War to the Restoration of the Monarchy: An Episode in Stuart England', Toynbee aspired to a worldview, and looked for clues across all cultures and civilizations. Because of this the more narrow-minded historians disparaged him and threw doubt on his efforts to identify in his 'challenge and response' theory the rise and fall of Empires. He had a passionate concern for integrity and inclusiveness – there was no 'restricted greeting' in his attitude to the human story in its manifoldness and diversity. Doubtless he made mistakes and trusted in too sweeping conclusions but his ambition was authentic and his erudition masterly. He had a deep concern for Persian life and history and a commitment to world peace and the diplomacy that might foster it. This was because so many of his young contemporaries at Balliol College, Oxford, had been killed in the First World War that he was for ever asking himself, 'Why – for what – have I survived?' This made him a workaholic for peace and the mutuality of nations.

It was my privilege to translate for him when a large, expectant audience gathered in Bishop's House. It was a formidable task, only somewhat lightened by the fact that I had been given his text in advance. Such speaking by 'interruption' (interpretation) is never easy, stopping and starting in jerky pieces, but the whole was very rewarding, as Dr Yarshater testified both as to theme and translation.

A different kind of visitor came in the person of Kenneth Cragg, who first reached Isfahan in 1957 as the Travelling Study Secretary of the (then) Near East Council of Churches. It was just after his well-known book, *The Call of the Minaret*, had been published in New York by Oxford University Press. From 1958 to 1966 he was the mainstay of summer schools in Jerusalem to which several of our people from Isfahan and Tehran went. He was several times among us again in the early 1970s in his other capacity as Assistant Bishop within the Archbishopric in Jerusalem, when he travelled extensively from Morocco to Muscat from his home in Cairo.

His experiences of Muslim theology and culture had begun in Beirut where he and his beloved Melita ran St Justin's House, a Palestinian Hostel within the American University of Beirut during the 1940s. There he had realized the significant common ground between mosque and church in respect of creation under God, creaturehood in 'dominion' (*khilafah*) as the divine entrustment of the natural order to human care and liability. This meant a divine 'omnipotence' that was uncoercive, ready to forgo sheer power and 'depute' to 'deputies' (you and me and all peoples) this strange management of the good earth by which 'cities and villages', as William Blake wrote, were 'in the bosoms of men' ('Jerusalem', lines 21–34, *Poetical Works*, 2nd edition). Because of this human dignity, the sciences could explore and exploit, control and technologize, while the arts

– in poetry, colour, design and music – could celebrate. Above all, worship had to consecrate.

Prophethood, law and guidance fitted exactly into this scenario of divine magnanimity and of human empire, because – just because of the trust – the trustees, men, races, nations, rulers, laboratory operators, etc. needed urgent direction how to use their autonomy and independence. It became more and more evident to him that these were precious truths common both to Islam and Christianity. If they were Biblical, they were no less Quranic. The common ground ought to be acknowledged by both communities without patronage or compromise or condescension.

It was then even more clearly evident how the two faiths of mosque and church differed radically – not about *whether* this was so but about *how* the human vocation was fulfilled. Was it enough that there should be law, *Shari'ah*, *Dhikr*, reminder and direction plus exhortation so that, being no longer ignorant and with the help that Islam with its Five Pillars would provide, we could satisfy the divine pattern? Or was there a deep need for a more radical answer? Might we not know well and yet fail to follow the law and thereby defy it? Paul in his experience had known all about this perversity at the core of the self, in the face of which law alone could only regret the wrong and punish the wrongdoer. In that event was not law itself defeated? Were we not in need of redemption, of a divine forgiveness? If so, was there not a sort of Islamic reason for looking to a Christ? And would not that Christ find his world cruciform if omnipotence was truly 'uncoercive'? Yet this deep contrast between Christianity and Islam arose out of, and belonged squarely with, all that we truly had in common. On the basis of this we could, and should, renounce 'restricted greeting' and strive for community even in partial truth, as a condition of mediating the ultimate gospel of 'God in Christ' across the old and stubborn apartheid.

This was something of the pattern of thought and witness that Kenneth Cragg brought to us and which I had to render into my best Persian. Initially I found it rather bewildering and riskily innovative, but gradually I realized that it was in line with all my own deepest instincts about the Islam that was still part of me alongside the Christ I had come to know. Cragg always made it clear that there was no proud dogmatism in this 'line' and that if others hesitated or annulled it, all of us 'to our own Master' stay accountable and 'where the Spirit is Lord, there is liberty'. So a steady friendship matured between us in which was a warm and mutual gratitude. We even consulted together about the as yet untitled *Design of my World* and a shared instinct took us to that Maidan of Isfahan, where I had the joy of being his 'town-guide'.

Two incidents from those visits remain vivid for me. I found him deeply impressed by our Islamic architecture and drawn into deep reflection in its presence. We were together in the captivating beauty of the Lutfallah Mosque on the Maidan, with a man from the Department of Archaeology to explain. Given the enchanting quality of tile and colour, dome and calligraphy, it seemed to him incongruous to find amid all this splendour a broken, movable wooden pulpit haphazardly leant against a wall. He said wearily, 'This incredible building! What does this shabby pulpit mean?'

When I translated this to the archaeologist, he replied, 'Tell him that neither this pulpit nor those who occupy it matter to us!'

Kenneth's reply was to ask, 'But why was this glorious building wanted so much by those who yearned for its erection?'

After Lutfallah we meandered through the famous bazaar of Isfahan and on to the portal of the School of Theology. On the lintel and framework were the *Asma' al-Husna*, the 99 'Beautiful Names of God'. As we were deciphering them, a seminarian came by and, seeing the European visitor, enquired if he read Arabic. 'Yes,' I said, and a conversation began which led to us going inside. Appreciating the invitation we entered; in the forecourt was a table where a number of students were sitting, and discoursing with a heavily bearded elderly teacher. Bishop Thompson was with us and three of us sat down, while Kenneth Cragg talked with the student who had brought us in. After a few minutes the teacher seemed to want to finish it, but the student said to the teacher, 'Do you realize what he is saying?' I will never forget the admiration in the tone of his voice. The conversation was about the meaning of the Cross and how it might be truly comprehended between our faiths if there was any will to gentleness of thought and an open heart. When we said goodbye to them, I felt I had experienced another occasion in which I had come across a teacher apt to meet my deepest mental and spiritual need of strength and wisdom.

His visit came at a point when, after eight years' almost continual ministry, I needed stimulus, some declogging of my heart and mind, a quenching of my inner thirst. Cragg's thinking and friendship were the refreshing breeze that came my way and I responded to how he seemed to feel a way into Islam that, with his gentleness and modest warmth of heart, I could emulate and, out of my own different antecedents, enlarge and enrich. Some of the inner contradictions and tensions I had known in my own past were resolved in fresh hope and purpose and a new harmony of mind and rest of heart. For the comprehending love between us we could both render to God thanksgiving as being, authentically, 'the fellowship of the Holy Spirit'.

These thoughts were confirmed in April 1958 through a large conference in Asmara, Eritrea, convened by the (then) United Presbyterian Church in the Middle East at which Kenneth Cragg gave Bible/Quran studies at the start of each day on Psalm 36:9, 'In Thy light we see light', later published in the Near East Council's study programme papers. There we had the first printing to hand of his English translation of Muhammad Kamil Husain's study of the crucifixion of Jesus, *City of Wrong*, now in its fourth edition and presenting the first significant and positive reckoning with the Cross from inside Islam as listening to the inviting words 'Behold the sin of the world . . .' without broaching the rest of the verse. The author thought Good Friday was 'the darkest day in human history', the Cross being a deed, at the hands of high religious

1. Wolf Cubs in Isfahan, 1928. White arrow shows author

2. Stuart Memorial College, Isfahan 1939

3. The author and his wife, Margaret,
1952

4. Author's ordination as Deacon in Isfahan, 1949

5. Second from left: Professor Arnold Toynbee followed by Bishop W. J. Thomson, Mrs. M. Thompson, Professor Ehsan Yarshatter, Author, 1960

6. The author with his father and father-in-law in Taft, 1957

7. St Luke's Church, Isfahan

8. Rev. Arastoo Sayyah in Shiraz Church, 1970

9. Author confirming a Zoroastrian convert in Yezd, 1964

10. Easter morning hymn singing by the Isfahan Khajoo Bridge, following the early Eucharist in St Luke's church, 1966

11. Author with His Holiness the Patriarch
Catholicos of the Church of the East,
Marshimon XXIII, Isfahan 1966

12. Professor Girshman with the author in the oil-fields, Iran 1963

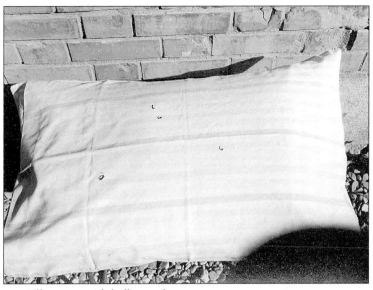

13. Pillow case with bullet marks, 1979

14. Bahram William Dehqani-Tafti in Oxford, 1978

15. Author's installation as Assistant Bishop in Winchester Cathedral, 1982, with Bishop John V. Taylor

16. Author celebrating 50 years in ordained ministry. Service held in Winchester Cathedral, October 1999. L. to R. Guli Francis-Dehqani (author's daughter), Bishop Iraj Mottahedeh (present Bishop in Iran), Bishop Michael Scott-Joynt of Winchester, Dean Michael Till of Winchester

17. Family gathering in Basingstoke on the occasion of the author's 80th birthday, May 2000

scrupulousness and proud political law-exerting, which epito-
mized the perversity of human institutions and the humans
within them. It is a book which still merits careful reading.

Consecration as Bishop

Some three years after the conference came the Diocesan
decision concerning the successor to Bishop Thompson who
announced his intention to resign during 1960. Prior to the
events of 1974–76 and the creation of the Province (to which
I will return) our Diocese was still within the jurisdiction of the
Archbishop of Canterbury, advised by our Diocesan Council,
routeing its ideas and wisdom through the Archbishop in Jerusalem who was still nominally accountable to Canterbury.

In that capacity, Campbell MacInnes came from Jerusalem
to Iran to consult widely with Church members across the
country. He conveyed our local thoughts to a wider circle of
concerned parties in the other parts of his jurisdiction, promis-
ing to return to us with further 'findings'.

In the event he had two proposals with a stated preference
for the first, which was for an interim appointment of a retired
Bishop, unfamiliar with Persian, in a holding operation. Only
after this met with strong opposition was the second proposal
made: that I should be nominated to succeed Bishop Thompson. Prior to all discussion or knowledge of this, I had been
asked to leave the room. After half an hour, I was informed
that the Council – 16 Iranians and 9 ex-patriates – had adopted
the option of my appointment. Archbishop MacInnes kept his
word to abide by the Council's will.

So it came about that I was called to the utmost trust the
Church has, the Church that I had so long before pledged to
serve till death. I could only ask the Council members to stand
and pray with me and for me in the fulfilment of that sacred
pledge.

Soon after the Council the Archdeacon left for leave in Australia and we went as a family to Tehran to take over the care
of St Paul's Church and the Diocesan business during the six

months prior to the Consecration in Jerusalem. Here, not entirely for the first time but now more demandingly, I had to give much thought and care to English-speaking ministry. The worshippers at St Paul's were very varied. There were diplomats, Oil Company personnel, British Council (cultural) staff members and many nationalities. There were also numerous technicians servicing the rapidly expanding technologies, civil and military, in and around the capital and beyond, and there were educationalists, academics and tourists, ministerial advisors and the Point Four people. It was no small effort to cope with an adequate response, both pastorally and spiritually, to so diverse and exacting a constituency. I had to take great care with my sermons.

I soon discovered how readily people could be offended or disconcerted, which may mean that the point is striking home. Once I was expounding the theme of 'silence', how in front of Pilate Jesus 'answered him not a word', stressing the place of quiet in an ever more raucous world. I was taken aback after the service when one Englishman said with a tone of sarcasm, 'So you Iranians are innocent of all noise and clamour?' He seemed to imagine that I had been scolding, or at least addressing, him personally rather than enlarging on a meaning that embraced everyone.

On another occasion, was an Eastern European present who had reached Iran via Russia and had faced much stress in his life, and of whom I was not aware until we met as he was leaving. I had spoken of how ready we are to blame parents, environments, accidents, and so on, for our problems in order to exonerate ourselves. I was about to shake his hand when he seized it, stared angrily and said, 'You do not understand anything at all.'

Yet another time I was bidding farewell to the British Ambassador who often attended with his wife. He asked me, 'Why, in praying for Heads of State, do you give priority to the President of the USA over your own Shahan-Shah and our Queen Elizabeth?'

I said, 'Iranians respect their guests and give them priority over themselves and their closest friends. I am an Iranian, Anglican

Christian, and in prayer to God list the Heads of State according to Iranian tradition, namely: the US President, the Queen of Holland, the Queen of England and the Shah of Iran.'

He seemed disconcerted, perhaps assuming that, though an Anglican Diocese, we should still follow the Prayer Book of the Church of England. He pursued the matter by writing to the Archbishop in Jerusalem who simply referred him to Bishop Thompson and that was the end of the matter. Moreover, I did not change my usage.

Sadly, though, that item of correspondence stayed in the files of Isfahan and when Bishop's House was ransacked at the outset of the Khomeini uprisings and documents filched, ignorant persons who had no knowledge of the niceties of correspondence or its essentially innocent content latched on to it; it seemed to their clueless minds to be conveniently incriminating about our role as the tool of Western powers. Great importance was made of it in the press that bore no relation to the liturgy involved – though perhaps they disputed my reading of Persian etiquette, and yet it would have been premature to pray for the Ayatollah as a Head of State. Would they have wanted me to give first priority to the Shah?

I had to take a courtesy part in the official visit to Iran of Queen Elizabeth and the Duke of Edinburgh at that time, when, happily, in addition to all their protocol duties they also toured the hospitals of the Diocese and the Blind School. In Shiraz they attended St Simon the Zealot Church.

These visits by the Royal party were arranged unilaterally through the auspices of Dr Peter Wild and the Diocese itself was not officially involved. I felt that a point needed to be made, namely that all ex-patriate people – doctors, carers for the blind at the farm project, teachers and clergy – were all members of the national Church, the Iran Diocese. We believed proudly in the Iranian identity of the Church which gladly embraced all but affirmed its Persian identity. Accordingly, I took up the point in *Nour-i-Alam*, the Journal of the Council of the Church, much to the chagrin of Dr Wild who had not thought to discuss such matters first with the church.

The half-year in Tehran gave me a welcome opportunity to renew old friendships as many of my University friends were still there. I gained much from the Persian congregation and it was well to have such wide international contacts.

And so to the consecration in Jerusalem, via Isfahan, leaving the three children in the care of their grandmother. St George's Cathedral is located in what was then Jordanian Jerusalem with access via the airport at Qalandiyyah, north of the Old City but south of Ramallah. The day was to be the feast of St Mark, 25 April, 1951. I spent time in meditation and prayer in 'razgahan', as we would say in Persian, and – on the advice of the Archbishop – pondered especially the First Epistle to Timothy with its emphasis on pastoral calling and 'seeking the face of the Lord' for my task ahead.

Among the tokens of office, I received a Bible bound in red leather from my consecrator, the Archbishop (sadly stolen in the events of 1979 in Isfahan), together with the episcopal ring with an agate stone to signify my office. For the pectoral cross worn as a symbol of self-offering I requested that it be in the form of that Persian cross my predecessors wore. To link its costly significance directly with our church I later invited Ali Darvish to engrave on it a flower design of Persian tradition, which he did superbly. The episcopal staff, in the form of a shepherd's crook betokening the pastoral care of the people, is the one that is now set by the Bishop's Chair in the pro-Cathedral of St Luke's in Isfahan. Bishop Thompson arrived in time to participate as a co-consecrator along with Bishop Najib Qubain and Bishop Oliver Allison of the Sudan which, at that point, was still within the Jerusalem Archbishopric. Many clergy, both Arab and expatriate, were present and, happily, representatives of the ancient Churches – Orthodox, Armenian, Coptic and Syrian, and the Latin Catholic Churches.

How does one do justice, whether in heart or by pen, to such a pivotal event in Christian vocation – what St Paul spoke of as 'that which comes upon me daily, the care of all the churches' (2 Corinthians 11:28)? It would be *all* those within our modest Diocese and, unknown to me then, those of the Province that would later be created.

Episcopacy was brought down to earth in a curious way by dint of a waiter in Tehran from whom I had also a salutary lesson about devotion to duty. En route back from Jerusalem we stayed two days in Tehran and a friend invited us to a meal in a restaurant. I was wearing episcopal attire, and as a result the traditional collar – unknown to me – was violating the custom of the place. A waiter came to tell me that ties had to be worn in that establishment. Evidently he did not understand my explanation. For he soon returned with an assortment of coloured ties from which I might choose. There was amusement all round save for the diligent waiter who persisted until finally our host betook himself to the manager to explain. At this point the good waiter came again to our table, this time profusely apologetic. He wanted to kiss my ring in the thrill of discovering what it meant. I reassured him and said that I approved how assiduous he had been in his responsibilities.

Installation followed in St Luke's on Ascension Day, 11 May, with a wide Christian representation and the Governor General of the city together with government figures, local and national, as well as College friends from far and wide. The dire events of nearly 20 years later lay far beyond the happy scene of that blessed day. Even so, halcyon as it was and memorable in the story of our church for the first time chief-pastored by a son of the soil, I took as my sermon theme the call to the taking up of the Cross with which Jesus had recruited his first disciples, in whose steps we followed.

My predecessor, and of course Mrs Thompson, had given 47 years of service to Iran, half as teacher and half as Bishop. His former students and many friends organized a farewell party and underwrote the cost of building a new hall in the Carr Secondary School, which was named after him as 'The Thompson Memorial Hall'. The Governor General attended its dedication. In later years, with the increase of our cultural programmes, a small room in the school, next to Bishop's

House on Abbas Abad, became a lovely chapel to be a further memorial to his ministry and a place of prayer and worship. That, too, like so much else in our precious heritage of intra-ethnic unity in Christ, was prey to the devastations that later overtook both place and people.

CHAPTER 8

My Tenure as Bishop

Hope's winding path I tread relying
Only on Your grace supplying.

Vahshi Bafqi

I was Bishop of the Diocese in Iran for 29 years, only 19 of which were in Iran itself. The remaining 10 years until my retirement as Bishop in Iran, perforce, and sadly, were passed outside the land I loved. Fully to recount the events of those crowded and momentous years would be too large a task for these pages. Accordingly, the narrative will utilize the archives of the Newsletter of the Friends of the Diocese, which ensures that the salient points will find due place, together with any personal recollections I can bring to implement them. This Friends' Newsletter has been published regularly from the time of the inauguration of the Diocese more than 80 years ago. It fairly reflects the many vicissitudes of the ministry of the Diocese during all that time, via letters from the incumbent Bishops and news items from many servants of the Church.

The Diocese: Jurisdiction, Work and Travel

It will be useful to begin with some outline of the jurisdiction, the churches and institutions in which the Diocese lived and worked, the relevant committees in charge of its ministries and how its administration operated. For it is the task of a bishop (*episcopos*, from 'eye' and 'sight' in Greek) to take all these upon his heart and devote himself to constant care for their integrity, unity and zeal.

In the city of Isfahan, St Luke's Church stood close to the

Christian hospital and nursing school of the same name. There was also St Paul's Church in the Armenian quarter of Julfa. Attached to the hospital was a clinic in a village, as well as an institute for the welfare of the blind, built up over many years. Ayin Noori was a centre for the education and training of blind girls and women, and Christoffel a similar establishment for boys. At 'Cyrus the Great', the farm project, there was training for the blind in keeping poultry, animal husbandry and agriculture. There was a bookshop, a kindergarten, four schools, and two hostels for boys and girls.

Tehran has St Paul's Church, with congregations speaking Persian and English. The Church of St Simon the Zealot in Shiraz had a small 'daughter' church in the village of Qalat, and also a bookshop. In Shiraz too was a 100-bed hospital. In Kerman was the Church of St Andrew; in Yazd was the Church of All Saints with (later) a clinic and also a worshipping group in Nosrat Abad in the Yazd area. In Khuzestan there was a Persian priest for Persian-speaking Christians; at Masjid Sulaiman there was an expatriate chaplain for members of the Oil Company and others speaking English.

These being its components, the Diocese had close links with the Evangelical (Presbyterian) Church whose base was in Tehran and also membership in the Khuzestan Church Council whose centre was at Ahvaz in the Church of the Good Shepherd.

One of my main duties was to visit and inspect these churches and institutions of the Diocese – a task I tried to accomplish twice yearly. It was during these many journeys that I tried to read as much as possible, for the steady study of the faith and its theology is vital to effective ministry. Sadly, pressures never gave me the space I really needed to keep abreast except when I could utilize the time taken in long travels being driven by someone. Though I knew Yazd, Tehran, Kerman and Shiraz well enough, it was always a delight to return; every journey brought new and fascinating features to light. Crossing wide, dry deserts, we would halt where some spring or well had laid a carpet of wild flowers. The mountain scenery, too, lent vistas that eased the weariness of the body and refreshed the spirit within. The high landscape responded to the shifting clouds, or patterned itself beneath jagged peaks, as the changing light played with the shadows. Those of the morning were long and luminous, but as they shortened through the afternoon they would soften into a gentler glow. Where the peaks seemed to kiss the sky their contours from dawn to dusk were bathed entrancingly in all the colours of the spectrum. You may guess my pride in my Iran, tempering my heartfelt praise of God, creator of its beauty.

Episcopacy in this territory was never shorn of childhood memory, specially going from Shiraz to Yazd via Abarqu and passing the Shirkouh mountains. When going from Isfahan to Shiraz the amazing ruins of Persepolis and Pasargad were on our flank, the ancient haunts of Darius and of Xerxes, and the mausoleum of Cyrus the Great. Pastoral pre-occupations lived and moved with heritage and history.

The oil-rich province of Khuzestan was less familiar. It excited me to see the burning desert landscape transformed into fields of cane and sugar beet and into groves of citrus fruit trees. From the 1960s onwards, through the length and breadth of Khuzestan, were evidences of development and promise: dams constructed for irrigation and barren areas set for productivity. Archaeology, too, had come alive there, with many excavations. Professor Ghirshman discovered the remains of a third-century Christian church and monastery on Khark Island in the Persian Gulf. Inland, at Bard-i-Neshandeh, near to Masjed Sulayman, he also located what he believed to be a desert temple of Aryan tribes dating from the seventh century BC, a place, probably, of the worship of Ahouramazda. At Haft Tappeh an ancient ziggurat named Choghzanbil had been uncovered dating from the Elamite period.[1]

These incidents of archaeological savour lightened my episcopal task and diversified my fellowship with my clergy. Thanks to the close rapport I had with Dr Ghirshman both I and the chaplain in Masjed Sulayman had occasion to appreciate the scholarly grace and integrity with which the Professor went about his work – the fine art of having the past yield up its secrets. It is good that the seekers should be reverent and courteous where stones possess mysteries. It was thrilling to bring Christian worship again to Khark Island when I flew there via Agha Jari. I once conducted a baptism there (a Philip Kirtley it was) – we had, it was noted, linked 16 centuries in 1.

I normally went by plane to this province of Khuzestan. However, there was one occasion when we decided to go by car from Isfahan. The venture took 13 hours! We set out in the small hours of 3 March 1965 through mountainous terrain and encountered heavy snow by the time we reached a village named Tiran. The snow persisted through Khoram Abad and beyond to Andimeshk, more than 600 kilometres in all, where snow had ceased. We then passed through flat terrain all the long haul to Abadan. How fascinating snow and peaks, dark ravines and glistening slopes are for a poetic eye! You will not be surprised that I am addicted to them all.

We had passed through winter, via spring, to arrive in the warmth of summer. The snowy, lofty panorama had given way to near tropical verdure and a lowly shoreline. It seemed to me an allegory of the vicissitudes of life, as the English hymn has it:

> Through all the changing scenes of life . . .
> The praises of my God and King
> My heart and tongue employ.

For me there was the glow of native pride in the grandeur, the immensity of the country of my birth and ministry.

To turn from itineraries to committees is a sober necessity. Soon after my consecration in 1961 the Diocesan Council met in Isfahan to plan ahead and review the whole situation. Around that time I ordained Khodadad Khosrovy, a young man of Zoroastrian background, as deacon after his studies in Bangalore seminary, India. There were two important anniversaries to be planned: the 150th anniversary of Henry Martyn's completion of the New Testament in Persian, and the fiftieth anniversary of the formation of our Diocese.

Our national and local celebrations of these two waymarks in our story were lively and joyous, but we felt it necessary to include also our friends in England and elsewhere. Accordingly, the Friends of the Diocese arranged for me to visit England. It was June 1962. I spent two months travelling widely across the country, despite the interruption of a week in hospital which immobilized me for a week. The main event was at St Margaret's Church, Westminster, where some 800 people gathered – all having some loved link or other with Iran. The epochal consecration of the new Cathedral at Coventry was included in my itinerary and in the adjacent ruins I renewed the deep lesson taken from them during my visit as a Cambridge fledgling in 1949.

The new edifice was no less striking in its imaginative shape, its radiant glass, its chapel of unity and its enormous open-glass western window wonderfully binding it into one with the ancient ruin to the south. These ambitious expressions of architectural praise were well matched in Coventry by the outreach of compassion and community, notably to the city of Dresden which had been comparably afflicted by 'saturation bombing', this time by British planes.

This commemorative journey quickly receded into a grateful memory after my return to Iran, because of the tragic earthquake that devastated parts of the north-eastern area of the country on 1 September 1962. Shocks were felt in the triangle of Tehran, Saveh and Hamadan. Many villages – Boin, Rustam Abad, Roodak, Esmat Abad and others – were engulfed, mud shacks shattered and buildings razed to the ground; the earth itself was rent with gaping chasms that broke across the roads and streets. I went at once to Tehran and flew in a small plane over the stricken area with the Chairman of Inter-Church Aid of the World Council of Churches, and a representative of the Lutheran World Federation. Through this horrendous experience, a Committee of the Council of Iran Churches was formed, chaired by Dr John Elder, to raise funds to help rebuild the shattered villages. After governmental consultation and referral to Geneva, the village of Esmat Abad became the responsibility of the Iranian Church Council.

A prominent part was played by Mr John McDouall of our Church, manager of the Irantour Hotel in Isfahan, whose plan was adopted by the WCC. The enterprise took its toll. A relative of the Assyrian Church Pastor, Ess-Haq, was killed in an accident en route to Esmat Abad as a member of our committee. He had a good knowledge of Turkish, the language of many in the stricken region. John McDouall suffered in a similar road accident but mercifully survived it.

Several times I took the opportunity to get to the village, and these were not without incident. I formed the impression that the plan of the new dwellings had two faults: first, in two rows on either side of the road, those on the south had sun but the other side, facing north, was sunless and this deterred the villagers; secondly, no plans had been made for livestock and animals so that the inhabitants had to improvise unsightly extensions for this purpose.

The heavy calamity of the earthquake and the trauma of the rural population that the agencies of compassion were seeking to serve seemed a strange commentary on our diocesan celebration of jubilee. But is not the intermingling of joy and pain, of celebration and commiseration, intrinsic to the Christian experience of grace? The sharp reminder we had in the earthquake of the precariousness and sorrow of human life, in its raw exposure to danger, made for realism in our assessments of well-being and rejoicing.

There was the same double aspect in another feature of the diocesan jubilee, namely the publication of commemorative books. One of them was a life of Henry Martyn, written by Vera Eardley and translated into Persian by Sohail Azari. A short history of the Diocese, with the title *Four Gardens*, written by H. R. J. Biggs, was published in English and a shorter pamphlet in Persian by Mansoor Amiri. The things that called for doxology had the mark of costliness on them in the expenditures of love.

Another, though different, feature of diocesan life both then and later was the reception of visitors. Episcopal hospitality is a large part of episcopal ministry. It is appropriate to recall that intriguing admonition in 3 John 6: 'You shall speed them on their journey worthily of God.' Part of the 'speeding onward' was the garnering of their wisdom. For lectures, talks and conversations were expected of them. Only seldom did they disappoint! Certainly not Max Warren or John Taylor, General Secretaries of CMS (though sometimes with their ever-gracious successor Simon Barrington-Ward I found myself wondering how and where his conclusion would come). It fell to me on these occasions to interpret in Persian – a fact which made my concern for the point in every clause more 'existential' than it might have otherwise been. Also, 'speaking by interruption' is not easy for the one speaking all the wisdom.

Max and his wife Mary spent three weeks in Iran, to bring the greetings of the Society over which he presided. They visited all our centres, including the induction of Iraj Mottahedeh as Vicar of St Simon the Zealot in Shiraz. In appreciation of Max's quotation from Hafiz he was presented with a superb copy of that poet's *Complete Works* and he also visited the garden near the famous Qur'an Gate of Shiraz where Henry Martyn had lived prior to his last journey through Turkey where he died. His Persian translation of the New Testament was published in Russia in 1815, three years after his death.

The General Secretary's visit to Kerman coincided with the induction of Arastoo Sayyah in St Andrew's, Kerman, where we visited the Christian cemetery with the graves of earlier servants of the Church: Dr G. E. Dodson, Revd Henry Carless and Mary Bird. Max Warren was followed some two years later by John and Peggy Taylor. John, as Bishop of Winchester, would later play a crucial part in the 'design of my world' following the tragedies then far beyond the horizon. Frequently it was part of our hospitality to introduce our visitors to the splendours of our history, the great ruins of Persepolis and the mosques and madrasas of Isfahan. Cultures as well as cuisine fall within the art of hospitality. As the psalmist said of the

Lord, 'You spread a table before me' (Psalm 23:5), and that table includes the panorama of nature and what time and history have done to it. The host's reward, of course, in part is in the delighted appreciation of kindred minds. Another such was Douglas Webster, Canon Theologian of CMS, whose books enriched my mind, notable among them, *In Debt to Christ* written in 1957.

In 1965 a group came from the same Society and made a highly acceptable film entitled *Spring in Iran*; this depicted both the charm of the land and the story of the Church. Three other visitors among so many may be mentioned for specific reasons. First, John Robinson, of *Honest to God* fame, who was en route to India for the Teape Lectures. His reputation drew a sizeable audience though many were puzzled by his approach. Of a different order, secondly, was the Primate of All-India, Archbishop De Mel from Calcutta, who was actually the guest of the Government of Iran. Aside from the wisdom of his faith, he was witty and convivial and charmed our children. Among his stories was that of the Persian Ambassador in India who refused to follow the rule of the Mughal Emperor that he should enter the Imperial presence in a bowing posture. Accordingly the Emperor had a door erected through which visitors would have to bend, the aperture – like that at the Church of the Nativity in Bethlehem – being extremely low. Not to be outdone, the Ambassador resolved to enter stooping backwards. The scene was enacted out by the Archbishop in his full regalia to the great delight of Dehqanis minor.

Thirdly, the Bishop of Massachusetts, Anson P. Stokes, Jr. His deep concern about 'Third World' poverty and the huge disparity between it and American affluence struck a deep chord in my heart. It confirmed what I had often felt in his country in my own travels, namely the 'dollar wall', the implicit 'patronage' in wealthy givers, the potential humiliation – or improper expectation – in the beneficiaries. I came to think that any Christian visiting the USA should strictly exclude any requesting as the condition of any true and equal relationship. The bestowal of gifts can make the giver sanguine and complacent, and the recipient a sort of dependent client. This compromises any genuine community. The giver needs the humility of receiving – as can often happen in non-monetary ways – while the receiver deserves the benison of being generous in turn. To give of life-experience or listening time and care is worth more than easy cash, which can be an alibi for costly love.

In relating these jubilee visits I do not forget our own ecumenical people, such as Archbishop Campbell MacInnes and Mar Shimun, Assyrian Patriarch of the Church of the East who came to us in 1966, though resident in the USA for the most part while caring for his community in Iraq, Iran, Syria and the American diaspora. He was assassinated shortly after that visit.

I interrupt this partial record of travel to and by the Diocese and the world to explain my long ambition during the 1960s to develop education, which relied considerably on ecumenical links and discussions. From my own youth I had realized the vital ministries of centres such as the Stuart Memorial College in Isfahan and Alborz College in Tehran, founded within the Christian mission. I was eager for our Diocese to emulate their example. (The subsequent expropriation of all these institutions was one of the saddest events in our country.)

It was urgent to take our work beyond primary school level. I wanted to see a high school with boarding facilities, one for boys and one for girls. The best hope lay through Inter-Church Aid. Accordingly, I went to consult them in Geneva and thence to Bonn where I discussed plans with the Evangelische Zentralstelle. They had clear and comprehensive conditions for any grant-in-aid. We would need to have the necessary means to offer one quarter of the cost of building and own the deeds for an adequate area of land, approved architectural plans and the prospect of competent local staff. The Dioesan Council was able to accept these conditions. Its Trust Association, registered to hold land and chaired by John McDouall, found a plot of land of adequate size, via Haj Mossaver-al-Molki who generously donated 20,000 square metres in north Isfahan.

The Ministry of Education granted the licence to build and run the school and CMS undertook to send a number of English teachers for some parts of the curriculum. Thus, after two years of effort, the Carr Memorial High School on Kaveh Street came into being with a boarding section. The official opening was a memorable event. Alerted during a visit to Australia by an old Cambridge friend to the importance of 'room for expansion', I decided to apply for a generous legacy from Miss Millicent Wood, who left £20,000 to the Diocese, to purchase the same number of square metres of land close to the school for a football field and possible future expansion.

Thus my vision was fulfilled and shortly afterwards via the services of Mary Isaac, a long-serving member of the Diocese who had acquired Iranian citizenship, our existing primary girls school was developed into a Girls' High School, so that the Diocese had a complete school programme available from primary to high school.

These and other factors meant much global travel for me on behalf of the Diocese both to inform and inspire the wider Christian community, sharing all that Iran could offer and highlighting the reality of Christian ecumenism. One such occasion was the Anglican Congress which convened in Toronto in the summer of 1963. With my immediate family, who were to stay in England, I travelled from Mah Shahr on an oil tanker, by courtesy of the Tanker Company. It gave me time for reflection, as well as many intriguing experiences for the children. Iraj Mottahedeh was my fellow delegate in Toronto who went by air directly from Tehran to Toronto. After duties in England, I travelled on *The Empress of Canada*, the relative luxury of which was in painful contrast to the time on the tanker. The Conference agenda on mutual responsibility and inter-dependence in the Body of Christ was very congested, and we delegates from Iran registered how disparate were the economies of the Churches represented; we also drew strength from the realization of the brotherhood to which our small Diocese belonged.

After the Congress a trip to the United States began with a mishap when my host caused me to miss the scheduled plane. Eventually, after some delays I arrived in Washington and was taken to the grounds of the Cathedral where a mechanic was lying beneath a large car, repairing it. The mechanic emerged and greeted me most warmly: it turned out to be Francis Sayers, grandson of President Woodrow Wilson and Dean of the Cathedral. At the National Cathedral in Washington after a sermon, who should accost me but Dr Charles Alexander King with whom I had lodged years before in Cairo.

Returning across the Atlantic I was involved in a seminar in Beirut on religious freedom, where I reflected on 'The Art of Being a Minority'. I stressed the vocation of Christ's disciples to live side by side with the majority faith and culture, avoiding any ghetto mind and seeking to participate creatively. Salt seasons food only by its (hopefully) minority presence in the pot!

After a meeting of the Episcopal Synod, also in Jerusalem, in that summer of 1965, studying the whole future of the jurisdiction, I headed for Australia and New Zealand, with all the accumulating thoughts of my months of absence in the West. Among them was the hallowing of the new headquarters in Waterloo Road, London, of the CMS. I recall the diplomatic reply of Queen Elizabeth on that occasion to my asking her opinion about the chapel of the HQ which had sparked heated debate. 'It is different, it is different,' she said evasively. I also attended the Billy Graham Congress in East Berlin and spent a few minutes with the great man despite the reservations I had about the accompanying razzmatazz, the noise and lighting fantasia which I found disconcerting and unreal.

In Australia and New Zealand, the time was hectic. I travelled via Perth (where I had a long talk with Archbishop George Appleton) to Adelaide, Melbourne, Sydney and Brisbane, and from there to Auckland and Christchurch. I preached in sundry cathedrals, visited universities, even farms outside smaller towns. I found some welcome respite at the home of Rachel, my sister-in-law, and her husband, before resuming my work in Iran.

I was invited to give some talks in Mashhad by the Evangelical Church there. It was thrilling to be with the youth of the church and, later, after using the talks in Tehran, to publish them in Persian under the title *The Costliness of Love*. I also managed a side trip to Dhahran, Saudi Arabia, at the invitation of ARAMCO, the Arabian-American Oil Company, where I celebrated Holy Communion and gave a number of talks before returning home to celebrate the birth of our fourth child and third daughter, Gulnar (Guli) Eleanor in June, 1966.

Events from the wider world were continually invading the pastoral care I would rather have been giving inside the Diocese, had there not been the duty to maintain the sinews of the global fellowship. The next such occasion came with the Lambeth Conference of 1968. It had grown immensely from its somewhat modest and controversial beginning in the 1860s. This eleventh conference took place in Church House, Westminster. The family travelled with me, though Bahram was already at Monkton Coombe, the school where his grandfather before him had been a pupil. Michael Ramsey, Archbishop of Canterbury, presided though he rarely spoke, despite his great reputation as a theologian. He rather relished, I think, the fact that his stooping gait and his balding head – not to mention his twitching eyebrows – made him seem more venerable than he actually was. It fell to me to be Secretary of the Committee on Dialogues with Other Faiths, the Chairman of which was Archbishop George Appleton. His eagerness for mutual relations perhaps made him too sanguine about the range of the spiritual issues involved, seeing how far all religions need an honest critique of themselves. 'Religion' and 'religious' can be very elastic terms, not always either admirable or desirable. George thought, one might say, more with the heart and soul, than with the intellect. How do we rightly interrelate them in the things of faith?

The concluding Eucharist, conducted by our Jerusalem Archbishop, Campbell MacInnes, was held at the vast White City stadium in west London. I was to be the preacher. It was an awesome experience – the congregation in thousands and me unfamiliar with using a microphone in such an expansive open-air venue. Repeatedly, too, planes flew overhead to and from Heathrow, commenting raucously on my deliverances. It was – at least for me – a relief to finish.

A contrast was the Royal Garden Party at Buckingham Palace which the Queen offered to the delegates. Through the wide courtyard we entered the elegant rooms en route to the broad lawns at the rear of the building. Tea was served and the Queen mingled with the throng conversing with those near at hand. It was a splendidly international, inter-racial scene.

A sequel to Lambeth took me to the USA for a second time. The emphasis was to be on the 'mutuality' of inter-relation between the Anglican Provinces in inter-cultural terms, via visits to schools as well as parishes, trying to interpret the theme of 'Christ in Iran' and of 'mission in diversity'.

In Boston, recalling the good Colonel Tremane of my army days, I tried to renew contact with him. However, a call to his wife brought the sad news that he had died. Elsewhere, after an illustrated lecture, a young acquaintance from those early years came to me, requesting to borrow my slides overnight. I now think he was an agent of Savak, the Secret Police in Iran, investigating me through the content of the slides. He had once come to me in Isfahan for Bible study. Maybe even then he was a police agent. However, he returned the set of slides the next day.

In Denver, Colorado, it was a joy to meet again Zirakzadeh, then of Boulder University and long before that a fellow pupil in High School. In Berkeley, California, I had a different sort of encounter. I had heard of hippies, now 'mine eye sees them' – unshaven fellows with unkempt hair, dirty clothes, and half-naked women of singularly unshapely form. They seemed out of place in a university setting. They reminded me of the dervishes I recalled from my childhood in Taft, with their long hair and wild attire who wandered around reciting poetry with a walking stick and kashkoul.

A sweet renewal took place in New York, where I met again my colleague in Tehran University during the War, Benji Zadeh

(I shared a flat with him). Now he was driving me through New York, reciting a Ghazal of Hafiz that brought a flow of tears to his eyes. So moving and eloquent is the Persian that it defies translation into English but something of its theme can be guessed from 'The Extasie' of John Donne, the seventeenth-century Dean of St Paul's in London. The theme is how the eyes of lovers 'negotiate' their joys and yearnings:

> Love's mysteries in soules do grow
> But yet the body is his booke . . .
> So must pure lovers' soules descend
> T'affections and to faculties
> Which sense may reach and apprehend . . .[2]

Elsewhere the same poet writes of how true love so sweetly and surely binds the twain that even in absence they are 'inter-assured of the mind,/by a love so much refined,/that ourselves know not what it is'. He then employs the image of the draftsman's 'compass' with its two feet circling, the one fixed the other making the circumference:

> And though it in the centre sit,
> Yet when the other far doth roam
> It leans and hearkens after it,
> And grows erect as that comes home.
> Such wilt thou be to me . . .[3]

The artistry of words across all literatures serves the lively imagination by which, in one kinship, they all rejoice. Benji Zadeh was a Christian of Jewish birth whose whole being responded – even, as then, with tears – to the thrill of poetry.

On another occasion in New York I was the guest of an old and learned friend, Dr John Moyne. He invited Dr Ya Shatter and a few other scholars to dinner, enabling us to share something of the erudition that underlay the *Encyclopedia Iranica*. By other writings, too, Dr Yarshater had contributed massively to the revival of Persian culture and its interpretation in the West.

There were always occasions in those international travels that were relevant to the needs of the Diocese. Returning from the USA in 1967, I came through Holland and spent some days with the Re-formed Church of the land – by now fully engaged with the Diocese in the project of the training farm for the blind.

Ours, as is well known, is all too frequently a land of earthquakes. That of 1962 in the north-east had its counterpart in 1968 in the area south of Mashhad. Again the Church Council of Iran through the Aid Committee of the World Council responded by donating and equipping a 35-bed hospital which was handed over in the presence of the Shah on the first anniversary of the disaster. I recall a dismaying incident when the Shah, at the official assembly, passed along a line of ecclesiastical and other representatives and, unhappily, quite ignored Paul Verghese, the WCC envoy with his long beard. We had expected a handshake and an exchange of greeting with thanks from the Iranian side.

From that ceremony in the Mashhad region I went on to visit the leper colony in the city. I was appalled at the dreadful conditions under which the patients lived, served only by the compassion of two or three young French women belonging to the Order of Little Sisters of Jesus – the Order parallel to 'the Little Brothers of Jesus' and dedicated to ministry where, all too often, others shun the conditions. The Sisters had a few simple rooms and a chapel in a corner of the colony. Their practical compassion seemed then to me more than ever a surer witness than theologians ever bring. I recalled the saying: 'Half a deed is better than 200 sermons.' Woe to us who preach so many, unless we share the other half of the deed! And, despite all that is authentic in our love to them, may not the same caution apply to poets with their flights of fancy, their bewitching words? Nevertheless, I took advantage of the visit to Mashhad to salute the tomb of Ferdowsi nearby and at Neyshapour to inspect the graves of Farid al-Din Aftar, and that old agnostic charmer, Umar Khayyam. Not all those who enjoy his imagery of taverns, wine and intoxication appreciate how far the imagery avails in Sufism as an analogy for the state of absorption into God and for the discipline that induces it.

Rapid Progress

I turn now to the enormous developments that were taking place in Iran throughout the 1960s, which were deeply affecting the task of the Church. Isfahan acquired a steelmill, fulfilling what had long been a goal. The railway had reached Yazd and Bafq and was extending to Zarand and beyond. There was extensive growth of agriculture, notably in Khuzestan. The burning dry desert between Ahvaz and Andimeshk began to wear a green face through irrigation and horticulture in field and garden. The University of Jondi Shahpour, a place of pride in the pre-Islamic era of the Sassanids but for centuries an almost forgotten name, had been renewed and was now full of promise. Irrigation has always been vital in Iran's economy. Dams were a new and crucial feature in the construction of those years. In doubtless a more sinister way, the army was being massively modernized with an influx of new technology and military hardware. The Shah was eager for all the gadgetry of modern warfare to correct what he saw as the weakness, the exploitability, the political victimization, of the nation as symbolized by that Tehran Conference of Western powers in our very capital.

The Shah took immense pride in these developments, seeing Iran entering – or re-entering – 'the gates of a great civilization'. All was a prelude to the coronation for which it seemed that both he and we were ready. It took place amid great splendour in 1967. The Shah received the nation's acclamation in celebrations across the land, with gifts of congratulation offered to him from a variety of organizations and institutions, educational, social and civic. Our Diocese presented a Persian Bible suitably prepared by local artistry.

In diocesan terms, too, there was much development, not

least in our educational and social ministries. The Carr Schools, both Junior and High, under Mir Mohammad Sadeghi, with competent teachers both Iranian and foreign, were establishing a fine reputation around Isfahan. Under Mary Isaac, the Rahmat Junior and High School for Girls was also prospering. The Christian hospital had been completely rebuilt to renew – on the same site – the healing ministry alive there for 100 years but now rehoused and re-equipped, with a fine team of medics serving its public well.

The churches in Tehran, Isfahan, Shiraz, Yazd and Kerman had fully trained and able clergy with bookshops and clinics reaching into neighbouring villages. The building of the headquarters of the Diocese in Tehran was happily completed with an adjacent school for the teaching of languages and crafts under Betty Gurney and Miss G. Nour-o-Llah, while back in Isfahan the training farm for the blind was fulfilling its purpose in the arts of husbandry, with livestock and poultry production.

The year 1971 was named 'The Year of Cyrus the Great', marking 2500 years from the institution of monarchy by Cyrus. Throughout the nation there were elaborate ceremonies of celebration in a lavish display of patriotic pride and fervour. The apogee was the great event at Pasargad in the empty tomb-chamber of Cyrus and also in the vast and awesome ruins of Persepolis.

Representation of the various world religions at the ceremonies had been planned but, as the nominated representative of the Archbishop in Jerusalem, I only received my formal invitation two days ahead of the great occasion in Pasargad. This meant a very hasty journey to Shiraz, to find a very varied group of religious Heads (if one may so speak respectfully – for it is hoped we have hearts as well) including Orthodox Christians, Buddhists, Confucians, as well as Roman, Protestant and other Christians, with Mormons, Adventists and even an Amerindian (Red Indian) Chief.

We were all staying in the Daruish Hotel on the first night. While registering there, I noticed, standing in a corner, Prime

Minister Amir Abbas Hoveida. While our eyes met and stayed so for several moments, I am unsure whether or not he recognized me. We had been together years before in the Officers' Training College while on military service. I did not see him again, until at the beginning of the Revolution, I listened to his words at the televised trumped-up trial he underwent. Unable to see his judge, he asked, 'Are you, in fact, Qarabaghi?' He was trying to identify his accuser. Then he added, 'The system has changed out of all recognition.' It was a tragic scene, as, in extreme danger, he deplored the travesty of justice that was being enacted. Later I was to see his body with that of other victims after his murder.

To return to the ceremonies: we were taken by bus the next morning from the hotel to Pasargad where we listened to the Shah's spirited words with their refrain: 'Sleep Cyrus, for we are awake!' A strange thing happened on the bus as we returned. A retired General, Mazahari, was in charge. He had the embarrassing task of explaining to us assorted ecclesiastics that our hotel rooms that evening would have to be vacated and that we would be flown to accommodation in Tehran, to be returned the next week. The reason was that some political and diplomatic delegates had brought larger entourages than had been anticipated and these had to be housed with their superiors.

Many in the bus were mortally offended and protested at what they took as a slight, a slur on their dignity and their office. They demanded to be taken to the Daruish Hotel where all their belongings were, in anger at the disturbance to their plans. Orthodox Bishops and some American priests were quite vociferous in registering their angry dissent at the perceived discourtesy. I felt embarrassed for the poor General, who was only doing what duty required. Accordingly, I got up towards the rear of the bus and said that, as Christians, we should be humbly ready to show the Christian spirit and defer to what was planned for us, and cease our reproaches and the unseemly wrangle. Some in the bus agreed but others remained restive and argued among themselves.

Whatever the protests, it transpired as the General had said. We flew to the Semiramis Hotel in Tehran and were brought back to Shiraz the next week. Some delegates collected their expenses and boycotted the ceremonies that followed. They missed the memorable march-past at Persepolis. I regretted their discourtesy. For is it not part of a true courtesy that you do not chafe at its opposite where you think you detect it?

The remaining delegates were placated the next day by an audience with the Shah. Some brought costly jewelled gifts to present to him. I presented only a detailed telegram from Archbishop Appleton in Jerusalem. The Shah handed it to Shojaidin Shafa to be filed in the archives. We were invited to be seated and I found my chair was next to the Shah's. I responded to his words in Persian. Astonished, he asked if I was Iranian. I said, 'Yes. I am the current Bishop of the Diocese in Iran whose institutions in Isfahan Your Majesty visited at the time of Queen Elizabeth's visit.' After that, the exchange ceased. It was as if he was disappointed to find that I was Iranian.

How different it all was from the florid speech of the Amerindian Chief, in his massive head-dress and colourful feathers, who bestowed on the Shah the grandiloquent title of 'The Leopard'. His sycophantic gesture was much reported in Tehran's evening papers.

The State authorities had requested that the nation's Christians should arrange their own festivities to mark the noble anniversary. A committee was formed of Roman, Orthodox, Armenian, Assyrian, Episcopal and Evangelical Churches. It decided to hold a service in thanksgiving to God for the reign and liberality of Cyrus the Great, with different clergy participating. The venue was at first to be in Karim Khan Zand street at the Armenian Church, but when its Archbishop demurred about my preaching in Persian (for the sermon had been assigned to me) we had to move. For he wanted only English to be spoken, Persian being forbidden in an Armenian edifice. I explained that the celebrations concerned Iran and that I must use its (my) native tongue. Accordingly we transferred to the Chaldean Church in Forsat Street. My theme took its cue from the several Biblical references to Cyrus and stressed his tolerance and how he had been designated 'God's servant and His anointed'. It was surely proper to salute the occasion in these cherished Biblical terms.

However, despite the dignity and enthusiasm at that time, all was not well with Iran. There were growing murmurs of dissatisfaction. Many of the Shah's grandiose schemes proved over hasty or were ill-grounded. There were many examples. Our ports had inadequate facilities for the massive imports they were meant to handle, or lacked storage and transport onwards for their cargoes. Although thanks to oil the national – and for many the personal – income had risen dramatically, so also had the price of goods. Inflation reached high levels until, for example, a professor's salary would all go on renting accommodation. Discontent began to be voiced on many sides. Fear of Savak, the Shah's secret police, deterred the media from reporting the real facts of deterioration, and rumour fed on the ignorance. Though the sheer lavishness of the anniversary celebrations was widely criticized outside Iran, at home it was the theme of endless adulation and eulogy.

It was in this atmosphere that the tapes of the exiled Ayatollah Khomeini wielded such influence. For they were shrewdly drafted to foster and foment anti-Shah feeling and anti-government unrest. The Islamic Communists, or 'People's Fighters', despite having quite opposing goals, collaborated with the Islamic revolutionaries, arousing both speculation and apprehension among the general population. There came a sense of gradually eroding confidence in 'law and order', and a malaise of psychic insecurity and fear. It appeared that even the will to normality was failing in the very heart of the nation.

Here are two examples. In the small town of Delijan, on the road between Isfahan and Tehran, an old Armenian had run a successful café which he managed with the utmost cleanliness.

He was attacked one day by a bunch of ruffians, his livelihood destroyed, and he was threatened with worse things if he complained. There he was – a homeless refugee in his own country, with no restitution or justice. The perpetrators went unpunished.

My old headmistress from Yazd days, Armenhoohi (Nouhie) Aidin, now retired was living in a small house in Isfahan. One night some thugs attacked her house, tied her to a bed and ransacked her belongings. Word of it was never published and there were no arrests.

These portents of tribulation ahead did not curtail the active ministry or my travels inside and beyond the Diocese. In early 1970 there was a Synod in Cyprus which gave opportunity for a courtesy call, with Archbishop Appleton, on the Ethnarch of Cyprus who was also President of Cyprus, Archbishop Makarios. In reply to my query why he had not come to Iran for the Cyrus celebrations he answered curtly, 'We were not invited.' There was also a dual episcopal consecration in Khartoum and advance discussion on the future of the Jerusalem Archbishopric when George Appleton's tenure would be ended around 1974 to 1975.

I made two visits to Pakistan and was intrigued to savour for myself the strong influence there of Persian language, culture and arts – thanks to Babur and the succeeding Mughals. In Lahore I met Bishop Inayat Masih and, via Edwardes College, Peshawar, made my way by bus through the Khyber Pass to Kabul, musing the while on Nader Shah and his campaigns through it.

The second visit came in 1970 when I attended the inauguration of the United Church of Pakistan, on behalf of the Diocese and of Jerusalem and the Anglican Consultative Council. I brought a chased brass plate which I presented for use as a church plate.

It was before these visits, while mercifully back in Isfahan, that I learned of the death of my father away in Taft. At once I set off but, instead of offering solace to a community in grief, my arrival caused disquiet to my brother, Yahya. He intimated that as they had already buried my father, my coming was unnecessary. He was insistent that I should go back to Isfahan. He then foresaw difficulties about my presence at the traditional third-day service following death. When I insisted that I must be there, he called the local religious leaders to the house. I found myself confronted by a dozen turbaned men who were unanimous in their verdict that my presence in the mosque would be intolerable. It was the mosque I had attended as a child. There was nothing to be gained by arguing. There was a deep anger in me when their leader recommended that I swallow the humiliation and return home forthwith. So I went and stood for a while by the door of the mosque in prayer and loving recollection of my father. Then I left for Isfahan.

Though some ten years before the Revolution, this bitter personal experience of the heartless power of the mullahs stayed in my own soul as a sharp token of a reality the Shah's regime was tragically ignoring, until its grim potential became all too evident. It was a potent inner force which, once effectively mobilized by crowd incitement, sufficed to topple his imperial throne.

That improvident attitude, despite the vigilance of Savak, came home to me when I visited Oxford to see my son Bahram who was at Jesus College, studying politics, philosophy and economics. Meeting the Economics Professor, I was interrogated about the Shah. 'He,' said the academic, 'invites us at great expense to go to Iran to advise on his economic options, but when we arrive we have to listen to his own views with no chance to expound our own – for what *in situ* they might be worth.'

That triad of politics, philosophy and economics might be loosely located in similar alliance with the ecumenical business of Christian mission. For inside ecclesiology, or study of 'being the Church', there is some trace of ecumenical politics, as well as a philosophy of mission and its sinews in finance. It was this triad that took me at the turn of 1972/1973 to a conference in Bangkok, Thailand, that was to sort out the future form of the old International Missionary Council, as a unit of world mission inside the World Council of Churches. Three hundred and thirty delegates came together with the theme 'The Meaning of Salvation Today'. They came from the West, from Russia, West and East Germany, Latin America and elsewhere.

It was soon apparent that there was a kind of consensus emerging against 'mission' and 'the West' on the part of local and national churches, vociferously claiming to detach themselves from all the alleged paternalism, the superiority complex they read into their western relationships. I was perplexed how the theme of 'salvation' could engender attacks on 'missionaries' as hirelings of their countries or 'lords over God's heritage' in Asia or Africa. I found myself at odds with many leaders, among them – symbolizing many more – a Burgess Carr from Liberia. To be sure, white missionaries had made mistakes but were not wholly at fault in that their governments had presided over empires. To tar all with the same brush was hardly Christian nor was it the study of 'salvation'. Such sentiments ignored or disparaged the vast outpouring of sacrificial love and ministry in the name of Christ by his evangelists. I said to Burgess Carr: 'But for the likes of David Livingstone and Albert Schweitzer the likes of you would not exist.' I was second to none – as all the previous narrative has shown – in my first affirmation of identity and culture, language and poetry in the Persian heritage. But I felt I had to be equally emphatic about the obligation to the decisive unity we had in Christ to resist all 'go-it-alone' rejectionism on the part of 'younger churches'.

That encounter has had many repercussions since, but 'keeping the unity of the Spirit in the bond of peace' has to be paramount over all pride of lesser belonging. I have held steadily to that principle of genuine, authentic '*inter*-dependence in the body of Christ', neither patronizing nor isolating, seeing that any 'sufficiency in Christ' is ours only in knowing that our own culture never suffices him in his inclusive grace.

Though my difference with the likes of Burgess Carr was deep, he was very gracious in his friendship when, later, I underwent such heavy grief and loss. I met him unexpectedly on one of my travels. He promptly hugged me and, with a warm kiss, consoled me over my loss and pain. I became then the more convinced that those missionaries in Africa had done a good job.

Imagine my surprise when one day in 1975 the office of the Governor of Isfahan informed me that Elizabeth, the Queen Mother, was to visit the city and would like to see the Nour Ayin Institute for the Blind. She duly arrived with her entourage and was warmly greeted by the blind. Margaret and I were invited to lunch with her in the Shah Abbas Hotel, with the British Ambassador, Sir Anthony Parsons, also present. My conversation with the Queen Mother was about the need for dialogue and friendship between faiths within what she held to be the common goal of all religions. We later received a signed portrait of Her Majesty prior to her departure from the city.

It was around that time that new responsibilities devolved on me because of the retirement of Archbishop George Appleton and the end of the arrangement by which Anglican jurisdiction in the Middle East had been organized since 1956. The former Bishop of London, Robert Stopford, became an interim Vicar-General to co-ordinate a new pattern by which a Province of Jerusalem and the Middle East would be created, to which body local autonomy could be passed from Canterbury, making our Church self-governing. That principle had been pledged at Khartoum in 1970. Long and arduous discussions were needed in the different areas before the plan was finally set in place. These brought Bishop Stopford to Iran where he spent some two weeks, forfeiting his penknife at the airport on arrival for safe-keeping away from his person till he departed.

The outcome was the launching of the new Province, made up of four dioceses of which we in Iran were one, together with Jerusalem, a reconstituted Diocese of Egypt and the two-limbed creation of 'Cyprus and the Gulf'. An elected President Bishop would exercise a sort of overall jurisdiction with, initially, a five-year term, renewable only once. It was this new and arduous responsibility to which I was elected after the formal inauguration of the Province at memorable sessions in Amman early in 1976. Election was at the hands of a Central Synod to which each diocese sent four members, those from Iran at that point being the Revd Arastoo Sayyah, Mrs Robabeh Shirvanian and Abdul Hussein Imani-Rad.

This new provincial dimension to my tasks was a heavy trust, entailing a pastoral concern for the whole area from far North Africa, Ethiopia, the long Gulf line of States from Muscat to Iraq, the island of Cyprus and the heartlands of Christian history in Palestine, Syria and Lebanon – all to be cherished in Christ in an Anglican fellowship that held each diocese both autonomous and contributory, the entire structure being itself innovative and untried. It was the sort of regional self-responsibility that had come to African dioceses much earlier but had hitherto been delayed, given the complexities in the Middle East. The Palestinian Christians of the Diocese in Jerusalem had long been ardent for the kind of autonomy it brought. For it was essential that their Western links and associations should not compromise the legitimate part that they had to play in the nationalism of their people, faced with the traumas – mental, physical and environmental – consequent upon their experience of a recovered Jewish nationalism in Zionist form in the land they called home.

The 1976 transition also meant that the new autonomous Province had to assume the role of Anglican representation in the Mother City of the faith and be ready to greet and facilitate the spiritual and study needs of those who came from the ends of the earth to 'a holy land'.

The new burdens I had to assume as the first President Bishop were simultaneously a deep joy and privilege, but also an exacting call, with precedents to be made and ventures pondered. One of these was the launching of occasional papers called 'The Presence', which might help to unify and inform the whole. This, and much else, demanded more office-based tasks.

In these I was ably helped by Jean Waddell, lately Secretary to Archbishop Appleton and the Vicar-General. She agreed to my request and moved across to Isfahan. It was also incumbent upon me to visit the four constituent Dioceses and meet their clergy. Links with the wider constituency of the whole Communion had also to be maintained and deepened in a mutual sharing of all that belonged between us in the unity of Christ.

Margaret and I, accordingly, visited the Episcopal Church, USA, after the inauguration, for three crowded weeks. I visited all the Churches of the Province twice during my first five-year tenure. That kind of itinerary is not hard for any reader to imagine. From Shiraz, for example, over to Muscat and the Shaikhdoms of the Gulf, Sharjah, Abu Dhabi, Dubai, Qatar, Kuwait and Bahrain, thence perhaps to Amman and Jerusalem and thereby over to Cyprus, or across to Cairo, not forgetting Ethiopia and Eritrea to the south, or Iraq en route homeward to Isfahan. Cairo would be a point of departure for the Chaplaincies to the west in Libya, Tunis and Algeria. I recall after one of these journeys that I had changed currencies 18 times, and currencies are at times more easily changed than passports approved or visas secured.

On these forays into the jurisdiction there were also encounters with history. Notably at Muscat I was thrilled to enter somewhat into the legacy of Thomas Valpy French by a visit to his grave in a lonely burial plot set in a cove between precipitous cliffs which can only be reached from the sea. He had been the first Bishop of Lahore, builder of its fine cathedral on the Mall. After retirement he went to Muscat in a lonely evangelizing venture, an old man yet full of ardour. He died exhausted from the heat within a few months, having refused the (relative) comforts of the British Consulate lest his Christian purpose might seem compromised. It may seem a forlorn gesture yet his story – in our annals as his heirs – stays both to rebuke and enthuse the heart. Earlier he had visited Iran and held both an ordination and a confirmation.

There was history of a different kind when in Cairo I witnessed the demolition of the large Cathedral of All Saints. Only consecrated by Archbishop William Temple (then of York) in 1938, its strategic location between the Nile and Sharia Rameses, Cairo's main artery, was urgently needed for the building of a massive six-lane bridge across the river. The arrangements, in their complexity, had taken many years but demonstrated the possibility of genuine mutual trust between a Christian community and a Muslim municipality. The site was enormously valuable. But instead of haggling over a purchase, it was agreed that the municipality would grant an equivalent plot of land and build to an agreed design at its expense. The overall dimensions both of the Cathedral and the dwellings would be identical – though of a different shape and pattern. The Church was to pay the architect and was invited to search around for the location it would like. Accordingly, in the little car they shared in those modest days, Bishop Kenneth Cragg and Provost Douglas Butcher went off and found the derelict site in Zamalek, behind the old Umar Khayyam Hotel, where the new Cathedral now stands. It was consecrated on St Mark's Day 1989, by Bishop Ghais Abdel Malik. The story was one of mingled grief and grateful satisfaction. I remember visiting my old friend now aged and housebound, Archdeacon Adeeb Shammas, and hearing his grieving thoughts on the whole protracted episode.

Worrying Times

These travels and experiences in the wider context did little to allay the fears I sensed when I came back to Iran – perplexities and anxieties stemming from the gathering sense of restlessness and dismay in the population at large. There was a feeling of confusion at the heart of things, with edicts arbitrarily issued (like the one that lost us our schools) and bungling in sundry forms. The school debacle was typical and meant I had to forego my long hope of recreating for a new generation the sort of excellence that had been achieved in the old colleges I had known.

A decree was issued that there were to be no more student

fees; all education was to be free. We acknowledged this as a sound idea, but who would pay our teachers? Enquiries at Isfahan were merely passed on to Tehran. There was no answer, so that decree entailed the handing over of the school to the government.

To deepen the dismay of these situations we had to endure the tragic loss in road accidents of Amy Hanson, the wife of the Director of the Christian Farm for the Blind, and of a young Australian surgeon, Dr Ian Thomas, and one of the nurses, who were returning from a rural clinic. Further, there were those long-time ruins of the Yazd Hospital (destroyed in a flash flood). Given the place Yazd had in my heart, they always seemed to affect me when I went there. So much so, that I had great delight when Dr John Coleman, who had earlier served in Shiraz, agreed to return from a period in England to resume medical work in Yazd in 1978. His ordination to the ministry was a help to the local Church in Yazd.

Overall, however, our sky seemed more and more to be oppressed with gathering clouds that were heavy with foreboding. It is one of those paradoxes of Christian experience that I have to associate the tragic with highpoints of personal and family joy. These had to do with the graduation of our son, Bahram, in Oxford and the thrill of the Lambeth Conference in 1978.

Bahram had postponed his formal Oxford graduation while at George Washington University. His eldest sister, Shirin, was returning from the USA, already having graduated from Demavand College, Tehran, and subsequently from the University of Texas in Austin, while her sister Sussanne was in training at St Thomas's Hospital, Lambeth. It was a proud and gratifying moment for us to be present as one family on Bahram's great day to share his joy in graduation at the Sheldonian Theatre. This glad event has been etched into my heart for his sake.

The ensuing Lambeth Conference of 1978 convened at the University of Kent in Canterbury, with 450 people attending from 25 autonomous Churches within the one Communion, and with a Wives' Conference alongside it. It was in these benign scenes that the sky of Iran grew darker still. A fellow bishop handed me a paper and asked, 'What is going on in Iran?' There was a picture of the Rex Cinema ablaze in Abadan, reports of daily riots, attacks on banks and shops, and demonstrations in the streets. It was a strange mental setting in which to debate 'Ministry in the Body of Christ'.

All the family except Sussanne returned to Iran after the Conference. Martial law was declared in Isfahan and 11 other cities the day after we arrived home. On the Friday of that week – 'Black Friday' – many were killed and injured when the army fired on demonstrators who had defied the curfew. Throughout the autumn the situation worsened until, on 16 January 1979 the Shah left for Egypt and 16 days later Ayatollah Khomeini returned triumphantly from Paris, from where his broadcasts had long been exciting the populace. Vain was the talk of Shahpour Bakhtyar as Prime Minister about restoring order. Soldiers returned to their barracks, while demonstrators and revolutionaries stormed the ammunition depots and effectively took control of the capital and other cities. The Ayatollah dissolved Parliament and appointed Engineer Bazargan as Prime Minister. The Revolution had triumphed. The Diocese, along with so many other bodies in the nation, sent a telegram of greeting to Khomeini and impatiently awaited the pledged restoration of freedom, justice and security – the sweet things he had promised.

CHAPTER 9

Watchman: What of the Night?

The story this chapter must tell might have many titles, drawn from those ever fertile poets with their imageries of 'trial by fire', of 'tides rising higher', of 'naught for your comfort'. Hafiz declares:

> Love's true fire is not the gentle flame that dances from the candle's gleam. It is the burning thing that draws the moth into its scorching self.

Only experience, as Sa'di knew, could know what sequels are. The sequel waits in what one undergoes. So,

> Beware the turning world, the changes and the chances of this life.
> Only that turning told what, turning, it would be.

But imageries apart, the ultimate truth is best found in the words of Jesus himself:

> If any would come after me, let him take up his cross and follow me. For whosoever would have his life will lose it and whosoever loses his life for my sake, he will find it (Mark 8:34–35).

I return to my diary from the start of 1979, the end of the winter of 1357 by the solar calendar, for a daily narrative of the traumatic events that followed the Islamic Revolution in my beloved Iran. It amazes me now how we tried to assume a degree of normality, despite the forebodings that translated themselves into cumulative tragedy as the days and weeks went by. We tried to carry on steadily with our work, aware of realities both grim and menacing, yet buoyed up with a paradox of hope, trying to believe the things the Revolution had said about freedom and truth, how oppression would be rooted out and terror ended. With tyranny and despotism gone, the people would be free to follow their religious and political beliefs. The poor and needy would be exalted and the rich and powerful abased. It might almost sound like The Magnificat. Deception and deceit would yield to honesty. Fraud and hypocrisy would end and sincerity and candour would take up the reins of power.

How could we know that these pledges would be swirled away in the flood of bigotry, wrath and demagogy?

I thought of Hafiz's lines, only that we were not 'on the shore', we were tossed in the flood; still, though, the question fitted the situation exactly:

> A mountainous sea, moon clouded o'er,
> By night the whirlpool's awful roar:
> How can they know our labour sore
> Who stay light-burdened on the shore?[1]

One might add to this the words of a great English poem about a sea of storm and drowning where there is one for ever abiding:

> I greet him the days that I meet him, and bless
>   when I understand.[2]

As things worsened we moved where the contemporary poet Nader Naderpour had been when he wrote:

> That earthquake that shook the house
> In one night everything destroyed,
> Like a flame it burned the sleeping world
> And filled the morning's ash with blood.

We tried to believe what they said when the agents of the Revolution brought to the house their manifestos inviting our co-operation against oppression, injustice and tyranny. We were far from ever imagining how dire the sequel would be. It never crossed our minds that they would bring to pass, as it were, Malekalshoara Bahar's lines in 'The Song of the Dawn Bird', familiar enough in their poetic terms:

> The cruelty of the cruel and the oppression of the hunter
> Have shattered my nest.

Though the events that ensued have been related in many an interview and set down with anxious care in *The Hard Awakening*, I must do so again here since so much in life's meaning and vocation turns on them.

Ominous Signs

The first blow, foreshadowing many more, was the brutal murder of our priest in Shiraz, our dear Arastoo Sayyah. Two youths whom he knew from discussions about the Christian faith, Nasihat and Kolahi by name, knocked on his door and were invited to come in. It was around midday. A few hours later, Arastoo's elder son, Kamran, went to his father's office and found his decapitated body. The two youths were arrested, held for one night and then released. The murder of an infidel was then no crime in Islamic law.

With a few friends I hastened to Shiraz on news of this dastardly deed. We held a service and, deeply mourning, buried our brother and returned in heaviness of sorrow to Isfahan. Before leaving Shiraz we went to see Ayatollah Mahalati, whose response was that the crime was the work of counter-revolutionaries – a standard cry at that time, divesting any and all Islamic fanatics of blame or implication. That reaction was in no way reassuring.

In Isfahan, however, with my colleagues Dr Ronald Pont and John McDouall I went to see Ayatollah Khademi, who

implied to us that we could continue our work without difficulty. He was out of touch and, indeed, so weak and ill that
he died shortly afterwards. The reality was that fanatics and
members of the Islamic Propaganda Organization were active
locally against us. After his death their activities increased.
False propaganda and trumped-up charges were levelled
against the Church and against me. They multiplied almost
daily. Even within our institutions came a few insinuations
from people serving in them; the circulation of these falsehoods
made normal working arduous and anxious.

On 31 March 1979 (1 Farvardin 1358) came the announce-
ment of a referendum for the setting up of a new government,
with the voters ostensibly free to vote for whatever sort of
government they wished. It was clear enough what the Ayatollah Khomeini and the Revolutionary Council had in mind: 'an
Islamic Republic', and that alone. I had no mind to vote that
way. For the sake of my duties outside the Diocese as President
Bishop I had to ensure the validity of my passport, etc. I was
told by friends that unless it bore a stamp as proof of my
having voted, return would be hazardous.

After much thought, Iraj Mottahedeh and I went to vote at
the Kazerooni Mosque opposite our house. Two armed men
sat with their guns on either side of the ballot box. In order
to satisfy my conscience, I wrote: 'Islamic Republic, taking into
account the Universal Declaration of Human Rights'. This, of
course, did not go unobserved by the armed guards.

Killing became so easy, so routine. Day after day we read
of persons shot – a Shahidi, a Kazerooni, an Eshraqi, and so
on. The corpses of the dead appeared daily on the TV screen.
Twelve people were shot on 11 April, including Mayor Neek-
pai of Tehran, a former student of Stuart Memorial College,
and on 8 May there came the report of 21 people executed,
including Gholamreza Kianpoor, a former Governor of
Isfahan.

These developments brought fear into the hearts of many,
especially children. The horror was sharpened by the sense that
true Iranians were capable of such acts of terrorism, being of

a calm and kindly disposition. How could our fellow countrymen be capable of such deeds? Some suggested that atrocities were the work of people who had been schooled in them abroad.

In this frightening situation some suggested that I should announce the temporary closing down of our work, of the Diocese, and that we should leave the country. Margaret and I could not agree to this, having in mind the words of Jesus:

> I am the good shepherd. The good shepherd lays down his life for the sheep. He who is a hireling and not a shepherd, whose own the sheep are not, sees the wolf coming, leaves the sheep and flees: the wolf snatches them and scatters the sheep. He flees because he is a hireling and cares nothing for the sheep (John 10:11–13).

That was how Christ saw things and the Bishop is called to be his under-shepherd. The duty of all of us was clear. At a meeting of the clergy and staff I announced that my decision was to stay but that others – after thought and prayer – were free to leave if they so chose. It soon became clear that the expatriates had no alternative but to go. Of the Persian clergy, two left and two remained. Staying was by no means easy. It is false to imagine that there is, in times of adversity, some gift of stoic indifference to danger, a sort of obliviousness that somehow makes a crisis unreal. On the contrary, the tensions are grievous and peace of heart can only prevail by the constant search for grace. 'I will think upon God' (Psalm 77:3), as the psalmist found, is no carefree attitude but rather what elsewhere he called a 'cleaving to the Lord'. To have heavy responsibility is to seek the Lord the more urgently in such stressful situations. 'O Lord, in thee have I trusted; let me never be confounded', had to be our prayer.

The tension and perplexity made me ill. I spent three weeks in bed, with a high fever. The clinical diagnosis was obvious enough: stress had prostrated me. The body had answered the weight on the soul. Medicine itself did not heal me but a new infilling of the love of God, and a peace that only a new sense of God's presence could bestow. The God of love was the antidote to my anxiety about the future, and enabled me to endure the present.

There were those in Isfahan we had always known were members of 'Islamic Propaganda', who styled themselves now as 'the Committee' and stealthily organized their hostility to our institutions. In the chaos following the breakdown of public order, they infiltrated our work, fomenting disturbance and expelling overseas workers, contriving to take the institutions over. One of their ugliest methods was to create division and suborn workers from their loyalty to management. Tales were spread engendering ill-will and disruption. They threatened one worker, Shahpoor Pourpeshang, with a gun, trying to force him to work against us. He was terrified and we transferred him to Tehran. Even there they harried him and he forged false documents to lay charges against the Church.

How these tribulations brought to mind the words of Hafiz:

The doors of the tavern they have closed, O God.
Let them not open houses of dissimulation and hypocrisy.

Another saying of his that was also appropriate was:

The nearer to the vine, the more bitter the cup.
The higher one climbs the more perilous the path,
The nearer to the Throne, the thornier the Cross.

We had to live through days of unpredictable developments, looking for wisdom and courage in each perplexity as we had to confront it.

On 11 June 1979 (21 Khordad 1358), just after I had travelled to Tehran, a group of people took over the Isfahan hospital, expelling all expatriate workers. The next day I took part in a combined meeting with the Presbyterians to discuss the role of Persian Christians in the Islamic State context and also the Church in Khuzestan. There were other consultations of great urgency, including a discussion with the British Ambassador, Sir John Graham, over the hospital take-over in Isfahan – half of the land was held in the Land Registry in the name of the CMS, a British-based body. We maintained worship and fellowship by all the means we could. Times of acute anxiety were lightened by the keen sense of peace I knew, if intermittently, in the knowledge of people in prayer for us.

Some days after returning to Isfahan and toiling over the hospital situation, John McDouall and I were asked to go and see the Governor of Isfahan. Some fanatical people were there, as well as the Director of the Department of Health. They demanded that I sign minutes of the meeting, effectively handing over the hospital to the intruders. John McDouall and I both signed adding: 'signature signifies presence, not agreement'.

Two days later we learned they had transferred its accounts to themselves and drawn moneys from them. When we referred the matter to the Bank, they told us: 'You are right, but what can we do with their guns pointing at us?'

It was difficult to spare time and effort, but I composed a document, and referred it to Prime Minister Bazargan; it concerned Persian Christians, their status and vocation in our country. Tensions were sharpened by attitudes in our inner circle concerning how best to preserve the hospital. These involved our leading expatriate medic, Dr Ronald Pont. The British Embassy protested about the hospital seizure as half of the land was registered as British. In Tehran I consulted Monsignor Bugnini, the Pope's envoy. The Tehran property was also under threat. To deepen our sorrow came word of the death of Dr Peter Wild in England, our former medical director. A memorial service warmed but could not solace our hearts. Then came word that the Shiraz hospital had also been expropriated. Having thought at first he might transfer there, Dr Pont now opted to return to England.

I found myself beginning to think that our institutions, so valued in the past, were perhaps a burden to the Church which would be healthier if divested of them. Were we now being schooled by adversity to think that way, or might the reaction be a response to the stress under which we worked? I was in no doubt, however, that we should take our stand against the gross injustice in their being taken from us. I protested strongly against lawlessness in the expropriation of Church properties and assets but, at the same time, made clear our readiness to comply with orders duly deriving from central government, not from what was mob rule. A strongly worded telegram to this effect was written by our lawyer Feshareki, sent to the authorities in Tehran, and followed by letters of protest to the government departments involved. We also informed the World Council of Churches in Geneva. This stand on my part against outright confiscation and lawlessness, as being contrary to Islamic law itself, only intensified the fanatics, emboldening them still more against us. But 'I could do no other', as Luther said at another time and place.

That August I was involved in Khalil Razmara's youth camp and sundry duties in Tehran, when word came that armed men had seized the Christoffel Centre for the blind. Then, back in Isfahan on Sunday 19 August, some 30 revolutionary agitators forced their way into our house, ransacked each room, and then stole from the Diocesan Office. They made off with our family albums, the lists of confirmed Church members, and archive copies of *Piam be Kalissaha*, the circular I had edited for 30 years. What they did not choose to take they dumped into the yard and burned. I could not but recall a verse about the Mughal invaders: 'They came, they killed, they burned, they stole and they went.' After drafting telegrams of complaint to inland and overseas centres I went to bed. Six days later, having travelled to Kerman via Yazd to see our clergy there, word came by phone that the church and centre in Tehran had likewise been attacked and ransacked. Returning in dismay and grief to Isfahan, I passed by Yazd to see the Colemans and at Taft ate with my brother Yahya. The following week found me in Tehran assessing with Shahpoor Pourpeshang what had happened there.

More attacks followed on the training farm, coinciding with

the 35th Diocesan Council and the priesting of John Coleman. On Sunday 7 October things became even more ominous. Karami appeared, a man whom Arastoo had baptized, together with Dr Azali and his son Jahanmir. The first said that he was a member of the Revolutionary Committee in Shiraz and that I was under orders to hand over to him the Diocesan Trust Fund. I answered that the fund was not mine to hand over to anyone. Before they left, Karami said, 'We'll be back tomorrow, maybe later tonight, to arrest you.'

The next day, they did return – Karami, two guards named Kharrazi and Ruhbakhsh, and a member of the Islamic Propaganda Organization named Vaezi. Going to the office to demand the money, they were told that I must sign the document. Eventually they arrested me. The Revolutionary Council detained me in a small room. I took off my cassock and sat on a small, half-broken chair I found there and began to pray. After a while I was taken out into a vast yard with young gun-men standing around. I did not then know that this was the area used for execution by firing squads. From behind a large metal door I heard voices and was informed that foreign reporters had arrived to find out what was going on. In the meantime, Demitri Bellos had gone to the Governor General's office to tell of my arrest (earlier in Tehran I had met a James Allan of the *Daily Telegraph*). It was that paper's correspondent who had come to investigate matters. The Governor had meanwhile informed the Prime Minister; he ordered my release on condition that I inform them at any time when I wished to travel abroad. While I had been in the detention area a note was passed to me from Margaret, with a towel and a toothbrush. It read, 'I am very proud of you for standing up for the truth.' This strengthened me enormously. The day before the arrest I wrote in my diary:

The day of testing faith . . . An hour during which I prayed (meditating) in the Thompson Memorial Chapel. I feel the presence of God within me and around me. Everything is in his powerful hand. He is the just judge and he is the

Almighty. So my prayer: 'O God, I thank you that you have given me this tiny particle of faith. As is needed, make that particle grow larger and stronger. Give me trust and tranquillity so that I may be a worthy ambassador for you. Grant me courage and trustworthiness so that I may never show timidity or weakness other than the weakness of the Cross, which is love to the end when faced with hatred, misunderstanding and the bearing of pain and suffering. O God, give me the strength to bear this. You are present in me, around me, and in all these events. So I go forward in your name and I entrust my dear ones, Margaret, Shirin, Bahram, Sussanne, Guli and the Church to you. Your will be done. Amen.'

All through October the crisis wore on. Newspapers from Tehran telephoned enquiring about the grim day of my arrest and I tried to answer them. There were issues about land ownership raised, with lawyers involved. Hushang was confirmed and our regular worship held central to our lives. Dr Azali from Shiraz phoned me daily urging that we give the Trust Fund money over to Karami. I had interviews with Tony Allan-Mills, the *Daily Telegraph* reporter, and licensed Paul Hunt to the care of St Paul's Church, Tehran, and pondered an order to attend at the Revolutionary Court in Isfahan, after consulting with Demitri.

The order had been signed by Hujatoleslam Omid Nadjafabadi, himself later executed, who – as I did not then know – had signed death warrants for several Isfahanis.

On 23 October Demitri came with me to the Court but I went alone into a room where Hujatoleslam Omid Nadjafabadi was seated at the head of the table, and round him a number of men, some of whom I knew, such as Vaezi, Baba Safari, Salamatian and Atrian. As I learned later, this was intended by them to be a court hearing at which, that very day, they would condemn me to death and execute me immediately. I was wearing my Bishop's cassock and kept quite calm when I answered them. After a while Hujatoleslam enquired what day I intended to travel abroad. I told him I was thinking of about five days later in order to attend church meetings in Cyprus in my capacity as President Bishop. The meeting ended and, amazingly, we separated politely and respectfully.

However, three days later, came the attack on Bishop's House. Around 6 a.m. three men climbed over the rear wall and forced their way in. They had asked my stepbrother, Hussain, who was living in the house, to give them the key of the gate to facilitate their escape, but he had refused. While one stood over him with a gun to prevent him moving, the other two came up to our bedroom on the first floor. I heard Margaret saying, 'What are you doing here at this time?' Then, as he leaned over my bed, I heard one of them calling my name. Opening my eyes, I saw the barrel of a gun no more than a foot away from my head. The next instant came the sound of shots aimed towards me. Margaret had thrown herself across me. Those who had fired the shots ran off. Margaret pursued them calling after them, 'Why did you do that?' They escaped by climbing over some railings against the wall. They later went to the hospital, making enquiries about my corpse.

My first thought was that my life's work was ended. There was a powerful sense of peace and release. Then, feeling my face and head, I realized that I was still alive. Finding no wound and no blood, I surmised that the ammunition had not been real: they had only meant to frighten me. However, when Margaret returned to the bedroom, I saw that blood was pouring from her left hand. I wondered if she had knocked it on the railings on the verandah. With typical Anglo-Saxon coolness, she replied, 'It seems I have been shot.' Then, glancing at the pillow, she exclaimed, 'Look at those bullet holes!' A semicircle of four bullet holes on the pillow marked where my head had been.

We took Margaret to the clinic near the house, where Dr Panahi stitched her hand. Returning to the house, we found it full of Revolutionary guards, police and others. One of them had retrieved the bullets from the pillow which he showed to me. I asked whether they were real and he answered in astonishment, 'Any one of these could have killed you.' That evening Iraj Mottahedeh led the weekly service and I said a few words about the incident. It was the last time I spoke in St Luke's Church, the home of my vocation and my Holy Orders.

Early the next Sunday morning (6 Aban), leaving Shirin and Guli in Isfahan, Margaret and I left for Tehran and gave our passports to Iranair as required for our flight to Cyprus. Paul Hunt led the evening service. The next morning I went with Demitri to the Department of Justice, to meet the Senior Judge of the Supreme Court, Sayyed Mehdi Sadjadian. He could only commiserate over what had happened, saying that, as the situation stood, he could do nothing.

Feeling that every avenue should be explored in our quest for justice over the confiscations and the threats, Demitri and I went to the Palestinian 'Embassy' in Tehran. It had only recently been opened following Palestinian links with Ayatollah Khomeini's movement. Failing to see Hani al-Hassan, its Chargé d'Affaires (he was either unwilling to meet us or absent), we met Qazi al-Hussaini and Abu Salam but to no avail. I hoped they would help us in the matter of a committee being formed in Cyprus, for aiding refugees. They were uninterested. I later met with several Catholic Bishops in Tehran who called to see me and to discuss the increasing apprehensions we all felt, and which were evident enough on their faces. The insecurity and repeated executions took their toll on everyone.

Three days later (11 Aban) with Margaret and Bahram, I went to Mehrebad Airport, Tehran. Even before the Revolution, leaving Iran had been difficult, in that the airline had to have passports for security checks ahead of flight time, to be given back on embarkation. (This meant uncertainty prevailed until one was airborne.) As Karami was still pursuing an expropriation of the Trust Fund, we might well be debarred from leaving on that account. He was countered, however, by the action of the Prime Minister, Bazargan. We were allowed to go. Kissing Bahram's forehead as we parted, I had no inkling that, in this world, we would not meet again. I will for ever recall the innocent eagerness of his newly bearded face, intelligent, sensitive and filial as he always was.

Travels Abroad

When we arrived in Cyprus in my capacity as President Bishop, we were met by Bishop Leonard Ashton of the Diocese of Cyprus and the Gulf, with a police escort. The Cyprus Police knew of the attempt on my life and gave us two plain-clothes guards throughout our stay. Two men had in fact come to Cyprus from Tehran to kill me but had been arrested and sent back to Iran by the Cypriot authorities. A surgeon at the British Airforce base attended to Margaret's hand. I took up my tasks as President Bishop, the first of which was the opening consultation on aid for refugees, the next, in Ayia Napa, the Standing Committee of our Church. News reached us of the take-over of the American Embassy in Tehran by students of 'The Line of the Imam'.

Early the next week, we left Larnaca for Amman where the four Bishops of the Synod went to the Iranian Embassy. With Ambassador Akhavan and Third Secretary Ahmad Ali Emami, we raised the matter of the Standing Committee's addressing a letter, through them, to Tehran. After some embarrassed prevarication a letter was, in fact, sent. As President Bishop I consecrated Elia Khoury to serve as Assistant Bishop in Amman, Diocese of Jerusalem, the service being broadcast on Jordanian television.

It was in that same capacity that I was due to attend the meeting of Anglican Primates in Ely on 26 November. Family greeted us in London. A surgeon at St Thomas's Hospital where Sussanne was studying nursing advised on further treatment of Margaret's hand wound (which needed massage every day for some two months and might have permanently impaired thumb movement) and we were besieged by enquiries about the recent events.

The Primates' Meeting lasted for three days. After much narration of events and reflection they unanimously decided to sign a letter of deep concern to the Iranian Embassy in London. No reply was ever received.

Leaving Ely and London, I went to Mombasa, Kenya, to a conference on Muslim–Christian relations. The venue was near a beach on the Indian Ocean. Kenneth Cragg, with whom I shared a room, went daily for a morning swim. I tested the water only once. I was greatly interested in the theme of the conference but Iran and its tribulations were never out of my thoughts, my radio yielding more grievous news and little 'for my comfort'. My yearning was for an improvement that would allow me to return.

We had one pleasant respite from the accumulating cares and perplexities of those weeks, in the welcome shape of a short stay in the English Lake District. There with Margaret, Sussanne and her fiancé, Andrew Lock – whose parents we met later – I walked, rested and sought a clear perspective of events. We were also able to discuss the wedding plans.

During those days we decided that Margaret would return to Iran and I would stay away. We had left with no more than a single suitcase, not as willing exiles. The Church in Iran wrote officially that I must be in no hurry to return. With the resignation of Bazargan and the siege of the US Embassy, the situation had deteriorated. My would-be assassins, I was assured, were awaiting my return. Bahram had been debarred from leaving the country. On enquiry as to why, he had been informed, 'Tell your father to come and hand over the money [the Trust Fund] and then you will have your exit permit.'

Despite the counter-advice of English friends, Margaret was resolved to go back. Bahram, Shirin and Guli needed her, not least with Christmas at hand, and there was the need of the Church. We tried to see the pain and uncertainty of separation within the larger cause and to be ready for what seemed to be 'the costs of the Kingdom'. The Lord is not one to waste his servants' pain. Four days before Christmas 1979, she returned to Iran with Diana Hunt and her two children, while I spent the festival with Sussanne's fiancé's family in Rochdale. It was a fine opportunity to get to know them better and to be

introduced to English football, when Mr Lock, Senior, took
me to see the renowned Manchester United play Nottingham
Forest. Afterwards I repaired to Margaret's mother's home in
East Sheen, West London.

Deep in my heart, as I brooded and wondered and prayed,
part of my sorrow came from the sense of betrayal by my own
countrymen of the best in our tradition. I asked myself how
fellow Iranians could prove so callous, devious and vicious. I
yearned for that soul-kinship of which Jalal al-Din Rumi had
written so sweetly in 'The Song of the Reed':

> Hearken to this reed forlorn,
> Breathing ever since 'twas torn
> From its rushy bed, a strain
> Of impassioned love and pain.
>
> The secret of my song, though near,
> None can see and none can hear,
> O for a friend to know the sign
> And mingle all his soul with mine.
>
> 'Tis the flame of love that fired me,
> 'Tis the wine of love inspired me.
> Would'st thou learn how lovers bleed?
> Hearken, hearken, to the reed.[3]

I felt as if those words were written for me. I was idealist
enough to think that Karami and others would have perceived
the sheer honesty and integrity of my position over the Trust
Fund, that they should have known in their hearts that it did
not belong to me, was not mine to surrender to them and that
their lust to gain it was a crime, reinforced as it was by violence
and deceit. I had an innate trust in the will of the authorities
to discern what justice meant and correct all denial of it. It
was to affirm the rights of the Church and to clarify the truth
of things at all costs that I had knocked on all doors and taken
the truth to all and sundry in hope of action, to friends and

foes alike. Surely there was an inherent justice – not to say love – at stake in the situation. 'O for a friend to know the sign and mingle all his soul with mine!'

The Ministry of Justice in Tehran had failed me. The Palestinians had been aloof. I wondered if anything could be done through international circles. So on 12 January 1980 I went to Beirut where Demitri from Iran joined me. Together we went to the offices of the Middle East Council of Churches for discussion with the Executive Secretary, Gabriel Habib, and also to the Armenian Patriarchate at Antelias where we met the Catholicos and Bishop Karakin Sarkissian. I also met Bishop Elia Khoury whom I had lately consecrated in Amman; as a Palestinian close to the PLO leadership he might exercise some influence were he to visit Tehran. He agreed to consult them and consider then what might be possible.

At the Iranian Embassy in Beirut, where I went to arrange certification of my written consent for Margaret, Shirin and Guli to travel abroad, I found total chaos. It appeared that a young revolutionary had taken it over, expelling the Consul, an honourable man. When I humbly requested him to sign and stamp the document, despite holding the actual seal, he declared that the seal was broken and I should return the next day. He was visibly anxious and confused. I replied that I was travelling and courteously begged him to stamp the paper, even with a broken seal. This at length he did and I left the building with that mission accomplished. The same day I gave a talk in the Near East School of Theology and answered various questions. It was a testing time; I had a lump in my throat and could not restrain the tears that came.

Demitri Bellos went back to Iran, and I made my way to Cairo where I was due for another Standing Committee of the Central Synod. I had a puzzling reception. My Iranian passport, although valid for Egypt, seemed to embarrass the officials and they put it aside. Despite urging them to take some action, I was left in a sort of limbo for three hours, until happily Bishop Fa'iq Haddad, also travelling to the Committee, spotted me and was able to get the passport released and stamped.

As President Bishop I chaired the sessions of the Standing Committee, sharing with the members the significance of the crisis in Iran. As for my own return there, while the hope of it was devoutly cherished, the Committee decided that I should remain in Cairo, fulfilling my duties from there as far as possible and awaiting any return to near normality. I was accommodated in the new guesthouse, following the prolonged migration from the old Nile Corniche location. There seemed to be some early teething pains in which I had to share.

Accordingly, I set myself to study Arabic with an Egyptian Christian in the hope that I could at least preside in Arabic at Holy Communion and fulfil other episcopal tasks in the languages of the local church. I could come by no experienced teacher for more basic study. I would walk by the great river, the river that gives being to Egypt from far-off Ethiopian mountains, noting the often dusty and uneven pavements and musing at the ever noisy, ever changing scene. Traffic in Cairo is notoriously bewildering.

An acquaintance also took me to the famous Al-Azhar University to tour the various departments. We visited 'Necropolis', the 'city of the dead', a grim kind of mausoleum where the bodies of the dead lie under rubbish, while children played, with dogs, among the rubble. Reacquaintance with some of the old Coptic Churches brought back to mind my brief sojourn in Cairo en route to my studies in Cambridge.

It was a strange and difficult hiatus I had to endure, happy as I was to become better aware of the Church in Egypt. I was ever on the alert for news, both of Iran and family, listening anxiously to my radio. Nor was the news cheering. I had word of the tragic death of Paul Ashton, the only son of my sister-in-law, Eleanor, and the Revd Richard Ashton, and a schoolfriend of Bahram, his cousin. He had been blown down from the cliffs in Cornwall in strong winds and killed. How do parents take the sudden grief that like a crevasse opens up before them? Grieving deeply with them I little knew we too would be enduring the same horror.

Hoping against hope about my return home, I took some

heart from what I saw and heard of Pope Shenouda, the Coptic
Patriarch. I attended the weekly Bible studies he gave in his
Cathedral at Abbasiyeh, Cairo, where some 2000 Copts came
and hung on his every word. He answered questions which
were put to him in writing from the previous sessions. I went
also to a programme of 'Son et Lumière' at the pyramids which
I found fascinating, with the ancient wonders brought into
focus by the technology of today. What thoughts did the sphinx
indulge in, bathed in that unwonted glow with voices around
speaking for him? Was he gratified? Was he insulted? Who
could say!

Letters that arrived still argued my continuing absence. I
heard that Bishop Elia Khoury was to go, and I hoped that his
meetings in Tehran and Isfahan would lead to a favourable
word to the contrary. As it turned out, he met only with one of
the Muslim clerics, and after a week's stay and a Confirmation,
returned to Jordan. He sent me a brief report from which it
seemed that false accusations had been made against me which
he was not able to refute. He had brought back photocopies
of two forged letters purporting to come from Sir Anthony
Parsons, the British Ambassador, and William H. Sullivan, his
US counterpart – or at least carrying their signatures. The
English text was full of misspellings and ludicrous errors that
could have deceived no one. I sent these on to the Foreign
Office in London and a complaint was made to Tehran.

Meanwhile, at the Synod of the Diocese in Egypt, I gave
devotional talks and explained things I had undergone in Iran.
I followed its agenda and listened to the issues arising from
the impending retirement of Bishop Ishaq Musa'ad.

In due course, in March 1980, I left Cairo for Germany to
meet leaders of mission there in Frankfurt, whose director,
Wilfred Blanch, had invited me. Here too it fell to me to recount
events in Iran, but I resisted giving media interviews fearing
the repercussions and also being dubious about whether the
translation would distort the truth, as the media are always
prone to do. In Bremen, north Germany, while in the home of
Herr W. Kahla, I was able to telephone Margaret and Bahram

who were distressed that not even President Bani Sadr had
been able to lift the order banning our son from leaving the
country. Bahram told me that when he approached the authorities in Tehran, stressing that he had done nothing to legitimate
any ban about leaving, they referred him to Isfahan where he
was again told: 'Tell your father to return and hand over the
Church funds and we will give you your permission.'

He added, 'When I say to them, "What sort of justice is that!"
they answer, "Watch out! You may put yourself in danger."'

I phoned Bishop Eliya Khoury, back in Jordan. He was vague
but doubted that conditions would allow my return. Those
with whom I spoke in Bremen had no better wisdom to offer
and no solution to our acute dilemma. Should my own continuing exile put in jeopardy those most dear to me? It was the
cruellest of dilemmas.

Meanwhile, back in England where I went after my short
foray in Germany, plans were afoot for our second daughter's
wedding. The hope was that Margaret, Bahram, Shirin and
Guli should come from Tehran for the occasion. Iranair duly
arrived in London bringing all but Bahram whose absence from
our otherwise joyful reunion caused deep grief in each of us,
though we did not talk of it. Through tears I read the letters
Margaret had brought with her. Renewed contact at that time
with Eleanor and Dick Ashton in the throes of their own grief
gave us a heartening, if also burdening, example of fortitude.

The wedding in Rochdale duly took place. We saw the proposed marital home in Bacup and I had the joy of taking part
in the service with the local vicar. In the brief interim after
Germany the enthronement of Robert Runcie as Archbishop
of Canterbury had taken place. I attended as President Bishop
representing the Middle East. It fell to me to read one of the
Lessons at the Eucharist the next day, preceding a meeting of
the Primates. It was here we first met Terry Waite who was
to play so central a part in our own hostage crisis of diocesan
personnel. These joyous events, familial and official, only
sharpened the inner burden that weighed down our hearts, the
burden of perplexity, anxiety and indecision.

Separated Once More

One decision did seem clear and was firmly taken. Margaret would return to Isfahan. Sir John Graham, who had lately returned to England from the Embassy in Tehran, received us at his home and his counsel, too, was against my going back. Accordingly, after prayer and further consultation, we decided that Margaret, Shirin and Guli would return while I awaited the developments that, hopefully, would allow me to join them. They would be a strength to the Church and to Bahram whose dangers and hopes were theirs also, in mutual comfort.

The pain and distress of separation in a situation of such chaos and unpredictable menace were hard in the extreme. One has to do what seems 'the counsel of God' and entrust all it entails to his everlasting mercy.

There was a distressing hitch at Heathrow when the three were initially barred from the flight on the false claim that their names were not listed. The plot was to give their places to other persons. Only the intervention of John McDouall who had connections with the airline enabled them to get airborne.

With a heavy heart I turned to my loneliness, the abeyance of my responsibilities and tasks in the Diocese and the larger Middle East. I was anxious and bewildered. All the factors from my childhood about a 'shepherd's devotion' to his flock accused me as an absentee. My conscience struggled with the predicament of survival by absence and the vocation to belong where call and duty lay. In my very loneliness and anxiety of heart, I wondered about finding a consultant, a kindred mind, one who might understand my situation and perhaps help me to find the answer, the divine will that, at all costs, I desired to obey. But, like Job: 'O that I knew where I might find Him' (Job 23:3).

Bishop John Taylor, now at Winchester, came to mind. I had known him as General Secretary of CMS, where – fully proven – his spirituality, gentle temper and penetrating intelligence had impressed so many. I sensed he might understand my deepest thoughts and be able to sift and search them towards a right discernment of the way.

On the day my three beloved left by air I went to Wolvesey, the home of Winchester Bishops. John Taylor welcomed me with the reassuring kindness I had anticipated from him and listened to the outpouring of my heart. His response in part was to refer to Paul in Philippians 1:21–24, where the apostle reasons with himself about 'departing to be with Christ', that is, taking the risks he faced, yet finding the need to live in order to serve being 'more needful' in the world. He said to me, 'If you return and are killed, you can no longer serve; while you live you are the Bishop of your people. It is better that you continue your ministry, your duty to the whole Church, by being at one of the centres there.'

I found his counsel wise but remained uncertain as to my decision. A meeting followed a week later at the Anglican Consultative Council, at which certain leaders together with CMS personnel and Bishop John Howe considered my situation but inconclusively. I also conferred at Lambeth Palace with Archbishop Runcie, pondering the course of events in Iran and the path of my duty. There was no clear light. Demitri Bellos came from Iran with the word that all our people there counselled against my return. Similarly a meeting at that juncture of the Friends of the Diocese yielded no resolution of my quandary, despite being a welcome occasion to renew fellowship and discuss the situation. It was then I saw for the last time my old teacher, Pat Gaussen. After a brief return to Oxford, walking in its famous meadows with Eric Hamburger, I was able to phone Bahram from London. 'We were in Oxford today,' I said.

With a sigh he answered, 'Here it seems so far away!'

He dearly loved the place and the three years he had studied there. He was teaching in Demavand College in Tehran and working as an interpreter with foreign correspondents. When I queried whether this work was risky, he assured me that there were several, 10 or 12, who were active with the press. It was the last time I heard his voice. The sound of it is ever with me and, as long as I live, will never leave me. He saw himself as a prisoner in his own land through no fault of his own. In the prime of his youth, open-minded and keenly intelligent, the injustice of it lay heavily upon him. He was unwilling to try to flee from his country though some suggested he should try to escape that way. The sense of a dear son's mental anguish only made my own heart-turmoil the more shattering.

The idea of locating back somewhere in the Middle East where I might fulfil the 'President' part of my duties was taken up by Bishop Leonard Ashton. He invited me to Cyprus with the suggestion that my secretary, Jean Waddell, might come across from Iran to set up a Cyprus office. What seemed a sound proposal was thwarted by a deed of violence. On 1 May, when I was readying myself for travel to Nicosia, an attempt was made on Jean's life. Two thugs went to her room, shot her and ran away. The story is told more fully in *The Hard Awakening*. Only a very able surgeon saved her from death. Margaret had only just got back to Isfahan. Leaving the girls and the house to God's mercy, she went straight to Tehran by the night bus to nurse Jean. Going directly from the bus to the hospital she did not leave Jean's bedside for a whole week, Jean later saying of her, 'She seemed to breathe strength and life into me. Even the touch of her hand had a special quality of healing and comfort.'

I left for Cyprus on 2 May and was warmly welcomed by Bishop Ashton, who introduced me to his clergy and staff. Later we went to Platres in the hills for the meeting of the Diocesan Synod. News came that evening of the SAS attack on the Iranian Embassy in London to release the hostages being held there.

The Fateful Evening

All unknowing the fateful day was near at hand.

> The melting candle takes the toll of burning flame.
> The flame we knew consumed the very heart.
>
> (Hafiz)

I was visiting the Orthodox monastery Kiko with the Synod members, close to the mausoleum of Archbishop Makarios. The air was warm and still. We walked towards the tomb, austere and imposing like his personality in robes. I stood there deep in thought and somehow my mind became engrossed with thoughts of Bahram, his hazards in Iran and the brave decision to go back to Iran from America where so much achievement might have safely come his way. I had urged him to complete his PhD course first, but he had insisted on returning. I was overcome with great physical weariness, left a meeting in mid-stream – as I had rarely ever done – meaning to ready myself for the next day's tasks, but soon fell into heavy sleep.

Near midnight there was a knock on my door that roused me. I was wanted on the phone. 'Was it from Iran?' 'No, from England.' There was a longish walk to the phone and some stairs – a fraught moment wrestling as I went with a medley of thoughts. At the bottom of the stairs Leonard Ashton passed the phone to me saying quietly, 'Bad news.' It was Dick Ashton, Margaret's brother-in-law, repeating the same words: 'Bahram has been shot and he is dead.'

In the utter numbness of the moment I said, 'He will be with your Paul now.'

Dick said, 'The reporters have agreed not to publish the news until you have heard. That was why we had to wake you.'

My hosts spared no effort, but in the face of such intense personal tragedy what sympathy can avail? I needed to be alone and returned to my room. In retrospect it amazes me that, in the immediate aftermath, no tears came. The fire of grief burns somehow within one's very soul before the tears that never end begin to flow. The awful mystery overcame me and the dread feeling arose that somehow my dear, dear son, in all his sweet promise, had been a substitute for me, his father. I felt an urge to write at once to Margaret whose grief so far away was one with mine and, by its crushing horror, making us ever more one heartache. Here are a few lines from that letter:

> I feel bewildered but very calm . . . May God forgive those who have murdered our son. For, plainly, 'they knew not what they did'. What had Bahram ever done to them? What have we done to them? . . . May God use the death of our dear son to free people from hatred and enmity in our country, in whatever way He knows. What an educated and cultured man our country has lost . . . The seed of this sacrifice somehow, sometime, somewhere in the whole plan of God for his world, will blossom and bear fruit. How and when and where we cannot know but we believe that the sacrifice will not be wasted. We must not have hatred in our hearts – only sorrow, pity, mercy and compassion, for those callous murderers. May God awaken their souls so that they realize the depth of their prejudice and hatred and so be saved from their sin.

Eventually around 2 a.m. I fell asleep and woke four hours later intending to give the talks expected of me in the programme. However, when people came forward to express their condolences, my self-control suddenly broke and those delayed tears began to flow. The programme went ahead without me.

My thoughts were constantly with Margaret, who was in the hospital nursing Jean Waddell when the bitter news reached her. As Jean later wrote, 'She did not leave my side until she had found someone else to stay with me to whom she could hand over the care of me.'

After four days at Platres, we all returned to Nicosia. That place in the hills is for ever etched into my soul as where, amid 'the peaks of the hills' – as the psalmist had it – 'out of the depths I had called unto the Lord' (Psalm 130:1). Did not he add concerning where the depths are, that 'the sea is his who made it'? The Christian community in Cyprus, Leonard Ashton and his people, richly fulfilled the reality of Christian fellowship and unity of soul in that desperate time. I learned anew 'the fellowship of the Holy Spirit in the bond of peace' and am for ever grateful.

What I had to endure in those days was not to be compared with the burden Margaret carried. She was determined to take the body of her beloved Bahram from Tehran to Isfahan. A woman in that society, up against officialdom itself in near chaos, faced formidable, daunting obstacles. Formalities had to be gone through with the gendarmerie, the hospital where he had been taken and the police. An ambulance had to be hired to take Bahram's body from Behesht-e-Zahra, the huge mortuary in Tehran. Mercifully, there were a few of our loyal friends on hand, notably Mrs Shahin Rajabnia, to help Margaret through these horrendous tasks and so sustain her own heroic courage, the composure through which she found a way to organize the journey amid the dreadful weight of personal grief.

The funeral service and the burial took place on 11 May 1989. St Luke's Church was full of mourners. Bahram's mother stood with one hand on her son's coffin and spoke for several minutes – words of pride and pain and of compassion and forgiveness. Shirin and Guli were present, grieving for their murdered brother. All were moved as, in his quiet probing sermon, Iraj Mottahedeh (presently the Bishop of the Diocese, then Vicar at Isfahan), voiced all the sorrow the participating congregation felt.

On that very day, the day of the burial, far off in Nicosia I wrote 'a Father's Prayer on the Martyrdom of his Son' in Persian. I dictated it over the telephone to Isfahan to be read at the service. It has become known worldwide, translated into many languages and made available in numerous books. Here is the prayer in English.

O God,
We remember not only Bahram but his murderers,
Not because they killed him in the prime of his youth
   and made our hearts bleed and our tears flow,
Not because with this savage act they have brought
   further disgrace on the name of our country
   among the civilized nations of the world:
But because through their crime we now follow
   more closely thy footsteps in the way of sacrifice.
The terrible fire of this calamity burns up
   all selfishness and possessiveness in us:
Its flame reveals the depth of depravity, meanness and
   suspicion, the dimension of hatred and the measure
   of sinfulness in human nature.
It makes plain to us as never before our need to trust in
   thy love as shown in the Cross of Jesus and his Resurrection,
Love that makes us free from all hatred towards our per-
   secutors:
Love which brings patience, forbearance, courage, loyalty,
   humility, generosity and greatness of heart,
Love which more than ever deepens our trust in God's
   final victory
   and thy eternal designs for the Church and for the
   world:
Love which teaches us how to prepare ourselves
   to face our own day of death.

O God,
Bahram's blood multiplies the fruit of the Spirit
   in the soil of our souls:
So when his murderers stand before thee on the Day of
   Judgement
Remember the fruit of the Spirit by which they have
   enriched our lives,
And forgive.[4]

All must surely understand how I ached to learn all that might become known about the details of Bahram's murder some-where in the outskirts of Tehran. There were two newspaper reporters with whom Bahram had worked as an interpreter who telephoned me with the details as they knew them. Here is their account:

> Two people, intending to murder Bahram, went to his house the night before the fatal attack. He awoke on hearing the noise they made and they then fled. Bahram went to a friend's home. The next morning he went, driving his driver's car, to Demavand College to teach, his own car being under repair.
>
> At lunch time he was called to the phone and when he returned – as the students noted – his whole demeanour was changed. He seemed under strain but offered no explanation. Probably it will never be known what the reason was or what transpired in the phone exchanges. One surmise is that they had given him false news about his mother or sisters to distract and confuse him.
>
> On the way home, two men in a car overtook him and forced him to stop. One of them went to the driver's seat and pushed Bahram over to the other seat. The car was then driven from the main road into a road heading towards the desert. The other car was following.
>
> On coming close to the infamous Evin Prison the cars stopped.
>
> A fourteen-year-old boy, passing at the same time, wit-nessed that he saw the two in the car talking. After he had walked well past them, he heard a shot and saw two, now in the other car, driving off at high speed. The boy at once gave information about what he had seen to the gendarmerie who came and took the body from the stationary car to the hospital. Bahram had died.

Shall we ever know what were the words that passed before the fatal shot? Given the seemingly rapid sequence – according

to the boy – it may well have been that they were demanding
money. Or had they a tape-recorder aiming to incriminate him,
or say something about his father, or even deny his Christian
faith? Much revolves on how long it was before they pulled
the trigger, the longer only the more dastardly, murder most
foul, in cold blood and from a fellow-countryman.

All these intimate details, to the near in kin so precious yet
so cruel to contemplate, remain unsatisfied speculation.

At the Criminal Investigation Department, all that Bahram's
mother and sisters were told had to do with ugly and offensive
pictures his murderers had planted in their victim's pocket. His
briefcase, containing his notes and other writings, was not
given back to his family. By that final act of hardness of heart,
depriving us of what we would so dearly have cherished from
his hand, they had still more brutally assigned him to the silence
of the grave. 'He, being dead, yet speaks.'

CHAPTER 10

Goodbye, Beloved Country

When Jesus came in sight of the city, He wept over it
and said, 'If only you had known this day the way that
leads to peace! But now it is hidden from your sight.

Luke 19:42

After the dreadful assassination of Bahram, it became evident
that Margaret and the girls should not remain in Isfahan, and
still more so that I should not go back – at least until, as the
psalmist had it, 'this tyranny be overpast (Psalm 57:1). The
only sane plan was for us to reunite as a family (all except our
beloved son) in England. I did not know whether they would
be allowed to leave.

On 20 May 1980, I went with Leonard Ashton to Nicosia
Airport in a state of acute anxiety. Through the good offices
of a BBC correspondent in Nicosia, Keith Graves, I was able
to ascertain that my wife and daughters were already on an
Iranair plane heading for London. How vividly I remember his
smiling face as he gave me the glad news: the sweetest news I
had heard in months of hard tidings and grim uncertainties.
With great thankfulness I boarded my own plane from Nicosia
for London and a reunion so near ahead. I had to disappoint
newspaper journalists wanting an interview, although a few
pictures were taken. One of them, which later appeared in
Time magazine, depicted me, prior to the blessed news, looking
deeply perturbed! Editors sometimes lack discretion – or is it
imagination? In that context, it mattered little.

Our two planes arrived at Heathrow not quite simultaneously. It was a tender yet loaded moment of reunion for
which we were all both blissfully and painfully thankful.

Margaret was pale and tired, wearied with the trauma through which she had passed; Shirin and Guli were dazed and weary too. The attendant throng of cameramen and correspondents did not help and we could only satisfy them with hasty answers and broken sentences, as we sought to escape to Margaret's mother's home in East Sheen.

Bahram's Legacy

It was heartening in the immediate days after our arrival in England to be so warmly and imaginatively welcomed by keen expressions of sympathy and concern. The very next day a beautiful bouquet of flowers arrived from Archbishop Runcie of Canterbury. Less benign than archiepiscopal flowers but still solicitous for us were two officials from Scotland Yard advising us on security and alerting us to possible dangers. We were also deeply moved to be visited by Oxford friends of Bahram's years at Jesus College – among them the son of the ex-President of Bangladesh, Kaiser Choudhury, who came with his father. A photograph of them together in Oxford is one of many treasured tokens of those student days. It was clear how affectionate a place Bahram had won by his gifts in drama and music and his role in College concerns during those halcyon days. We had to assuage our grief by thoughts that could only sharpen it. Whenever in loss we are invited to celebrate where we can only mourn, we hold past and present in a paradox of time. We could never be other than parents, gratefully proud and agonizingly bereaved.

There were correspondents and journalists to give interviews to, among them Baqer Mo'in of the BBC Persian Service and the representative of *The New York Times*. Several TV programmes were arranged and over 500 letters came from worldwide sources, many referring to Bahram. Some of these his mother collated and gathered into a book with the title *Bahram* published by Sohrab Books, Basingstoke. It achieved a wide circulation, was reprinted and spoke to many. Among the letters was one from Bruce Laingan, the US Chargé d'Affaires, himself incarcerated at the time with some of his staff in the building of the Ministry of Foreign Affairs in Tehran.

There was an onus on the Persian Church, and on our family, an onus of honour and of grief – namely to interpret the meaning of Bahram's death and, though grievingly, to celebrate his part in the redeeming fellowship of Christ as his father's prayer had told it. Accordingly, in St Dionis's Church, Putney, south London (a venue that had come to be a London home for the Persian Christian community through the vicariate of Dick Ashton), some 400 friends gathered for a Thanksgiving Service and Archbishop George Appleton preached. Over the Chancel Screen were the words: 'The leaves of the tree are for the healing of the nations' (Revelation 22:2) – how eloquent they seemed in that context! 'The tree of life' from which they are taken grows beside 'the river of the water of life' running – just like a Persian garden – through 'the street of the city'. The seer of this last book in the Bible surely realized, and made us realize, that life yielded up in sacrifice has within itself a healing power, a virtue by which the wounds and fevers of enmity and hatred yield up their malady. There, and ever since, my prayer has been that Bahram's sacrificial death might avail in God's eternal purpose to bring healing to our country and our people.

Later, a memorial plaque was erected in St Dionis's Church commemorating Bahram's life and death. His name was entered into the Book of Martyrs held both in Canterbury Cathedral and St Paul's in London. At the Church of the Epiphany in Washington, DC where Bahram had belonged while studying for his MA at George Washington University, another commemorative service took place. Here is an extract from a prayer used on that occasion:

Heavenly Father, even as we mourn for Bahram, we thank thee with deep thanksgiving for his short but rich and loving life, for his keenness of intellect, for his love of family and for the affectionate kindness of his spirit. We praise thee for his imagination and creativity and for the delight with which he enjoyed the beauty of life and enhanced it . . . in nature, in art, in music, in the theatre and in people.

Remembrance beyond these occasions was made at Jesus College, Oxford – where so much in his budding career had been created – by the setting up of a Memorial Trust by his contemporaries there and those from George Washington University. By the terms of the Trust an award is made annually to the best student in 'Modern Greats', that is Politics, Philosophy and Economics, the degree course he had followed. The Trust also gives a prize for the best essay in a set subject and a travel grant to a deserving student who wants to travel primarily to further a musical interest. Publicity is given to the successful recipients so that the memory of Bahram and the reasons for the ongoing encouragement to scholarship are kept in mind. That it is – and should be – so brings continual cheer to family and friends, in the way our poet Sa'di said:

Lasting his legend whose fair name survives.
After him his memory shall by fame endure.

These practical measures taken in his old College to perpetuate his stay there are indeed 'measures' of the place he occupied in its closely knit society of letters, song, choirs, plays and laughter. The time spent at Oxford is short-lived, and so undergraduate companionship is particularly intense. If a College, its lawns, hall and chapel are a fit place for nostalgia, Bahram's legacy certainly belongs there, and we are glad it is so.

To underline the point, a tradition has been established by which a sequence of musical concerts in the Chapel has been maintained – so far four in all at intervals of about five years. The Music Society and Choir of Jesus College, with help from our family, have planned and carried out these events. It has been delightful for his musical sisters to celebrate their brother in this way and the occasions have drawn a warm response from within the College and from the audiences who have participated in them. In this way we feel that Bahram's name and story are somehow tied into a longevity far beyond our own, such as an ancient foundation can expect. As one of our Persian poets has it:

> Make no search for where we lie in earth when we are
> gone.
> Our burial place is in the hearts where scholars dwell.

The monthly letters I mentioned earlier that were circulated in the Diocese were continued when our exile began, and were entitled 'Message of Love' (*Nāmeh-i Mahabbat*), meant now for a larger constituency both in Iran and beyond. A regular column in Bahram's name was begun, open for his friends and others to send in their poems or recollections. It also enabled us to cele-brate other martyrs and sufferers for Christ, such as Arastoo Sayyah-Sina of Shiraz, H. Sudmand, Mehdi Dibaj, T. Michaelian and Mehr Hovsepian. Then came an enquiry from Isfahan about what to inscribe on Bahram's tomb there. We decided that it must be the words of Jesus: 'Greater love has no man than this, that a may lay down his life for his friends.' (John 15:13). For the words exactly expressed our whole understand-ing of his death at those violent hands. It was fellow Persians who took his life away: it was for Christ, his Church and the land of his birth that he had been at risk amid the malice which they so hatefully vented on him with their ambush and their weapon. And so for us in the long aftermath of sorrow, how apt the words of the contemporary poet, Nader Nader-Pour:

> On a tombstone they inscribe the name of one they
> loved –
> They who in their ageing cleave with broken heart.
> Their tears are like a bleeding in the soul –
> Their lifespan reaping what they never sowed.

He was searching, as we were, for words to describe the pain of surviving, of going on 'in the land of the living', in the wake of an event which, when fully known, can hardly be 'survived'.

This reality will explain why I have dealt so frankly and so fully with the care of his memory and his significance that had to follow the tragedy of May 1980, that dark hour on the edge of Tehran etched like an eternity into our family story.

The Reality of Exile

But what of that time to come in Nader's lines, the future in exile we had to face and say 'goodbye, beloved country'? That 'life has to go on' is often the sympathizer's crude solace, a comfort too glib in grief, yet too evident as a simple truism even though putting it that way resolves no anxieties. Ours were multiple.

Yet was it, could it be, exile? Initially, as the poet said, 'Hope springs eternal'. We did not think we would not see Iran again. Rather, we wistfully hoped that conditions would change, that the chaos, confusion and savagery would end, that something like normality would return. We had great faith in the long majesty of Persian history, the charm and sanity of its culture, the resilience of its people. Moreover, Christian faith required a *nil desperandum* of the Spirit that refuses to capitulate to something like despair. Yet even courage has to be resourceful in the meantime. Steadily it became clear that exile – for the foreseeable future – it would have to be. And I had to deal with the reality that what had befallen us was what 'Iran' in its Khomeini terms had done. It was useless to dream our tragedy other than rooted in the Persian scene. Hafiz our poet had our situation right when he said:

I will not further moan to blame those foreigners.
Our own the hands that did the dire deeds we underwent.

Moreover, the news that came was increasingly ominous and harsh. Bishop's House had been looted and expropriated. My half-brother, Hussain, and his wife had been expelled. My books were stolen. Protest, needing to be made for integrity's sake, was always fruitless in that climate of indiscriminate violence.

As the realization that it would be a protracted absence became more and more clear, the issue was how to fulfil my episcopal duties and also those of the President Bishop even in absentia. There was the added problem about where to locate as a family, and a base for an office. It would be some 18 weary months before we reached the glad solution that would take me into the Diocese of Winchester as an Assistant Bishop. There is much to tell of the 'gypsy-like' interim we had to spend in uncertainty and travel, in exploration and *non sequiturs*, only that these were in no way the innocuous type that come in philosophical debate. They concerned the hidden will of God and the compassion and imagination of his people. At first, still in England, I made sorties here and there, consulting this office and that, but finding only goodwill and hope with no specific ideas.

In mid-June 1980 we went as a family to Cyprus and Jerusalem for Provincial meetings and ministry. There was a long delay and much altercation at Ben Gurion Airport near Tel Aviv. For reasons that I could not understand, the officials wanted endless details which I could not supply, the reason for which they would not, or could not, clarify. I said with some controlled anger that I had their State's visa which they should process accordingly. Only then, after much unhappy suspense, were we allowed through to join our waiting friends.

In the conferences we encountered much concern and sympathy from colleagues wanting to share our sorrow. A visit to the Sea of Galilee with the then Dean of St George's Collegiate Church, the late David Elliott, was a wonderful occasion. The charm of the Lake was enhanced by the celebration of the same 'eucharist' Jesus had planned for his disciples on the same shore. The shape of the Sea of Galilee has been likened by some to a harp, by others to a tear. Maybe both are right. The service meant everything to us as a family for whom 'communion' such as this had been so often forgone through separations. We returned to Jerusalem via Nazareth, Nablus and

Ramallah and went three days later to call on His Beatitude Benedicto, the Catholicos of Jerusalem, a veteran of 93 years. I found him thoroughly alert to events and fully informed about what had happened to our Church in Iran and to ourselves as a family. He cheered me by this lively fellowship of heart, the more welcome for his few words in Persian, and his blessing as we left.

At the end of June we returned to London and during the ensuing month were occupied with TV interviews in sundry locations, and still inwardly pre-occupied by the inconclusive how and where of the days ahead. Three moving encounters of that month I must mention. Mrs Abby Weed Grey, a long-time family friend, made a special journey from St Paul, Minnesota, despite undergoing treatment for cancer, in order to hear from us at first hand and share our grief. Sadly it was also to prove an earthly farewell, but nevertheless buoyed us up greatly.

A long-time lover of the Church in Iran and a devoted exponent of Persian language and culture, Professor Ann K. S. Lambton invited us to her home in Kirk Newton, Northumberland, where her family had its ancestral roots. It was a delight to have such respite in so charming a setting and to savour again *in loco* her massive contribution to Iranian studies and Irano-British fellowship – a fellowship of scholarship and soul in the sort of intellectual integrity academics do not always seek or find. She had been Press Attaché at the British Embassy in Tehran during the Second World War, and was then Professor of Persian at the University of London.

Dr Lambton took us to visit her cousin, Sir Alec Douglas-Home, former Prime Minister, with whom we had lunch. When, quite soon after, word came of the Shah's death in Cairo, I thought of the strange contrast between political fortunes in the two countries. He was the fourth Shah to die outside Iran and find 'a grave in foreign soil'.[1]

Professor Lambton's scholarship was matched by a lively Christian allegiance. We found that she was an active lay-reader in her local church where she preached from time to time and which we attended with her. In Iran she travelled far and wide, sometimes on camel, gathering data for her two volumes *Landlord and Peasant in Persia* and *The Persian Land Reform*. We found her house replete with Persian lore and books, so heartening for me to appreciate as an anxious exile. Her work on Persian grammar has long been a standard text. To her haven for all things Persian come scholarly enquiries and enquirers to call on her expertise. They find also what St Paul once described as 'the simplicity that is in Christ' (2 Corinthians 11:3) – that is, 'single-mindedness'.

Our third significant visit that month was to Grimsby, Lincolnshire and to the home there of Iris Sayyah, the widow of Arastoo of Shiraz, and of their sons, Kamran and Keumars – sharers with us in the martyr travail of our Church.

Meanwhile the quest for 'how and where onward' had to be pursued 'in a glass darkly'. Bishop John Robinson, then Dean of Trinity College, Cambridge, and our visitor en route to his Teape Lectures in India, invited us to Cambridge in his concern to offer us a constructive suggestion. It was that we might live in Cambridge and write a book about all that had happened. The Principal of Ridley Hall, the Revd Hugo de Waal, with this in mind, offered us a flat in my old haunt for a nine-month sojourn. The proposal and the offer seemed sound and at the beginning of August we moved there.

Professor Charles F. D. Moule – with characteristic generosity of spirit – agreed to vacate the flat for us and move into student quarters, pending his anticipated retirement. That gesture, over which we were never allowed to feel embarrassed, and the availability of a place for all four of us, were heartening. John and Ruth Robinson arrived with a car full of household equipment and utensils, and thus hugely facilitated our stay in the place where, just 30 years before, I had lived through such trauma of soul and had the blessed succour of that other son of Trinity College, Stephen Neill. One thing I had not needed earlier, however – the Cambridge Police came by to advise us about security.

We had hardly taken stock of dear old Cambridge when heavy tidings came. My secretary, Jean Waddell, had been arrested and confined in Evin Prison. Following on from her long recovery from her wound, she had gone to collect her exit visa where the Police referred her back to Isfahan. She had gone there with a British Embassy official but instead of a visa, she was arrested and the official snubbed. He returned to Tehran empty handed, she went to the infamous prison.

This dire news was soon followed by word of the arrest of Archdeacon Iraj Mottahedeh who was taken to the same prison. Soon after, it was Demitri Bellos, then Dr John and Audrey Coleman, and the Revd N. Sharifian who were put under house arrest in Tehran. Apart from the turmoil of mind these events brought on us, they also led to a spate of enquiries for interviews by an ever-interrogating media.

We registered a deep – even angry – sense of disquiet and of resentment against the fanaticism, the violation of some Islamic norms themselves in these acts of barbarity and injustice against innocent parties, especially with one of them still convalescing from an earlier outrage. It almost seemed as if our very Persian identity was degraded and besmirched, so that we could hardly look fellow humans in the face without shame. I resolved to write a letter to *The Times*, setting out in full the confiscations, murders, injustices and crimes to which the Church in Iran had been subjected at the hands of the Islamic Revolution. It is there in the edition of 20 August 1980 for archivists of the future.

Early in our Cambridge sojourn I responded to an invitation from Germany to give interviews in Frankfurt. At one of them an odd exchange took place. There were ten senior theologians but from their questions and concerns I derived the clear impression that they had little interest in Christian relations with Islam. In some frustration, I said at length, 'Why ever have you invited me here?'

They responded drily, 'We were interested in you!'

I felt rather like a specimen, an exhibit, or a piece of evidence in some laboratory. Later, I had better and longer talks with Herr Blanch and others about the outreach of the German Church. From Frankfurt I went on to Geneva to meet officials of the World Council of Churches who listened sympathetically to our story but felt unable to offer any practical help for fear of jeopardizing further the ancient Oriental Churches of the East, the Assyrians and Armenians. The General Secretary, Dr Philip Potter, was very hesitant. I was forced to recall the poetic lines:

> Wheresoever I stretched my hands for help, help there was none.
> Majestic mountains their appearance was – behind all-wasteland.

I was well aware that ecclesiastical diplomats need caution and have a mind for what is expedient in every situation. Nor did I fail to appreciate their inability to be of direct help. Yet I could only deplore the resultant inaction, the implicit silence about injustice and the violation of all the fine obligations of religion, mutually observed as between church and mosque.

Lest, in our inward selves, we should become like rudderless boats in a troubled sea, Margaret and I actively sought ways to maintain continuity against the grain of hard reality. The circular, mentioned earlier, was one item we sustained. We also resolved to organize a monthly event in London for Persian Christians and any others who might wish to join in, where, after tea and talk, we could conclude with Evensong and a short Eucharist in the Persian tongue. St Dionis's Church, which held Bahram's memorial, was the obvious choice of venue. The whole project was facilitated by Margaret's wide correspondence and diligent contacts by telephone. A lively sense of fellowship was generated and the half-days there on Saturdays (the first in the month) became the focus for a strong upbuilding of the Persian Christian community, where friendships were nourished or created and precious ties renewed.

Some participants became lay-readers and social workers in the London area. The venture helped to assuage the forlorn feeling we often had that might easily have degenerated into

despair or self-pity. We were careful to stress that we were not
creating some new Church, but rather fortifying and informing
existing memberships in sundry parishes. Numbers attending
would fluctuate between 35 and 80. After repaying St Dionis's
for heating and lighting costs, etc., the offertory was divided
among different charities by vote of those attending.

The first of these blessed occasions took place on Saturday
6 September 1980 and they continued until 1995. Wherever
we might be, they took priority in our programme and no
other task or appointment was allowed to displace them. By
1995 it seemed appropriate that we should relinquish the joy
of organizing it and for two years it lapsed, only to be reconstituted by its lively members at St Luke's, Redcliffe Square, in
west London, with John McDouall taking the major responsibility for it. We are still intimately involved. From the outset
I made a practice of including an item of Persian poetry for
recital at the beginning of the liturgy. It was important to keep
making clear that one's Christian faith lives in steady rapport
with one's culture. New birth in Christ in no way discards
original identity and culture. On the contrary, it requires it as
the place where the newness belongs. In John 3 Nicodemus
had not initially understood, when he asked 'how new birth
could be' when he was already 'adult'. Like Paul, who always
remained the man who 'sat at the feet of Gamaliel' (Acts 22:3),
Nicodemus brought all his earlier being into 'the newness of
Christ'. We of Persia likewise bring our glory and honour into
the Kingdom of the Lord, the welcomer, the arbiter, of every
culture.

Returning to the literary impulse and at the instigation of
the SPCK, I took up the writing of what became *The Hard
Awakening*. Each week, Myrtle Powley, one of the editors,
came to collect what I had drafted, returning the next week
for discussion of her editing. The whole thing was ready after
three months' work in this way. It was our eldest daughter,
Shirin, who suggested the title we finally adopted after many
surmisings of what would fit best. 'The hard awakening' trans-
lates a line of Persian poetry, one of Hafiz's sonnets in which

he muses on the perils and hardships of love in distress. The words were those of Professor A. J. Arberry's rendering of his Persian master lyricist: 'Love seemed at first an easy thing but Ah, the hard awakening.'

Meanwhile 22 September 1980 brought round the birthday of Bahram, the first since his assassination. It would have marked his quarter-century. Our constant thoughts of him intensified. Nor was the brutal world relenting. That same day word came of the Iraqi attack on Iran, the bombing of Ahvaz and Abadan that aimed to destroy the oil resources. Baghdad was doubtless calculating that Iran would be enfeebled by its Revolution and thus present a vulnerable target. The upshot, however, could only be rivers of blood and bitter internecine enmity between two Muslim neighbours with their ancient histories reaching back beyond Sennacherib and the great Darius.

It was hard mentally to have these oppressive events cohabit with the academic calm of Cambridge. Several requests came from Colleges wanting interpretation of the situation in Iran and our experience, everything in the strange drama that was Iran's Khomeini and our Bahram. It could be lunch or dinner, tea or even breakfast and anything between. I preferred to have a free discussion rather than a set lecture. Similarly in church services and groups. There were also academic offerings I could savour, among them, I remember, C. F. D. Moule on the Epilogue of the Fourth Gospel. There was also a fortnightly seminar run by John Robinson in his rooms at Trinity under the rubric 'Fringe Theology'. One of his noble forebears' portrait hung in his room. The theology was a mixed fare to which I had mentally and orally to relate realities as I knew them from Isfahan. John Robinson would expatiate on books he had written. Then one evening the renowned Don Cupitt from Emmanuel College was invited to expound a publication of his own that bore the title *Taking Leave of God*. He was starting from a sentence from the German mystic, Meister Eckhart, who seems to have meant that we should abandon certain concepts of God by refining our sense of some celestial 'crutch' on whom we feebly leaned (if such idea we ever harboured) and enter into mystical 'union' where 'duality' between 'human' and 'divine' was transcended. Cupitt seemed to be re-editing this into some disclaimer altogether of what he called a false 'realism', that is, thinking of God as objectively 'other'. It seemed to neglect the entire issue of creation, human 'dominion' and why we and anything should exist at all. Perhaps I quite failed to understand. What I could register was that it was all a long way from Evin Prison where our cherished friends were gaoled.

When November came it was time to go to the Central Synod convening in Cyprus when new elections of the membership took place. I was re-elected as President Bishop for a second five-year term, which – by statute – would be my last. The Middle East Council of Churches also held its Assembly around the same time. A motion was agreed and relayed to Iran affirming due religious freedom and asking for the immediate release of the Church personnel imprisoned without charge. This, though fruitless, was a necessary loyalty to that basic principle of human society and any self-respecting State.

Questions were raised in the British House of Lords about the imprisonment of our personnel in Evin Prison. We were invited to be present and took a keen interest in the workings of that august body, but at that junction, hardly 'august' enough in terms Iran could understand. More active and risk-fraught measures had to be taken than elegant debating from crimson benches under high, grandiose ceilings.

The venture of Terry Waite was about to begin. We had met him briefly when he greeted our arrival at Canterbury when we went for the enthronement of Robert Runcie. It was on Christmas Day 1980 that we went to see him at his home in south London and at great length discussed the plans he had to go to Iran as envoy of the Archbishop of Canterbury to seek release of the prisoners. We returned to Cambridge the same night and on New Year's Day 1981 learned that he was back in England. On the phone to us he indicated that he felt he should make another trip to Tehran.

Our Persian poets are prone to strange metaphors, to analogies as striking as they are remote. As 1981 dawned I saw our bewilderments and anxieties rather like those of the unknown poet who wrote:

> As night by night I mused and thought,
> My mind was now riding like a moon at the full,
> And now again a slender crescent on the wax or wane.
> Was I the ball in play, or perhaps the hand that held the
> stick?

How they captured our physical, emotional and spiritual situation in those stressful days! The words had come my way through a friend's postcard while visiting the Paris Louvre, where he had seen them in a sixteenth-century Persian painting in exquisite calligraphy. How could one fail to be in debt to the Church, its travail and its cruelly tried people? Inwardly I was like a fragile bark tossed about in a heavy storm. With *The Hard Awakening* written and at the printer's, our Cambridge interlude was due to end when the flat would revert to Ridley Hall's own use.

The numerous events through which we lived, interesting and valuable in themselves, did nothing to resolve our inner turmoil. There was, for example, the intriguing dialogue in Great St Mary's Church, Cambridge, when the Vicar, Michael Mayne, later Dean of Westminster, set up two pulpits on either side of the nave, after the pattern of Oxford's famous Divinity School. Archbishop Michael Ramsey, just retired from Canterbury, was to engage with Billy Graham on issues of evangelism and theology. As I remember, each had an opening ten minutes, after which there were questions. As a 'performance' it had its appeal; as a mind-encounter I did not find it a marked conferment of wisdom, though on the Vicar's part it was a laudable initiative.

Two days later came news of the end of the US Embassy siege after 444 days, but no word about our incarcerated people.

It was around this time that I was pressed, by phone and otherwise from several quarters, to abandon publication of *The Hard Awakening*. My response was to refer them to the SPCK with whom I had a contract on which I could not renege. Moreover, the text had already been printed. The SPCK promptly responded that, in a free country, they would not countenance surrender to such pressures. It seems that Terry Waite, while in Tehran, had been 'advised' to get the book aborted. It seemed, further, that he had agreed to do so and pressed his point strenuously, this being that his interlocutors in Tehran had made its suppression a condition for the release of the hostages.

Clearly here was a taxing issue. Was one to capitulate to such blackmail, surrendering liberty of publication and also the facts of a criminal story? SPCK decided to have the impasse considered by an *ad hoc* committee. As Chair of the Friends of the Diocese of Iran and, in her own right, a formidable academic, Professor Lambton sustained me in the view that to withhold the book would be wrong. The Society took the same view but a compromise was reached by which it was agreed that the publication would be deferred until those imprisoned were released.

This glad outcome finally happened around a month later. On 23 February they were set free – our Archdeacon Iraj, the Revd N. Sharifian, Demitri Bellos and the three Iranophiles from Britain. We went later to Heathrow to welcome Jean Waddell and the Colemans but were denied the privilege of actually doing so. It was a painful manoeuvre in diplomatic logic. Margaret had devotedly nursed Jean through her ordeal of near assassination. As for me I was still their Bishop and the person most involved on every score of authority and emotion. It almost seemed as if I was wanted out of sight – if the paradox may be allowed. Or was it political expediency displacing spiritual bonds?

With the releases came a public dismissal of all the charges levelled against the Church and its people. Accusations as to forging of documents and misuse of funds were explicitly withdrawn, and declared null and void. Such was the chaos, however, that almost at once the very personnel thus entirely vindicated were put again under duress, the charges reinstated and their personal freedoms withdrawn, including exit visas for travel.

Lacking all direct knowledge of what transpired between Terry Waite and his interlocutors during negotiation, I would be unhappy had he in any way hinted or conceded that the mission of the Church had no place in Islamic territory. Triumphalism and crude evangelism, of course, have no place in the Church that believes itself entrusted with the Gospel of 'God in Christ reconciling the world'. But that Church must never abnegate the vocation to serve, to witness and to hold itself open that 'whosoever will may come'. Mission – either Islamic or Christian – is an important dimension of freedom of faith and of movement of faith, without which societies and their systems become virtual prisons at least for those who, in integrity, find truth calling them, truth to which their minds assent and their wills must respond.

Such convictions about the duty of any faith to hold itself modestly open to access and welcome are basic to the very being of the Church. There is nowhere outside Galilee where Christianity was ever native or original. Everywhere it was brought in. The New Testament itself as a document with letters and Gospels would be inconceivable except as the offshoot of mission. Name any Christian saint or leader from Paul, via Patrick, Boniface, Augustine, to Martin Luther King, you will find they are in debt to those who told them, as these too in turn spoke only out of debts earlier still. A faith that is not on outward offer is not on inward fire. I recall that John Bunyan did not buy freedom with any vow of silence and I did not want to ignore that brave precedent.

It has always been in precisely this context that I have laboured for genuine respect and humility in inter-faith encounter. For mission in these terms never denigrates or polemicizes. Christian faith demands the utmost participation in the culture of one's birth and this, in turn, means a high regard for all within that culture that has made it historically what it

is and what it will remain. Such loyalty is no compromise of
witness rightly understood. In all the trauma of that laden
year 1981 I was often depressed by what seemed to be the
disparagement of the faith and Church around which, essentially, our whole tragedy had gathered.

Thus it was deeply troubling when voices were heard, in
circles that I had long trusted, that seemed to prevaricate about
what, to me, was the very *raison d'être* of our Persian Church.
The 'dialogicians' sometimes sounded vague and woolly in
their stance, as if the tension there must always be between
dialogue and witness was somehow elided, like the music on
a violin whose strings are limp.

So I was sometimes dismayed when Christian scholars and
leaders seemed to imply that mission was somehow no longer
authentic or that it should take the form of compassion only
in social and material terms without the 'preaching' dimension.
The first Apostles had indeed ministered in kind and cared for
poverty in their midst and across the lands. Was that 'collec-
tion' for Jerusalem not a centre-piece of Paul's story, indirectly
costing him his freedom to evangelize, since his going to Jerusalem gave the Romans a chance to arrest him? But there was
no silencing of his *kerygma*, his being a 'herald' of Christ.

I had to recall these New Testament realities when doubts
invaded my mind on this score. Would not any abeyance of
witness to Christ that – albeit reverently – sought discipleship
disqualify the costly decisions made by generations of new
recruits to the Lord across the lands and down the centuries?
How could we, in our time, de-validate all that had made us
what we were, as if ours was the last generation to be invited
into Christ?

Had I been wrong in resisting what the fanatics had been
doing to our Church? 'Turning the other cheek', as we had
done, did not mean that they were exonerated from the wrongs
they had committed. Protest had to be made, and made firmly,
against cumulative evils – hooliganism, cruelty, false accusa-
tion, usurpation of property and forging of documents, assassination attempted and achieved. How, from the outset, could

I ever rightly have surrendered to such actions thus to preserve my skin and that of my people, and so obviated all the afflictions we suffered? Peace at any price was no part of the Lordship of Christ. To have thought or allowed it so would have betrayed the blood of Arastoo and Bahram, of others who had given their lives under persecution, like Dibaj, Sudmand, Michaelian and Hovsepian of other Churches in Iran.

Amid the intrusion of thoughts of dismay, even cynicism, that this issue occasioned for me, I knew I heard in the core of my being the voice of God assuring me that sacrifice like theirs would never be in vain, that sincere love and service would always find fulfilment in creation.

For my Church's sake, I and mine had indeed been where Wordsworth was – however differently – when he wrote:

Through months, through years, long after the last beat
Of these atrocities . . .
I scarcely had one night of quiet sleep,
Such ghastly visions had I of despair,
And tyranny and implements of death,
And long orations which in dreams I pleaded
Before unjust tribunals, with a voice
Labouring, a brain confounded, and a sense
Of treachery and desertion in the place
The holiest that I knew of – my own soul.[2]

I came to know that the only way to fight against hate and suspicion is to suffer the pains they cause and let love, trust and understanding rule the heart and the situation. When the popular mind harbours wrong notions – ignorant or wilful – about Christ and Christianity, the only way is to absorb the hate and injury and go on in love and service. This is the very essence of Christianity. Were I to deny or fail this, I would deny the very *raison d'être* of my being.

After the release of the prisoners the time came for the publication of *The Hard Awakening*. SPCK arranged for a press interview but due to a hospital visit it had to be cancelled.

The *Daily Telegraph* printed a summary and pictures. It was translated into Danish (a best-seller), German, Arabic, Finnish and Icelandic. Two years later it appeared in Persian. I was hospitalized for five weeks, a time which was saddened by one event and greatly gladdened by another. The former was that I learned of the death of Nouhi Aidin in Isfahan – the dear teacher who had first taught me the Persian alphabet. The latter was that we were informed of a public tribute to the bravery of Margaret, to be awarded by the Ross McWhirter Family Foundation. To commemorate Ross, his family had established a trust to honour courage against the sort of hatred that had been vented on him by terrorists in Northern Ireland, in November 1975. The award was made by the Foundation in London, in the presence of Margaret Thatcher. With the prize Margaret purchased the piano we now have in our home.

There followed a memorable journey to the United States, mainly in response to an invitation from friends of Bahram at George Washington University. It was a matter of special pride and poignancy to us to meet with them and fulfil engagements they had arranged. There was also the happy matter of an Honorary D.D. bestowed by the Virginia Theological Seminary and a stay in New York with Bishop and Mrs John Allin, the Presiding Bishop of the Episcopal Church. Returning to Cambridge early in June 1980, we attended a lecture by the former Archbishop Michael Ramsey. I recalled how I had first met him when, accompanied by Bishop Thompson, I had called on him at Lambeth in what turned out to be an almost silent 20 minutes after an exchange of greeting. On the podium his great learning came across but I also remember more the strange fascination of his jerky syllables and the up-and-down movement of his bushy eyebrows.

Winchester Diocese

These travels, occasions and ventures apart, there was still the problem of a more permanent pattern of ministry. There were consultations aplenty and much goodwill but little practical wisdom. We might have likened the situation to that of a speaker, introduced by some chairperson with the stock formula: 'Our speaker today needs no introduction', to which he adds, fending off any longwindedness, 'but he often needs a conclusion'.

Eventually my mind turned to Bishop John Taylor of Winchester who had comforted me earlier with his advice about 'abiding in the flesh' being 'better', according to Paul, for the Church in Christ. He and his wife invited us to Wolvesey, their home in Winchester. After supper he listened to my story and concluded – as I had done – that I must pursue my duties to the Jerusalem and the Middle East Province and to our Diocese in Iran from a base in England. That base, he suggested, could be in his own Diocese as an Assistant Bishop. I would be available to him as Diocesan for any duties the Diocese sought from me, on condition that my other vocation had due scope and fulfilment. Winchester Diocese would find a suitable house and the stipend could be drawn from funds held for Iran by the CMS.

The proposal seemed eminently sound and we were greatly heartened by it. A meeting was held at the office of the Secretary General of the Anglican Communion, Bishop John Howe, together with Archdeacon Ralph Lindley of the Jerusalem and Middle East Church Association and some others. They were unanimously happy that the plan should be implemented. Time was necessary before an abode could be secured within the Diocese of Winchester, so we tenanted an empty vicarage in Luton by invitation of the Bishop of St Alban's for a period of six months prior to moving to 1, Camberry Close, Basingstoke, destined to bear the Persian name of 'Sohrab House'.

Meanwhile, the circulation of *The Hard Awakening* in Danish brought an invitation from the Danish Churches. Leif Munksgaard, who had served in Iran in bookshop organization, was my host. The first task was a press interview in which I was able to enlighten my hearers about Iran, realizing how little opportunity they had to know about its culture and the Christian presence there. We found Denmark delightful in its hospitality and warmth of heart.

So to that house in Basingstoke, convenient both for Winchester and for London. We had, by the kindness of the Diocese, the option to choose from four then on the market. For the most part the decision fell to Margaret who had eyes for practicalities. The house has now been hallowed by well-nigh a score of years, a haven of family unity and hospitality and a 'warehouse' for the production and distribution of 'Sohrab Books'.

Books recall for me a visit to St Paul's Cathedral by invitation of Canon Douglas Webster, himself a lively author. His *In Debt to Christ* had meant much to me in earlier years. We were with him, the whole family and Mrs Thompson, and during our time we inspected the Cathedral's Book of Martyrs. I preached – with some trepidation – in the Cathedral after looking for a long time at Bahram's name on the open page. By an old St Paul's custom I received a bottle of the Cathedral's sherry but it was too late to put more spirit into my discourse. As for the contents, my mind went to Hafiz – as often it did.

> Friend, whose face shines there, mirrored in the cup,
> Does the sheer and durable joy of our drinking come into
>   your ken?
> Bread and water, I trow, on Judgement Day 'twill be!
> Halal and haram, by shaikh's order we'll see!

After a week's visit to Cairo concerning the retirement of Bishop Ishaq Musa'ad and other Synod business, the hour of the end of our homelessness drew near.

Winchester Diocese announced that our future abode was ready and promptly we resolved to move from Luton, undeterred by heavy snowfall in that 'bleak midwinter'. 'Frosty wind' made no moan in our soul. 'Water like a stone', in the Hampshire we would come to love, would melt inside a home. We were warmly greeted on arrival by the then Archdeacon Geoffrey Finch, his wife and other friends, who helped us settle in. As the psalmist had it: 'The sparrow finds her house and the swallow her nest' (Psalm 84:3). Again old Hafiz came to mind:

> To gladness yield your sorrowing heart,
> Embittered never be.
> Be stilled the tumult in your mind
> Let sorrow cease its mourning way.
> Though heaven's turning cycle
> Did not your purpose serve a day or two,
> It moves in varying rote another day
> Your grieving mood to cancel into joy.
> From sorrow turn away.
> O heart of mine, though flood tides flow
> And seemingly extinguish all,
> Like Captain Noah of old
> From sorrow turn away.
> The path you tread with danger fraught
> Has end unseen ahead –
> No road that ever was did endless stay,
> From sorrow turn away.

In such renewal of morale, such evidence of God's provision through the unity in Christ, I began to take up my new duties. Hafiz again knew how to strike the note.

> O heart of mine, go – sheltering with God
> From tribulations past you had from harsh religious
>   hands.

The poet described those hands as 'long in hand and short in sleeve', in reference to power the mullahs wrongfully exercise – power that had deprived us of the place to serve Iran and made us fugitives and wanderers. Yet the mercy of God had led us to a beautiful realm in England, where there was a Diocese that ended my orphanhood, if only in part. In the November 1981 issue of *The Winchester Churchman*, Bishop John Taylor introduced me to the Diocese with a brief account of our story, and on 23 January 1982 I was installed as Assistant Bishop in Winchester Cathedral, in the presence of many friends, both Persian and British. The Archbishop of Canterbury had approved my being a voting member of the House of Bishops while the Diocesan was eager for me to be a full working member of the team, consistent with what I also owed to Iran and the Middle East. I was to attend the weekly staff meetings in his house, though I could not always well relate to items on the business agenda. When I enquired if I could economize that time and apply it to writing in Persian for Iran, his answer was that attendance would help the other. It was a wisdom I later appreciated. I needed to be fully integrated.

This is not to say that some of my duties in the English context did not daunt me. Beyond speaking tasks about Iran, there were Confirmations across the Diocese, meaning the preparation of sermons, of the right vintage for the occasions, as well as the monthly Persian service and its newsletter.

Margaret proved more than equal to what partnership could bring. She became expert with the map of Hampshire, locating the previous day the place we had to reach, often in the dark, in order – as the old song had it – to 'get me to the Church on time'. Like John Taylor, I believed in simplicity of ritual and quiet decorum, without prelatic ostentation, or over-indulgent – and weighty – sacerdotal robes. He knew of our tradition in Iran. As for 'cope and mitre', he advised that, sadly, there were parishes that would think the service subtly 'not right' unless I wore these, uncongenial as I found them. Accordingly, the Diocese had a cope and mitre made for me. I took a long time to get accustomed to these – the mitre especially. It was all part of 'loving the people of God' as they were.

I was sometimes asked about how we were received in Hampshire. With unfailing courtesy and kindliness, was the answer. When Bishop Taylor retired in 1985 and went to live in Oxford, his successor, Bishop Colin James, maintained the role with warmth.

Hoping against hope to return to Isfahan and my own Diocese, we strove throughout to keep in touch and to nourish the Church by prayer and pen as far as we could, writing letters, in Persian and English, both to Iran and associates around the world. 'The Message of Love' reached issue 445 when I retired from the Diocesan Bishop's role in 1990. Sustaining the activities of the Friends of the Diocese also took much time and energy. The Friends was begun in 1912 by Bishop Linton, and continues to this day. After the dire events of 1979–80 its name was changed from *Iran Diocesan News Letter* to *The Flame*, then later to *The Mustard Seed*. It was a hard task but was one of the best ways of serving the cause *in absentia*. Increasingly, we had to reconcile ourselves to an exile that would be long and perhaps permanent. As a contemporary poet has written:

> That yearning for sight of home again
> You now can only quench.
> All that remains of it
> Is what has been destroyed.

Given the reality of things, I had to face the spectre of retirement and ponder how a new Bishop for Iran might be inaugurated in all the vexing circumstances of my own absence and the near chaos in the country. What of ongoing episcopal care and ministry among the 'faithful remnant'? It had been made possible for some Confirmations to be held – thanks to Chrismation, a procedure approved after discussion at the Primates' Meeting in Limuru, Kenya in 1983. But the very continuity of the Diocese, of ordinands nurtured, of future guidance, as well as day-to-day love in pastoralia demanded that a Bishop be found. How to achieve this was the aching puzzle.

In Basingstoke on 1 August 1985 I gathered together an informal group whom I knew to be committed to the Church in Iran and conversant with the issues involved. Their unanimous counsel was that we should take steps to consecrate Archdeacon Iraj Mottahedeh as my Assistant Bishop. I then referred the plan to Lambeth where Archbishop Runcie signalled his approval on the condition that, as Anglican rubrics always required, a minimum of three Bishops – Anglican Bishops or Bishops in communion with us – should carry out the consecration. That, we knew, would be a hurdle we had somehow to clear.

The next step was reference to the Church in Iran. Happily, this – perhaps an insuperable problem otherwise – was made feasible through a trusted Persian friend, Yoosef Ganjavi, who had freedom to travel to and from Tehran and Isfahan and England. It was to be made clear that a new Diocesan was not being indirectly organized for them. They would remain free, whenever the time came, to elect as they wished. In the meantime, episcopal ministry needed to be provided. Unanimous agreement followed.

Our Provincial Constitution made it necessary that the approval of its Central Synod should be sought and given. It was due to meet in Cyprus in January 1986, when the new President Bishop, Samir Kaf'ity, received a Mandate from the Synod to consecrate our nominee. Deciding not to go to Iran himself, he gave me his Mandate to make whatever consecration arrangements I could. It was agreed that the plans should be concerted without publicity.

The difficulties were formidable. The CMS West-Asia Secretary, John Clark, and I were eager to have bishops from Asia and/or Africa. During a visit to Pakistan, I sounded out Bishop Nazir Ali of Raiwind, who agreed to go if a visa were given. Letters to Western Malaysia and Delhi proved barren. I realized that I should find one bishop and ask him to muster two others. The name of Archbishop David Penman, of Melbourne, Australia, came to mind. I had known him years before in Beirut when he ministered to students. He agreed to go and, as an Australian, succeeded in securing the visa, as – in the end – did his retired predecessor, Archbishop Robert W. Dunn, the Chairman of the Australian Board of Missions, Bishop Bruce Mason, and the Bishop of Raiwind in Pakistan.

Consecration Day was fixed for the Feast of St Barnabas, 11 June 1986. Tehran (St Paul's) had the largest congregation in the capital city. Mandates were sent in both English and

Persian and a copy of the recent Consecration Service of Bishop Ghais in Cairo, to be translated with modifications into Persian. A memorable occasion was completed amid deep hope and gratitude and the four Bishops left Iran two days later. Under God and by grace, they had made history, and a heavy burden was lifted from me. In my enforced absence the Diocese would be in good hands. Bishop Iraj served faithfully in this assistant capacity until my retirement in May 1990, when he was unanimously elected Bishop in Iran. After approval by the Central Synod he was officially installed on 12 October 1990, in the Pro-Cathedral of St Luke in Isfahan. He and his wife, Minoo, have proved to be God's gift to the Church in Iran through several stressful years. Their courage, fidelity and tireless ministry have greatly consoled me in our exile and are a steady theme of gratitude to God.

Continued Travels

Returning to my time in Basingstoke, it fell to me then to try to bring a sense of unity to the Churches in Cairo, Cyprus and the Gulf, and across the Diocese in Jerusalem. There were also many requests for explanations and interpretations of events in Europe, and across the Atlantic. Thus I visited Denmark, Holland, Ireland, Spain, France, East Africa, Canada and the USA. When leisure allowed I was able to indulge my love of painting among the entrancing scenes available for those who carry easels in places all across the British Isles as well as in our – as it was becoming – 'native' Hampshire.

When in 1982 the Archbishop of Canterbury invited Pope John Paul II to that city, I was invited with many other Heads of Churches to share the occasion, meet His Holiness and be present at a Service of Holy Communion. When, as part of the service, celebrated martyrs of the Church were remembered, Bahram's name was quietly added in my heart. I still vividly remember the expression on the face of Prince Charles when I met him there. He had heard of Bahram's murder and my exile. There was genuine grief in his look and in his words: 'I hope you will be able to go back home again.' I felt that he understood.

In Jerusalem in 1982 I presided at the Consecration of Samir Kaf'ity as Bishop in succession to Fa'iq Haddad. The occasion gave me the opportunity to visit the Hebrew University to meet Dr Soroor Soroory, whose scholarly interest in Persian poetry and in Christianity I had long admired, and with whom I had at that time a very rewarding discussion. On another occasion, I went to Haifa to see the Bahai Centre and the 'Persian Garden', where the Bahai community has the shrine of 'The Bab' and Abdul-Baha' – its two holy figures whose story reaches back into the complexities of the Shi'ah story in Persian Islam. The approach is designed so that the visitor has to come on foot, treading reverently on rough pebbles where no wheels can go. For a time Bahaullah had lived in nearby Acre (Akku), which we also visited.

In the spring of that crowded 1982, while still adjusting to the ministry in Winchester, I spent some time in Rome. It might seem that I was touring religious capitals! The Rome visit, by invitation of Canon Howard Root, its Chaplain, was to the Anglican Centre where a group was to hold a seminar in the context of its concern for Anglican–Roman Catholic relations. While there, and visiting St Peter's, my deepest impression was the message of Michelangelo's *Pieta*. With Bahram's cruel death still close in time, as it will always be, the imagery made a lasting impact on my heart and mind. The serenity of which it told drew me back several times simply to gaze upon it and be still. The body of Jesus in the lap of Mary seemed to enshrine for us the giving and the guarding of our son. I acquired a large print of the statue for Margaret who framed it to hang in our room in Sohrab House.

I was present in the square fronting St Peter's when the Pope emerged to meet the throngs. It had been arranged for me to be positioned in order to meet him. He shook my hand warmly and listened to my brief story, which he seemed already to have known. I told him what great help to me his Nuncio in Tehran, Monsignor Bugnini, and Archbishop Barden had been and he nodded in recognition of my recollection and of their role. His personality impressed me as lively and warm. One thought that crossed my mind was that each of us had been shot at, reflecting, too, that he – having no wife – had been hit by the bullet(s) himself, whereas I, a married man, had let them hit my wife!

Another memorable occasion was the Triennial General Convention of the Episcopal Church, USA, which in September 1982 met in New Orleans, Louisiana. We had been invited by Presiding Bishop John Allin. I had the opportunity to expound the experience through which the Islamic Revolution had drawn us, its events and meanings. But I think the deeper impression was made by Margaret's narration of all that she had undergone during our work in Tehran and Isfahan. The simplicity and quiet emotion in her narrative deeply moved all who heard it.

The Convention was also addressed by Archbishop Desmond Tutu of Capetown on the theme of race relations and the liberation of all victims of oppression. His words were reinforced by the calm eloquence of the widow of Martin Luther King, while in a different milieu of conflict and human strife, Archbishop Eames of Armagh told of the troubled jurisdiction which straddles the border between the political south and north in Ireland.

Limuru is a village near Nairobi, the capital city of Kenya. There the Primates of the Anglican Communion met in the month following the General Convention. I attended as President Bishop from Jerusalem and the Middle East and had to make my way there from London, via Frankfurt and Rome. It was a joy to be more deeply acquainted with the joyful style of African worship, so different from the careful decorum of the English in Winchester. I warmed to the sound of their large choirs and their rhythmic 'body language'.

It was in this meeting that 'Chrismation' was discussed as a way of caring pastorally for the Church in Iran during my enforced absence. It consisted of the use of oil, previously blessed, as a substitute for the laying on of hands by the bishop.

Eighteen months after these distant travels came the occasion, in May 1984, of the Consecration of the new Bishop in Egypt, Ghais Abd al-Malik, under my presidency. Canon Brian de Saram had taken great pains over the arrangements. The service was attended by Egyptian dignitaries of the State and the Coptic Church and a vast congregation. Brooms were busy in last minute diligence to perfect the hallowing of the new home, long years after the previous Cathedral had been surrendered to the Cairo Municipality to make way for bridge-building.

We took the opportunity to visit the Rafaʿi Mosque in Cairo where the body of the late Shah of Iran rested. Going soon after dawn to avoid the Cairo traffic, we found the Mosque not yet open and returned disappointed.

As if these several journeys were not enough of an Ibn Battuta existence – he who travelled for 25 years from Tangier and back via China, meeting a boy of 12 in Damascus on his return journey whom he had fathered on the way out – at the instigation of friends, we set out on a round-the-world venture. It lasted 41 days. Just before our departure came word of the passing of Bishop Stephen Neill, my wise counsellor and friend in my Cambridge distress and later a valuable consultant in working out the fledgling Province and its Constitution. We joined with many in Christ Church Cathedral, Oxford, in grateful salute to his ministry and with pride in every remembrance of his powers of mind and grace of heart.

One hope of the world journey was to meet and encourage friends in the Persian diaspora that had followed – and indeed more happily long preceded – the Islamic Revolution. This hope was early fulfilled in our first stop, Paris, where we found an old Isfahani friend through whom we encountered a horrifying testimony to the bitterness of the Khomeini years. It was in the form of a painting of the Ayatollah by an eminent Persian artist living in exile. The face was recognizable at once but on closer inspection was seen to be entangled with scorpions, snakes and deadly reptiles. It transpired that the artist's son had been arrested at the outset of the Revolution. The Ayatollah had ignored the father's pleas for him and the son was executed. Though there were angels of light representing, I suppose, the grace of God, the rest was the bitter image of sorrow and barbarity.

Travelling with this dark symbol in our thoughts, we reached New York, to find an old Yazdi friend Dr J. Moyne and through him the distinguished editor of the *Encyclopedia Iranica*, Dr Ehsan Yar-Shatter, an exile and Professor at Columbia University, and other scholars in his circle. Then in Washington came the occasion to renew old friendships dating back to Stuart Memorial College and Bruce Laingen, former Chargé d'Affaires in Tehran. Thence to Los Angeles where in the company of the late Dr Yahya Armajani and Ros Moore, Chairman of the Friends of U.S.A., we called at Westminster Gardens where a number of retired Presbyterian missionaries lived in community, folk who had given years and their gifts of mind and heart to the service of the Church in Iran. Among them was Dr J. Cochrane, born in Urumiah where his father and grandfather had served. Arrangements were made then for the American edition of *The Hard Awakening*.

From California, via Hawaii, we headed for Auckland, New Zealand, crossing the international date-line and thus 'losing' a whole day. I had numerous duties in the New Zealand Churches prior to a short stay with Margaret's sister, Rachel, and her husband Bill who lived on a sheep farm in the south island. We watched the sheep-shearing in amazement – New Zealanders make the activity a kind of competitive sport. Word of Desmond Tutu's award of the Nobel Peace Prize cheered us greatly and warranted cabled congratulation.

From there, via Honolulu and Tokyo, we went to Hong Kong to be guests of the Anglican Diocese in return for a sermon in the Cathedral and several other lectures around our experiences. We were received with great warmth and embarrassingly generous hospitality. What a tumultuous place Hong Kong is – great skyscrapers, crowded streets and teeming throngs, the bursting economic energy, the incessant buying and selling of the capitalist agenda. Leaving our host, Bishop

Peter Kwang, we travelled via Bangkok, Delhi, Karachi and Frankfurt to reach Basingstoke in those 41 days.

Almost immediately after our return came an occasion of great interest to me and which raised again the issue which I mentioned earlier, namely, converse between faiths and the criteria by which we rightly hold together mutual concerns and contrasted convictions. It took the form of a conference of scholars at St George's House, in the grounds of Windsor Castle, arranged by the House in conjunction with the Institute of Inter-Faith Studies, founded in Amman by Prince Hassan of Jordan. Both he and the Duke of Edinburgh were present. Margaret and I were invited and it seemed that our presence and participation were unacceptable to certain Muslims in the group. They objected to sitting in our vicinity and we moved to another part of the room as requested. At this, others among the Muslim representatives protested and insisted we return to our seats. It is a trivial incident better ignored, but its mention here is only to underline the impression that also came from the debates, namely, how far-reaching are the emotions that attend inter-religious efforts to mediate meanings and establish genuine openness of mind and heart. Was the 'apartheid' wanted because I represented a discovery, from within Muslim life and culture via Persian birth, of the magnet of the Cross of Christ as the ultimate index, for me, of the reality of God? Ought that to be seen as unforgivable by some law of so-called 'apostasy' when my love of Persia and its Islam was unimpaired? If so, what of there being 'no compulsion in religion' as the Qur'an had it (Surah 2:256)? For such *ikraha*, 'compulsion', remained if allegiance was not, continuously, an open option. To be unable to think oneself outside a heritage must mean that it has become a prison. Irrespective of personal hardship or ostracism, the principle of religious freedom deserved to be kept in steady view for Islam's own sake and the integrity of its faithful.

Yet it is hard for those on whom, in personal incidence, this issue falls, seeing that it is undergone – as they say in Latin – *pro bono publico*. We took part in these seminars twice at Wind-

sor and once in Amman, and tried to set forward the many things
at stake – doctrinal, spiritual and cultural – that belong with
these efforts. It was also important in these academic and discur-
sive situations, perhaps in a measure also elitist, to mention the
sinister aspects of religions (of all of them) that had left so deep
and dark a mark of tragedy on my own story. The unlovely ugli-
ness and enviousness of religion when, in its institutional forms,
it is not kept humble, need to be part of the agenda when dialogue
is under way. The meetings had their counterpart in other similar
ventures at University College, Oxford and in Lahore, from
which I profited greatly.

It was always a joy to turn from these exacting times and
from the regular activities of the Winchester scene to savour
the charm and variety of the British landscape. Long a lover
of the vistas of Persia, I delighted in the utter contrasts and
the strange affinities of the two lands, relating Yazd to Llang-
ollen or Mount Demavand to Glencoe. The mutability of the
English climate is well known. 'Perfidious Albion' will be sunny
here and cloudy or wet a few miles away. I always long for
the utterly clear skies of Persia while appreciating the cloud
formations of my adopted northern world.

As opportunity allowed we took extensive journeys, to
Snowdonia, for example, and the Scottish Highlands. There
were endless places begging for brush and easel, the watercolour that could capture their fleeting imagery in the changing
lights of dawn and dusk. The will to paint – as I found in
Glencoe – needs a gentle patience, waiting for persistent mists
to clear before capturing the panorama they teasingly hide for
hours on end.

Sometimes they never did lift and one would have to abandon the exercise or be content with a rough sketch. It was
always important to remember how the light had been if one
wanted to complete the picture from memory another day.
The Isle of Skye, in the north-west of Scotland, intrigued me.
For the mountains were not so lofty, yet their bare roundedness
in the cloud-play of light and shadow was entrancing. I thought
of Edwin Muir's lines about his childhood in the Orkneys:

Grey tiny rocks slept round him where he lay.
Moveless as they, more still as evening came
The grasses threw straight shadows far away,
And from the house his mother called his name.[3]

I came to love the English Lake District, famous for its cluster of 'meres' and 'waters', reflecting the towering peaks of Skiddaw or Helvellyn or nestling under crags like those of Langdale. The ever-changing cloud panorama harmonized with the hues on lake and moor. There I found an artist's paradise and realized why it was the loved haunt of so many who had gone to live and paint there away from the hubbub, the grime and dust of inner cities. Yet, indulging such rural privacies I had to remember how Samuel Johnson, a robust city-lover, had observed that 'he who is tired of London is tired of life'.

In the Yorkshire Dales, too, I found broad and charming landscapes for painting, as well as picturesque market towns. We also enjoyed England's canals, dating from the seventeenth and eighteenth centuries and running through meadows, then threading their way through the heart of great cities like Oxford, Birmingham and Manchester. One summer, with Margaret's sisters, we spent five days on the Oxford canal in one of the traditional narrow boats. In a similar journey Robert Louis Stevenson could write of having the same steeple in sight almost the whole day long, so gentle was the pace of things. We learned how subtle was the art of lock-manoeuvring. Was there any analogy here for inter-faith dialogue where one needs to be humbled if one is ever to rise to the occasion? Or should we think it a metaphor for the 'up' and 'down' of life's transitory way?

A notable landmark in those terms came with the twenty-fifth anniversary, on 25 April 1986, of my Consecration as Bishop in Iran. Bishop Colin James came from Winchester to our Parish Church of St Michael in Basingstoke for the celebration.

That happiness was overtaken a year later by the distressing news of Terry Waite's captivity in Lebanon at the hands of the people with whom, in good faith, he had been trying to arrange the liberation of their hostages. It was a cruel fate to become one of their number, in solitary confinement. Initially, when no word of his efforts or his whereabouts came through, there was agonizing suspense until the worst fears were confirmed. I was asked by the Archbishop to go to Lambeth for consultation, with John Lyttle also present. He was sadly to die before seeing the fruit of his many visits to Iran during Terry Waite's long incarceration. Having just returned from the Middle East, I could only report how ill at ease the Churches were at some implications of the negotiations Waite had been conducting and the propriety of the linkage there seemed to be with American arms deals and military transactions. Asked about the prospects of release I could do little to reassure the Archbishop whom I found deeply concerned over the fate of his envoy.

It was around this time of tense sadness and suspense that the Diocese of Iran was able to formalize a Trust Fund in the UK. A modest sum had been garnered prior to and after the death of Bishop Thompson in 1975, which stood only in the name of the Bishop of the time. Feeling this a less than ideal form for it, I was able to gain agreement with financial experts in CMS, whereby trustees were to be appointed, with the Trust becoming a registered Charity in the UK. This measure brought much relief to me and much reassurance to the Diocese as to its future viability.

The Twelfth Lambeth Conference came round in July 1988. For the third and last time, I attended as Bishop in Iran. I was able to tell the assembled Bishops about the events in my country in the years since 1978, the seizing of properties, schools, hospitals, homes and the false accusations against Church members and officers, as well as duress against the Diocese, withholding of travel permits, disowning the legal identity of the Church, and the failure to trace and prosecute the murderers of our two martyrs.

By its Resolution 88/25, the Conference requested the restitution of properties and the redress of the wrongs inflicted on us. It represented my last effort to gain justice for our hard-pressed, suffering community. The appeal remained almost totally unheeded despite the worldwide concern it had expressed and the liberties Muslims enjoyed in the lands from which the Bishops came. The usurpations remained.

In January 1989 I participated in a seminar, organized by the (British) Royal Institute of International Affairs, in concert with The Johns Hopkins University (Baltimore) on the theme 'The Iranian Revolution after Ten Years'. It was held in Chatham House, London, and lasted two days, with expert papers from specialists. Among them was John Simpson, senior correspondent of the BBC and author of *Behind Iranian Lines* (1988), debating with an American journalist. They discussed whether the events had been a 'revolution' at all. After the official debate, during comments from the floor, I intervened to argue that, 'revolution' or not, it had been an insurrection, that is, an uprising grounded in anarchist plunder and murder, entailing grim suffering by many innocent citizens. It had not been a 'revolution' if, by the term, one meant to identify any reforming enterprise, repairing injustice and renewing hope, tolerance and compassion in society. I saw the whole cycle of events as a tragic collapse into an extremism of a religious kind, when what had been needed was a patient correction of the secularization and flaunted Westernism which had tempted the previous regime away from the surest traditions of Persian culture and identity. All had not been well before and there were legitimate grievances, but the will to 'correction' had catastrophically over-reached itself and had unleashed a barbarity of fanaticism and wild violence that degraded the fair name of the culture of Hafiz and Sa'di, of the architects of Masjid-i-Shah and the glory of Lutfallah in Isfahan's Maidan.

Retirement

After my Consecration in 1961 I gave a sealed envelope to a friend and wrote on it 'To be opened in 1985'. When 1985 came, against all expectations, we were in Basingstoke. But the friend in Iran dutifully opened the envelope and reminded me of its contents: it read 'You are 65 years old. You have had 40 years in the diocese, 24 years of it as Bishop. Retire now, no matter what your friends say.' Although the thought of sticking to the decision of 1961 was very strong, we felt we could not leave the Diocese in the lurch, in the situation as it was then. Margaret and I, and indeed our daughters, have always had the strong feeling that Bahram gave his life to enable us to stay on outside the Diocese and serve the Church in its greatest time of need. We stayed on. In 1986 Iraj had been consecrated and appointed as Assistant Bishop. If we had not been able to do anything else, it was worth staying on to arrange for that important event and to be at hand to support him in any way we could. But now the time to go had definitely arrived. According to our Central Synod's Constitution, 'A Bishop may retire at the age of 65 years, but shall retire not later than the completion of his 70th year'. I would be 70 on 14 May 1990, and so I announced my retirement as from that date.

When the news of my retirement was published, I was met with a barrage of protests both from the Diocese and from outside, including our President Bishop at the time, Samir Kaf'ity; protests such as: 'How can you leave them at this uncertain and difficult time?' 'They are like people in a small boat on a rough sea. You are switching off the only visible lighthouse they have.' 'The Assistant Bishop is still stop-exited, and cannot represent the diocese on the Central Synod. The House of Bishops, with one absent among four, will lose its balance.' 'The relationship between you and the small flock has been so strong and personal that in spite of all the difficulties, the life of the Church has continued.'

My answer to all these was that no one is indispensable. 'I will have to go one day, why not go according to the Constitution of the Church at the age of 70? What is the point of carrying on for another few years?'

The answer was 'In order to buy time. In another few years the situation may become quite different.'

Then came a letter from Bishop Iraj himself, in which he said, 'I heard the news of your retirement with great concern. It came in a time of great anxiety . . . there are active demonic forces behind the scenes, trying to manipulate, to corrupt and to destroy the tiny flock. Humanly speaking, I know that it is cruel not to let you go . . . I believe you are fit still to go on for at least two or three more years . . . The situation in which we are called to live is so irregular and unpredictable, that the ultimate validity of a binding regulation is made questionable. Where the need is acute and immediate, grace minimizes and subordinates the demands of the "Sabbath" . . . The ultimate decision, of course, is yours. But I beg you to let these few lines be made known to those whose sacred duty is to decide . . .'

Tension in me rose and I was in turmoil. Once again St Paul's words to the Philippians, which had convinced me not to go back to Iran in 1980, came to my mind: 'I am pulled two ways; my own desire [to be relieved from the burden of responsibility] . . . But for your sake . . . [to stay on].'

After 29 years, with all that we had gone through together, I could not refuse their request outright in their time of need. But the text of our Constitution was clear, and I had announced my retirement according to it. The only thing was to take it to the Standing Committee of the Province which was to meet in January in Cyprus. I attached Iraj's letter to my report and submitted it to the Committee, and stayed in the meeting. With the risk of being misunderstood on the basis of personal ambition, I tried as hard as I could to explain the situation and to put forward the small flock's point of view. But I failed and I was misunderstood. Bishop Iraj's request was refused and my offer of what I thought to be love was rejected. How does one bear the rejection of love and the misunderstanding of motive? Only by quiet trust in the victory of the Cross.

I have written at length about this subject because I do not want the little flock and their friends around the world to think that I have not heeded their request and have deserted them when they felt they still needed me. Here I want to take the opportunity of asking forgiveness for my many mistakes during my services as Bishop, and President Bishop for two terms in the formative years of the Province, and to thank those who accepted me gladly and supported me warmly, without whose help I could never have done the job.

The Friends of the Diocese of Iran marked my retirement in their spring meeting (April 1990) by asking Kenneth Cragg to preach in the setting of a Holy Communion Service. Bishop Cragg, using the phrase 'But Now' from several passages in the New Testament, went through the different stages of my life: nurture, conversion, calling, marriage, ministry and tragedy, with an extraordinary insight characteristic of him, ending with words of encouragement, hope and thanksgiving. Some two months after that Holy Communion celebrating my retirement, Margaret and I met Gulnar, our youngest daughter, outside the same church, on our way to her home in nearby Putney. The suggestion was made that we should first look inside the church hall where, she said, there was a display of old books, always a bait for booklovers such as us. However, on entering I found myself in a well-laid trap. The church hall was crowded with friends, Persian and local, gathered from far and near. It was Gulnar's mischievous scheme to celebrate my seventieth birthday. Reminiscences were recalled with much humour and we were presented with a silver teapot. Knowing the skill and pains that had gone into its organizing, we were greatly heartened and, like the apostle Paul on a rather different occasion, 'thanked God and took courage'.

Retirement came – though with tinges of sorrow – as a welcome relief from the sense of pressure that always accompanies responsibility. While a weight had been lifted many things seemed still the same: duties in Winchester and sundry 'volunteer' tasks needed doing.

We went, for example, to Cyprus where, in Kiko Monastery, there were five young men from Iran taking part in study, prayer and corporate worship. It was a gesture of hope for the future well-being of our Church, pending fuller training for them later.

A visit to the Passion Play at Oberammergau when its ten-year cycle came round in 1990 left me with mixed feelings, apart from the hectic way in which visits had to be accommodated in the tiny Bavarian village. It was bewildering to relate them to the Persian Passion Plays I had known as a child in Yazd that had re-enacted the martyrdom of Hussain at Karbala'.

There was a visit, too, to exhibitions in St Petersburg. What Persian could not muse over the vast presentation in the museum there of the life of Alexander, our erstwhile epic conqueror, once master of Persepolis and much recalled in Persian miniatures and celebrated in verse and legend, even into the Qur'an itself?

Periodic visits to our daughter, Sussanne, and family in their home in Florida apart, my major preoccupation through the 1990s was 'Sohrab Books'. I had always desired to write at length about the long interaction of Christian faith and Persian culture, to detail the reality of their fusion in past centuries. It was vital to correct the frequent impression that these were two separated, even incompatible, entities, or that Persian identity was exclusively and unanimously Islamic. That might be how many saw Arabism, with the Prophet supremely *the* Arab *par excellence* and the Qur'an the ultimate Arabic eloquence. Persia, mentioned in the Qur'an (Surah 30:2), had a long antecedent story prior to that book, and in that story Christian faith had played a part.

Much had, indeed, been written but mostly by Western pens for subsequent rendering into Persian. I was keen to produce directly from Persian sources and also to translate worthwhile foreign texts into a more idiomatic Persian than, perhaps, foreigners would do. I was much encouraged in these hopes by Archbishop George Appleton. So we set about literary production. A fund was set up, to be administered by CMS Treasurers, and with a few advisors to monitor our efforts Sohrab Books became a sort of publishing outfit in our garage.[4]

It was thus that a trilogy took shape under the theme 'Christ and Christianity amongst the Iranians', beginning with a general survey, then covering the classical period and finally contemporary poetry, prose and art. Twenty-one items have been published in the first decade, either reprints or new works. Margaret's splendid energies have taken over practical matters of distribution and accounting in liaison with CMS. The market stretches worldwide and, not least, far into the Persian diaspora. Some books have even found their way into Iran!

One feature of old age is that 'arresting sergeant, death' coming to cherished friends. One of my first mentors, a man of deep impact on my mind and heart, Geoffrey Rogers, died in June 1991. Lady Marygold Graham, wife of the British Ambassador, Sir John Graham, was killed in an accident. They had both been a source of strength in our tribulation as people of lively faith. I was asked to say prayers at her memorial service in Winchester Cathedral. When his predecessor, Sir Anthony Parsons, died, it fell to me to take part in a memorial service at St Martin-in-the-Fields, London, when many from Iran were present. He was a very perceptive writer on foreign policy issues and knew Iran thoroughly.

That famous syllogism with which most lessons in logic begin, notes that 'All men are mortal', adds 'Socrates is a man' and concludes, 'Therefore Socrates is mortal'. It is a bizarre way of taking the fact to heart oneself. It seems that around the time of my retirement, I had taken Socrates to heart and discussed with Bishop Colin James, while still in office, the question of our final resting-place. He consulted the Cathedral Dean and Chapter and then informed us through a letter dated December 1994 that we could anticipate burial in Cathedral grounds where, normally, only Bishops, Deans of Winchester, and their wives, had the privilege to lie. We were very sensitive of their generous initiative, a sort of posthumous seal on all the warmth and integrity of the long friendship. I thought of some Persian lines of Hafiz:

The fire that never dies is in our hearts alive,
So where the fire of worship burns our bones may cherished lie.

Still, gratefully very much alive, we came at length to a Winchester celebration of 50 years since my ordination in Isfahan in 1949. The Cathedral played host to some 300 worshippers, Persian, English and others from Europe and America. Participating were the Bishop of Winchester and his two Suffragans, Bishop Iraj from Iran, and the choirs of St Michael's Basingstoke, and All Saints' Basingstoke, and members of our family made the occasion musically rich and joyous. It fell to me to be the Celebrant of Holy Communion, but our youngest daughter, Gulnar, now a Revd Dr, preached the sermon most fittingly. She sounded a jubilee note, in a review, at once sombre yet joyous, of those tumultuous years.

So draws to a close, with all its frailties and gentle victories, the story of my vocation in Christ, my destiny with Iran. My beloved parents lie in the soil of Taft, so far from the differently hallowed soil of Winchester. Is it macabre to think of merging soils, dust of the high plains of Yazd in the earth of an English shire, symbols of all else about the living Church, a parable of the sheer strangeness, the apparent contradictions, of my life? As any reader knows now full well, there were times when I mourned like the psalmist: 'I am a stranger upon earth . . . a sojourner as all my fathers were . . . I am become a stranger to my brethren, an alien to my own mother's children' (Psalm 39:12, 69:8).

Yet, through many tumults and trials, that language had to give way to how Paul told it to his Ephesians: 'You are no longer aliens in a foreign land, but fellow-citizens with God's people, members of the household of God' (Ephesians 2:19).

I have asked, 'Have I forfeited my identity, lost my soul or have I found my true self?' I have no doubt of the answer, despite all the hazards and the burdens, the pitfalls and the perplexities of the path I have trodden. It was a true self, a new self with the old, that I found in the reality of God in Christ; that wholeness of personality that is the credential of 'the children of God', as in him we become them. I live by the truth of the affirmation of St John's Prologue: 'To as many as received him he gave the right to become the children of God

– those believing in his Name.' In Christ, as Paul found, 'the
new has already begun'.

Let those who will think that I have dreamed my story,
taking haphazard eventualities as 'the design – God's design
of my world'. That my life has been a mission in divine trust
is the surest reality of a long and grateful retrospect. As Charles
Wesley memorably sang of One coming from above, 'the pure
celestial fire to impart' had 'kindle[d] a flame of sacred love
on the mean altar of my heart'. Or in the different imagery of
our Shirazi Hafiz:

The very intoxication of love, though tending to our ruin,
Makes the fullest life to flourish out of ruination.

Editor's Postscript

When the text is ready
Leave the annotation
To posterity.

So runs the advice from a contemporary Urdu poet, rehearsing the legends of Jamshid, the ancient Emperor of Iran. Texts, once written and published, are at the mercy of the readers they reach. Such are the hazards that authors risk. Sometimes they stay to haunt them.

What need, then, for annotation now that the text is complete? Is it not enough for the author to say in words from the same Urdu verse:

> We chiselled a song from the story heard
> And from that music learned a new thing –
> How to muse.[1]

Even so, musing being a very personal art, there might be a point for a postscript wondering how reflection might go, anticipating its direction without trespassing on its freedom.

It will surely need to occupy itself with three themes, for they emerge very clearly from all the foregoing: first, the cruel tragedy which the Khomeini Revolution visited on the small Iranian Church; second, whether a Christian initiative should have lent itself to what proved so costly an initiation; and third, the ultimate sacrament of human biography.

These three issues take up the whole meaning of a 'designed world'. The first queries whether what happened was, or was not, the doing of Islam. The second asks about the legitimacy of mission whereby a mother's faith came to sanction a son's experience in such tension with family and culture. The third explores how the texture of a lifetime gathers into its threads a significance from God after the sacred pattern of 'the Word made flesh'.

Were the murderous things in the story done by Islam? Was the deception 'Muslim' that could visit a priest in his study on pretence of spiritual enquiry and brutally kill him in the very sanctuary of his Christian calling? We will never know whether, en route there, the killers had walked under the Qur'an Gate for which their city is famous, by the road that skirts the garden of Henry Martyn, or whether again the holy text under which all Shirazis pass there was enough warrant for them.

There is, to be sure, a dark history of treachery and enmity in all faiths. The question whether 'they' in themselves were responsible is always elusive. For what 'selves' they are is always ambiguous. Accents in the Medinan part of the Qur'an might have 'justified' the bitter hostility, where 'killing' is seen as a lesser evil than *Fitnah*, or alleged divergence from Islam. In the longer Meccan period, however, Muslims in the Qur'an were innocent of all power-politics and lived on the receiving end of much adversity themselves.

The Qur'an, at that time – and even later – seemed, as in Surah 22:34, to validate a diversity of 'rituals' divinely 'given' to different 'peoples', so that, arguably, a mutual tolerance should exist between them. If so, any case against violence stemming from Islam's own experience of its pain and heart-ache came to be seen as overborne by the perceived necessities of belligerent statehood.

It has been basic to all religions to think themselves ultimate, being possessed of truths that ought to prevail. That posture belongs with their claim to finality. The question, however, has always been this: in what terms should such prevailing be sought? In the Meccan years, Islam was ever and only persuas-ive, not coercive. It knew itself as *balagh*, a thing to be preached, a theme about God and his unity, waiting on hearers. It was in the circumstances of Hijrah, or emigration to Medina, that the preached Islam fused its religious cause with physical means in a power equation, ensuing from the negotiated terms in which, in coming to Medina, the Prophet had undertaken a certain role in and for it as a monitor of its factions. In all the centuries of what thus became 'the years of the Hijrah', Islam has held to the legitimacy of force as properly counter-balancing the legitimacy of faith. That perception, amid the passions or the chaos of those late 1970s, may have allowed, if it did not inspire, what the Church underwent as its victim.

The ambiguous answer, then, to the first question stems from the inner tension between Quranic persuasion and Quranic power. There was ambiguity, too, in that the Revolution, set against an ostensibly 'Muslim' regime, raised vast issues as to the true identity of Islam itself. That of the Shah came decisively under the veto of the Revolution as an instrument implementing the deep Shi'ah doctrine that all *taqiyyah* by which aberrant regimes may be both 'tolerated' and 'denounced' inwardly as long as they are irreducible, must be forcibly confronted when they have become utterly ripe for terminal rejection.

The necessary passion of that conclusion – a passion the Ayatollah fed from his exile and finally enlisted the masses to vent on the Shah-dom – would likely be caught up in the excesses that so tragically victimized the Church. From these, then, Islam could not be exonerated. Yet, in the 'Islam' to be accused, there were deep and vital elements of an 'Islam' disavowing the violence of the other one – the Islam of that famed Shirazi, the poet Hafiz, or of the Baghdadi Al-Hallaj, in AD 922 himself the Muslim victim of other Muslims. There is nothing unique to Islam about this tangled situation of versions forever condemned by versions that deny each other in their deepest wretchedness or noble worth.

Nor are these contradictions all unravelled. Revolutions, we might say, have no idea of their own communal, cumulative ego-hood even though their perpetrators are able to register one within their private selves. Are not such inner tensions also characteristic of faiths as well as of revolutions? Their histories require believers to practice a self-scrutiny and be critically alert about themselves. By the recent story of Islam in Iran this seems urgently the case.

If sufferers at the hand of Islam, or even detached observers of its current history, are compelled to ask themselves about its image and identity (because these look so darkly ambiguous) can the faith itself refuse due self-interrogation? That there is a crisis of integrity about the 'right' Islam no one can doubt. The issue is in Muslim hands and minds. It is one that engages the wellbeing of all, one to which this life-story might contribute.

'To let God be God' is to let mercy prevail. Divine sovereignty was calculated to silence and subdue all raucous, censorious, fist-clenching violence in the streets, when the passion in 'Allahu akbar' translated into 'Islamu akbar'. The Islam that is indicated in what befell the Church might have stayed its hand by counsels no less claiming its name. Certainly *an* 'Islam' was guilty.

What 'annotation', then, of the second question? The mission of a church from England might be seen as an unwarranted intrusion in nineteenth/twentieth-century Iran. While reaching for, and in no way ignoring, ancient Christian elements in Iran's long story, it brought a Western tongue and a church tradition that had not earlier belonged. It fulfilled an earnest desire to evangelize and could not thereby avoid or renounce its culturally 'alien' aspects. Thus it was inevitably risking an inter-cultural encounter that might sharply vex all local, personal response.

Moreover, it used teaching and medicine to foster its religious hope of conversion. The healing it could offer, and the learning chances it afforded, both serviced the faith it brought. In the eyes of cultural dignity so richly present in Persian identity, did it thereby compromise itself in not being present by the sole quality of message-content? Yet, in a context of much deprivation, physical and scholarly, ought it to have refrained from active ministry in order to be solely 'spiritual' – a posture which on every count would have been never Christian?

At all events, a future bishop's mother was drawn to the Christ-community in the setting of nursing training and skill and drew from it a Christian ambition for her son that came to be sanctified by her premature death and the devotion to her memory of those in the mission who prized and cherished her vicarious desire. Thus was set in train the tussle within the motherless family concerning her son's education and his discovery of a Christian vocation. The father found himself caught in the pressures of society pitted against a sacred aspiration. Happily, there came, at two crucial points, 'the providence that shapes our ends', in the positive results of Qur'an consultation. How much we would love to learn in what form they were adjudged!

But might a detached – and perhaps faithless – observer conjecture that the taxing destiny should never have been broached in such painful terms through much tribulation towards a 'kingdom of heaven' so beset with cross-cultural stresses? 'Might-never-have-beens' are always impossible to measure or compare. The sure answer has to be that selfhoods everywhere, and from whatever source, deserve maximal access to meanings they may potentially come to love as their liberation and their 'light of life'. This must be true on every hand and from whatever angle, seeing that freedom of recognition of truth is inalienable in the right of personality, however excluded from it multitudes of humankind may be by factors of poverty, ignorance and deprivation.

To be sure, the mission within the call traced in these pages did not come in such abstract terms. It came to 'preach Christ' but, in the simplicity of its coming, it brought into ready, if costly, access criteria of omnipotence divine, and significance human, that – for all their arguably 'alien' auspices – had their warrant in their worth alone and could translate their credentials into every culture. They were of a sort in turn to enrich themselves – as here – from their reception, so that what might seem alien in its incidence was locally authentic in its fulfilment.

Such must be the final rationale for the legitimacy of mission as penetrating – not intruding – with a human birthright, of accessibility by each and all, into the trust with truth it brings and leaves. *The Unfolding Design of My World* becomes, then, a study in the vindication of a Christ made available to faith and of a faith brought persuadedly into Christ. Beyond all the tensions, the whole was a truly inter-human transaction in which mission was exonerated of all imperialism, and discipleship came to leadership in the integrity of shared culture. 'Of such is the kingdom of God', where none have prior rights and all have common claim.

Between religions there are so many factors, from history and in the psyche, making for a kind of apartheid which, sanctioned by community, then constrains each to treat the other with suspicion, wariness or enmity. They are then inhibited by loyalty from recognizing the things that might positively relate them. Muslim and Christian have long suffered from this impulse to disallow the other, so that what is genuinely and significantly at stake between them is rarely truly and hopefully broached by mind with mind or heart with heart.

It would be fair to say that the clue to what is at stake has to do with divine omnipotence, with what is – and can be – meant by the sovereignty of God, of Allah. The fact of it is mutually affirmed but the terms in which we find it imaged or denoted differ. For both of us, it has to be consistent with the human delegacy over the good earth, the dominion/khilafah humankind exercises in nature and history by the fact of God's bestowal of it in the cosmic order which underlies all culture and all civilization.

Must not this suggest a quality of sovereignty so great as to be ready for some relinquishment of its absoluteness in the will, and the ability, to grant creaturehood a partial autonomy able for an answering wonder and gratefulness? It is the limited kind of power that has to stay jealous of any concession, any magnanimity in its operations, lest it be misread as weak. Is there not already in our human experience of dominion what Christians see as *kenosis*, or self-expending, in the nature of divine omnipotence? May not that belong truly with Allah enquiring in the Qur'an, of us humans (7:172): 'Am I not your Lord?' and awaiting the answering: 'Indeed, we so acknowledge'?

We could perhaps locate the whole issue in that divine Name (in the *Asma' al-Husna* found in the Qur'an once at 59:23) – *Al-Mutakabbir*. Do we read it as 'overweening', 'overwhelming', or even 'arrogant' and 'utterly proudful'? These would be inconsistent with the Creator whom we find the creation tells. That fifth root of the Arabic verb 'to be great' indicates where the simple meaning is made intensely self-aware. If, then, *Al-Mutakabbir* is read as 'cognizant of great power' there would be room for an inner prerogative determining the shape in which it might conceive its ends, the ways by which we discern its outward exercise. Thus sublime self-limitation could be within its very majesty – not as some compromise of how great it was but as the norm and mind of an undoubted greatness.

It is just this conviction that Christianity understood in the *kenosis* that goes further than human delegacy into the human fellowship of 'the Word made flesh'. *Kenosis* was Paul's word in Philippians 2:5–11 to express this 'self-expenditure' in the very nature of God as love. It is the distinctive note of Christian faith but it has expressly to do with the very 'omnipotence' Islam makes so central to its theology. It is the Christian measure of God, 'self-given to the world in Christ'. One might make the case in two lines from the poet Hafiz about a theist imagining God as only a far-off spectator of our griefs:

> Poor sufferer – and God was with him all the time
> Who knew Him not, and glorified remoteness![2]

But, some readers may ask, does it matter how our faiths think of God and differ over the meaning of his omnipotence or the dimensions we assign to it? It matters vitally. One reason must be that to posit a totally arbitrary deity plays into the hands of secular minds dismissing God altogether. For that sheer arbitrary 'power-girt-ness' contradicts the strange guesthood we find ourselves enjoying in our technology. Then the God we must reject contravenes the God we must acknowledge. Nuclear physicists and genetic engineers must not be left to be as 'little gods', replacing a tyrannical One their sense of power can never acknowledge, when all the time their power tells them of a magnanimous One they ought to recognize.

The other reason, even more importantly, is that the Christian faith as to divine *kenosis*, told in creation, in Christ and in the ever patient ways of the Holy Spirit, becomes the sure sanction and the enabling of its human counterpart in a love that cares, gives and shares – the love of which mission has been the costly sign. The light by which human love moves and acts, its staying power to continue so, are ours only thanks to the paradigm in God. 'We love because He first loved us.' For 'love is of God' and comes only into our living while it lives in our theology.

Thinking this way has brought us already into the third concern, which deals with the sacrament of biography. From the Latin *sacramentum*, 'minded-sacredly', the word is characteristically Christian. There are several ways in which we can capture the meaning in seeing life-story as a sacrament. One is how form and content fuse in the flow of music or in the shape of a poem. Theme and pattern make a sweet marriage as they do in inspired architecture where what is wrought tells what was willed. 'Design' is always of this double order whereby the story carries the meaning because the meaning adopted the story.

We can think of the interplay of things human and things divine by this analogy of metaphor, provided that we remember how the metaphor was also history. 'The flesh was for the Word' because 'flesh the Word became'. Language takes from one realm what can carry another, because the two are congenial to each other. In borrowing, the one does not forfeit or lose itself in the borrowing; nor does the borrowed in the significance it lends. On the contrary, either gains in the association which, employing freely recruits and, in being employed, dignifies and enriches.

In these ventures in communication a 'theme-word' takes up a 'loan-word'. So doing it tells itself more vividly. Each is fulfilled by the inter-association. Examples are legion:

As for his bounty, there was no winter in it (Shakespeare).

We are tapers too, and at our own cost die (John Donne).

The grave's a fine and private place,
But none, I think, do there embrace (Andrew Marvell).

A fool might ask: What do these mean? A lively mind knows very well. We see a generosity killed by no frost; we sense mortality like a candle shortened as it burns; we visualize the grave as 'fine' ('narrow', 'final') and lifeless.

So Christian faith reads the 'theme-word' of 'God in Christ' in the 'loan-word' of the Jesus-story. What a metaphor might do in language was there done in fact, in a real event. God authored the person, work and suffering of Jesus-the-Christ as does a dramatist his drama. Who he is in his eternity is there by his own Self-disclosure, and is for us 'the light of life'.

Read thus in its own clear light, our faith as to 'God in Christ' means that the divine is not averse to being known in the human – as Islam would suspect. Nor is the human unworthy of divine employ. It follows that this central truth – 'told in flesh the Godhead see' (to adapt Charles Wesley's carol 'Hark, the herald angels sing') – can yield a paradigm for all human personality. A biography can carry significance for God as giving visibility through time and place to the grace and compassion of God. Through the once-for-all, and only, 'Word made flesh', all Christ's people may be bearers of his image and 'loan-words' for his meaning.

If this be so, we know the meanings we should find in the story this book has told. How dark a pain it was that enmity should claim the life of Bahram in the proven promise of his youthful gifts. How desperate a travail that a father should have ground to fear that the son had undergone what was meant for the absent father. How grim the burden of an unwanted exile from the loved place of ministry – an absence made more heavy by every frustrating turn of circumstance.

Only by setting all things inside the contours of the gospel could they be either sustained or understood. It follows, therefore, that the courage and patience which did set them there become further proof of what those contours are. It is in this way that we are all called, in some measure, to be metaphors of the love of God, even as the 'bread and wine' of the Eucharist were hallowed to be the sacrament of our redemption.

We can sum up that whole truth in lines composed by General Orsborn of the Salvation Army. They were inspired by some words from a sermon of Augustine of North Africa: 'It is the mystery of yourselves which is laid upon the Holy Table: it is the mystery of yourselves that you receive.' So the General wrote:

> My life shall be Christ's broken bread
> My love His outpoured wine,
> A cup o'erfilled, a table spread
> Beneath His Name and sign,
> That other souls, refreshed and fed,
> May share His life through mine.[3]

Notes

Introduction: The Design of My World

1. Ismail Nouri-Ala, *Key to Thunder: Ninth Anthology of Poems in Persian* (Denver: Persik Publications, 1997), p. 13.
2. Alexander Solzhenitsyn, *One Word of Truth: The Nobel Speech on Literature 1970* (London: The Bodley Head, 1972), p. 16.
3. Thomas Hardy, 'Moments of Vision', in his *Collected Poems* (London: Macmillan & Co., 1932), p. 401.
4. William Cowper, 'Vicissitudes in Christian Life', in his *Poetical Works* (London: Macmillan & Co., 1889, p. 423.
5. Thomas Traherne, 'Salutation', in his *Centuries, Poems and Thanksgivings*, II (ed. H. M. Magoliouth; Oxford: Oxford University Press, 1958), p. 6.

Chapter 1

1. 'Persia' and 'Iran' can be used interchangeably. Iran is the ancient name meaning 'the land of the Aryans'. Persia relates to the southern part of the country called Farsi or Pars. The dominant language of the country is Persian which is also spoken in other regions of Central Asia. It has a vast and worthy literature. Although in Persian the language is called 'Fars', in English the term 'Persian' is used to respect its universality and literary heritage.
2. Sayed Abdul Hossain Pooya, *Research in the Ancient History of Yazd* (Persian) (Yazd – Department of Islamic culture and guidance, 1989 [1368 Persian Calendar]), p. 14.
3. The following diagram illustrates the use of the Qanat:

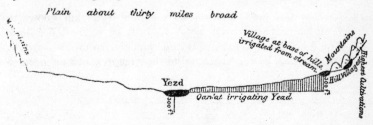

From Napier Malcolm, *Five Years in a Persian Town* (London: John Murray Albemarle St. W. 1905), p. 35.

4. Research into the local traditions gives Qal'at al-Majoos ('Dezh Gowrie' in Persian) or 'Castle of the Magi' as its [Taft] ancient name. This popular local name, which links the Wise Men and the tradition of a Christian monasticism together, suggests a Christian presence in my native ground centuries before Islam.

5. For the history and technique of this craft, see Hans E. Wulff, *The Traditional Crafts of Persia: Their Development, Technology, and Influence on Eastern and Western Civilisations* (Cambridge, MA: MIT Press, 1966), pp. 228–29. See also Muhammad Ali Islam-i-Nodooshan, *Roos-ha*, I (Persian) (Tehran – Yazdan Publications 1984 (1363 Persian calendar)), p. 35.

6. A chador is a sheet of cloth worn over the head and whole body by a woman.

7. 'Mullah' is a word very like the term 'clerk'. It is generally used of the clergy, but it is sometimes a mere courtesy title, and also can mean a man or a woman who can read.

8. 'In 1911 she had returned from a visit to England to care for her aged Mother, and Yazd was her location for around two years, till 1913 when she transferred to Kerman...' See Gulnar E. Francis-Dehqani, 'Religious Feminism in an Age of Empire: C.M.S. Missionaries in Iran 1869–1934, (PhD Thesis, University of Bristol, 1999), p. 130.

9. In habitable places where water passes through underground channels (Qanats), in order that people may be able to reach the water stream, a steep path with steps would be cut from the surface of the place to the bottom where water flows. This is called 'Pakaneh', a compound noun made up of *Pa* (foot) and *kandan* (to dig). Where the Pakaneh goes deep, the temperature differs greatly from the surface.

10. The first day of Aban normally falls on 23 October.

11. In Persian, 'he has salt in him'.

12. Every parish has a space, usually outdoors, where religious ceremonies take place; often a mosque is attached to it.

13. The members of the Prophet's family.

14. The eighth Imam in the succession of the 12 Imams honoured and revered by the Shiites.

15. Mullahs used the Qur'an for 'consultation' by a 'skill' known to them whereby pages were 'good' or 'bad', or 'neither'. The Book would be opened ceremonially and verdict given on the issue the enquirer had, by the 'character' of the page to which the opening led.

Chapter 2

1. William Wordsworth, *The Prelude*, Book 1, ll. 301–304 (Oxford, Oxford University Press, 1905), from *Poetical Works*.
2. 'Salat' is a Muslim prayer.
3. *Epistle to Diognetus* 5.1, from Maxwell Stansforth (trans.), *Early Christian Writings* (Harmondsworth: Penguin Books), p. 176.
4. Robert Browning, 'Easter Day', in his *Poetical Works* (Oxford: Oxford University Press, 1949), p. 409.
5. It may be of some interest to know how the government paid the cost of Alborz College, which had vast grounds and numerous buildings. The grounds were adjacent to one of the most famous streets of the capital. A few yards of the expensive grounds alongside this street were sold, and the money paid for the cost of the whole college. Alborz College was soon to be granted University status, before the American College in Beirut. However, it was the latter that would soon become one of the most important universities in the Middle East.

   Robert College in Istanbul was also one of the American Missionary Colleges, and later became an important Turkish educational establishment. In 1952, during my trip to India, I enquired about their schools. I was told that there were about 500 colleges belonging to different missionary societies, and they were all in the process of being run by Indian nationals. It is possible that one of the reasons why India has been able to keep democracy is due to the influence of such colleges. Compared to this, my country, as a result of dictatorship and the ignorance of government officials, lost the benefit of such schools. Thus it closed a window to world culture and civilization.

Chapter 3

1. Olive Suratgar, *I Sing in the Wilderness: An Intimate Account of Persia and the Persians* (London: Edward Stanford Ltd, 1951).
2. John Keats, 'Endymion' Book 1, lines 1–5, in his *Poetical Works* (ed. H. W. Garrod; Oxford: Oxford University Press, 2nd edn, 1958).

Chapter 4

1. James Morier, *The Adventures of Haji Baba of Isfahan* (London, 1824).

Chapter 5

1. A. E. Housman, 'Last Poems IX', in his *Collected Poems and Selected Prose* (ed. Christopher Ricks; London: Harmondsworth, 1988), p. 106.
2. Sayed Ahmad Hatef of Isfahan, Poet died 1783, in E. G. Browne, *Literary History of Persia*, IV (Cambridge: Cambridge University Press, 1928), p. 296.
3. Forooghi of Bastam, Poet died 1858, in Browne, *Literary History of Persia*, IV, p. 337.
4. Farid-Din Attar, 'Conference of Birds', in E. G. Browne, *Literary History of Persia*, II (ibid.), pp. 513–15. See also Ann Baring and Thetis Blacker, *The Birds who Flew beyond Time* (Bath & Boston: Barefoot Books Ltd, 1993).
5. Sayed Ahmad Hatef of Isfahan, in Browne, *Literary History of Persia*, IV, pp. 293–94.

Chapter 6

1. E. G. Browne, *A Year Amongst the Persians* (Cambridge: Cambridge University Press, 1902), pp. 394–95.
2. Robert Frost, 'Devotion', in his *Complete Poems* (New York: Holt, Rinehart & Winston, 1949), p. 308.
3. William Shakespeare, *The Merchant of Venice*, Act 1, Scene 3, ll. 33–34.
4. William Shakespeare, *Hamlet*, Act 5, Scene 2, ll. 299–301.
5. Browne, *A Year Amongst the Persians*, see 'Exordium'.
6. William Wordsworth, 'Kings College Chapel, Cambridge', in his *Poetical Works* (ed. T. Hutchinson; London: Oxford University Press, 1903), p. 451.
7. Related to Ahura Mazda, the name of God in Zoroastrianism.

Chapter 7

1. Mowlana Jalal-a-Din Muhammad of Balkh (Rumi) (1207–73).
2. George Eliot, *Adam Bede* (London, n.d.), p. 258.
3. Kermit Roosevelt, *The Struggle for the Control of Iran* (New York: McGraw-Hill Books Co., 1979).
4. Roosevelt, *The Struggle for the Control of Iran*. See also Nikki R. Keddie, *Roots of Revolution* (New Haven: Yale University Press, 1981); and Mohammad Reza Pahlavi, *Reply to History* ([Text in Persian], London: KVC, Paris: Mitra Organizations, 1979 [1358 Persian Calendar]), p. 73.

Chapter 8

1. 'Ziggurat' or 'Zikurt' is a Syriac term meaning a height or a peak. It is a pyramid-shaped structure on top of which a temple is built.
2. John Donne, 'The Extasie' (ll. 71–72), in his *The Poems* (ed. H. J. C. Grierson; Oxford: Oxford University Press, 1933), p. 48.
3. John Donne, 'A Valediction: Forbidding Mourning' (ll. 25–28), in *The Poems*, p. 45.

Chapter 9

1. A. J. Arberry (trans), *Fifty Poems of Hafiz* (Cambridge: Cambridge University Press, 1947), p. 84.
2. G. M. Hopkins, 'The Wreck of the Deutschland', in his *The Poems* (ed. W. H. Gardner and N. H. MacKenzie; Oxford: Oxford University Press, 4th edn, 1970), p. 53.
3. Jalal al-Din Rumi, 'The Song of the Reed', in A. J. Arberry, *Sufism* (London: George Allen and Unwin, 1950), p. 111.
4. This prayer can be found in *The Hard Awakening*, pp. 113–14; also in George Appleton (ed.), *The Oxford Book of Prayers* (Oxford: Oxford University Press, 1985), pp. 135–36.

Chapter 10

1. Mohammad Ali Shah Qajar is buried in Italy. Ahmad Shah, the last of the Qajar dynasty, is buried in France. Reza Shah Pahlavi died in Johannesburg; his body was brought to Tehran and buried there, but his son, Mohammad Reza Shah, took the body with him to Cairo when he left the country in 1979. It is kept in Cairo with the hope of a reburial in Iran. Mohammad Reza Shah's body is also kept in Cairo with the hope of burial in Tehran one day. See Yann Richard, *Shi'ite Islam* (trans. Antonia Nevill; Oxford: Basil Blackwell, 1995), p. 108.
2. William Wordsworth, 'The Prelude', Book 10, ll. 400–9 in *Poetical Works* (Oxford: Oxford University Press, 1905).
3. Edwin Muir, *Collected Poems* (London: Faber and Faber, 1963), p. 239.
4. A list of Sohrab Books publications is given at the end of these notes.

Postscript

1. Muhammad Daud Rahbar, *The Cup of Jamshid* (Cape Cod: Claude Stark Inc., 1974), p. 78.

2. *Hafiz of Shiraz: Thirty Poems* (trans. J. Heath-Stubbs and P. Avery; London: John Murray, 1952), p. 42.
3. Hymn 5:2 in the Salvation Army Hymn book.

List of SOHRAB Books Publications

Life's Journey (Persian) (translation of George Appleton, *Journey for a Soul*, Collins (Fontana), 1974

The Hard Awakening, SPCK (Triangle), 1981

Moshkel-i-Eshq (Persian), SOHRAB Books, 1981

Chimes of Church Bells (Persian), SOHRAB Books, 1987

Questions and Answers (Persian), SOHRAB Books 1990

Christ and Christianity in Persian Poetry, SOHRAB Books, 1987

The Costliness of Love (Persian), Nuri Jahan, 1962, SOHRAB Books, 1981

Christ and Christianity amongst the Iranians. I. A Short Historical Survey, (Persian) SOHRAB Books, 1992; *II. The Classical Period of Persian Poetry*, (Persian) SOHRAB Books, 1993; *III. Contemporary Poetry, Prose and Art* (Persian), SOHRAB Books, 1994

39 Persian Hymns with Music (with cassette), SOHRAB Books, 1993

Bahram William Dehqani-Tafti, SOHRAB Books, 1981

Divine Suffering (Persian), Nuri-Jahan, 1958, SOHRAB Books, 1995

Hymns, Persian and English: With Words and Tunes in Common, SOHRAB Books, 1996

Three Radio Plays: Birth, Death and Resurrection of Christ (Persian), (translated from Dorothy L. Sayers, *A Man Born to be King*), Nuri-Jahan, 1947 SOHRAB Books, 1996

Anxiety and Peace (Persian), SOHRAB Books, 1997

The Faithful Remnant (Persian), Nuri Jahan, 1952, SOHRAB Books, 1998

Yek Chah o Do Cheshmeh (Persian), SOHRAB Books, 1999

Like unto Him (Persian), (translation of Stephen Neill, *Christian Character*, World Christian Books, 1955; and translation of William Temple, *From Palm Sunday to Easter*, Student Christian Movement Press, 1942

Index of Names and Places